EMBRACING A DICTATORSHIP

Embracing a Dictatorship

US Relations with Spain, 1945–53

Boris N. Liedtke
Deutsche Morgan Grenfell

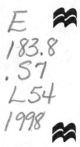

First published in Great Britain 1998 by
MACMILLAN PRESS LTD
Houndmills, Basingstoke, Hampshire RG21 6XS and London
Companies and representatives throughout the world

A catalogue record for this book is available from the British Library.

ISBN 0–333–71077–0

First published in the United States of America 1998 by
ST. MARTIN'S PRESS, INC.,
Scholarly and Reference Division,
175 Fifth Avenue, New York, N.Y. 10010

ISBN 0–312–17492–6

Library of Congress Cataloging-in-Publication Data
Liedtke, Boris N.
Embracing a dictatorship : US relations with Spain, 1945–53 /
Boris N. Liedtke.
p. cm.
Includes bibliographical references and index.
ISBN 0–312–17492–6 (cloth)
1. United States—Foreign relations—Spain. 2. Spain—Foreign
relations—United States. 3. United States—Foreign
relations—1945–1953. I. Title.
E183.8.S7L54 1997
327.73046'09'044—dc21   97–12036
                                                        CIP

This book is printed on paper suitable for recycling and made from fully managed and
sustained forest sources.

10   9   8   7   6   5   4   3   2   1
07 06 05 04 03 02 01 00 99 98

Printed in Great Britain by
The Ipswich Book Company Ltd
Ipswich, Suffolk

For
Gerlinde and Kurt
Tanja and Patrick

Contents

Preface and Acknowledgements

Over ten years ago I had the opportunity to attend a US military air show at the American Torrejón airbase near Madrid. The display of fighter planes was far less stimulating than the change of cultural environment one inevitably experienced upon passing the checkpoint. Here was a place in the middle of Spain, barely an hour away from the capital, which resembled in many aspects the American way of life. Low residential bungalows, large Chevrolets and American football games had replaced Spanish architecture, culture and entertainment. I was intrigued by the coming about of this strange arrangement and decided to investigate the historic and diplomatic background to it. Since then I have accumulated an enormous amount of debt which I owe to those who over the years have helped me in completing this study.

It would be almost impossible to name all those friends who have encouraged me to push ahead with the investigation when I had lost a sense of direction. However, I always knew that I could rely on the support from my family which was crucial before and during the work. I would like to thank Dr Spackman and Dr Pettigree who encouraged me to start my work in the first place. At the same time good friends like Simon Hankinson, Richard Murray and Penelope Simpson were always willing to help out and motivate me whenever I needed it.

On the academic side I am grateful to all those professionals who have made it possible for me to obtain the necessary documents. In this respect I am very thankful to Jo Ann Williamson and Kenneth D. Schlessinger from the National Archives in Washington, DC, and to Colonel Clayton R. Newell, US Army, Chief Historical Services Division, for their help with the declassification of US diplomatic and military documents. I am also grateful to Sir Frank Roberts for finding the time to talk to me about his experiences in the Foreign Office. At the same time I am indebted to three academics, Dr John Hulsman, Dr Enrique Moradiellos and Dr Paco Romero, who helped me develop many of the ideas and thoughts expressed in this book.

Finally I would like to thank Paul Preston who, throughout my work, gave me outstanding professional advice. He always found the right words to rekindle my enthusiasm. I am certain that without his help I would not have been able to complete this study.

B. N. L.
London, 1997

List of Acronyms

CIA	Central Intelligence Agency
CNT	Confederación Nacional del Trabajo
ERP	European Recovery Programme
FY	Fiscal Year
IBRD	International Bank for Reconstruction and Development
ICAO	International Civil Aviation Organization
IMCO	Intergovernmental Maritime Consultative Organization
IMF	International Monetary Fund
INI	Instituto Nacional de Industria
ITT	International Telegraph and Telephone Corporation
JMST	Joint Military Survey Team
JUSMG	Joint US Military Group
JWPC	Joint War Plans Committee
MDAP	Mutual Defense Assistance Program
NATO	North Atlantic Treaty Organization
NSC	National Security Council
OECD	Organization for Economic Cooperation and Development
OEEC	Organization of European Economic Cooperation
POL	Petrol, Oil, Lubricants
PPS	Policy Planning Staff
SACEUR	Supreme Air Command Europe
SHAPE	Supreme Headquarters Allied Powers Europe
UGT	Unión General de Trabajadores
UN	United Nations
USAF	United States Air Force
USCINCEUR	US Commander in Chief Europe
USIS	United States Information Service
WHO	World Health Organization

Introduction

This is a study of the relations between Spain and the US from the end of the Second World War to the conclusion of the Madrid Agreements. In the 1940s, almost as soon as the Western democracies had solved the fascist challenge to their social and economic structure, an old enemy, Communism, renewed its claim as a plausible alternative to the capitalist economy. The struggle between the two systems, which engulfed almost the entire world, was unique in that the decisive battles rarely involved soldiers. More often they were fought out by diplomats, economists and industrialists all over the globe. The two superpowers continuously tried to extend their respective influence to as many countries as possible. In this context Spain, guarding the entrance to the Mediterranean, was of particular strategic importance.

The first part of the book, covering Chapters 1 to 7, sets the international context for the attempt by the US to bring Spain into the Western defence structure. Chapter 1 analyses the coming about of the tripartite statement: a weak condemnation of Spain as a fascist regime. For both historic and economic reasons, France felt more antipathy towards the Franco regime than either Britain or the US. The Quai d'Orsay resolved to force the two other Western allies into a condemnation of the Spanish government. However, Britain and the US were unwilling to jeopardize their cordial diplomatic relations with Spain. They succeeded in watering down French demands to such an extent that the ensuing statement had little real impact upon Spain herself.

One of the developments that emerged following the statement was the discussion of the Spanish problem at the UN. The way in which Communist countries tried to exploit the situation at the UN forms the topic of the second chapter. After long talks throughout 1946, the UN passed a resolution which condemned Franco and, amongst other things, recommended the withdrawal of ambassadors from Madrid.

The new-found willingness on the part of the Western democracies to speak out against Franco did not last. In the third and fourth chapters we see how economic, commercial and strategic interests in the US and in Britain encouraged a *rapprochement* to Spain between 1947 and 1948. Over these two years the US State Department, fearing possibly adverse diplomatic effects of close ties with Spain, was slowly pressurized by the Department of Defense and several influential Congressmen

1

into accepting their point of view. The international developments during 1949 and early 1950 led to a new official US policy towards Spain. The fifth chapter looks at the influence which the growing conflict between East and West had on US policy towards Spain. The outbreak of the Korean War added to fears of policy makers in Washington. In the sixth chapter the importance of this uncertainty is emphasized. Spain was quickly reintegrated into the international community and the UN revoked its own earlier recommendation to withdraw ambassadors from Madrid. Furthermore, the National Security Council initiated a revision of its policy, stressing the importance of promptly making use of Spain's geographic, military and strategic position. As becomes clear in Chapter 7, the emerging US policy called for immediate talks with Spain, ignoring the diplomatic, military and moral concerns of its European allies. In June 1951 this policy was issued and authorized by the President. The background was then set for the two countries to come to a mutually beneficial agreement.

The second part of the book concentrates more on the diplomatic relations and negotiations between the two countries than on the global context. Chapter 8 analyses the first Spanish–American talks between General Franco in person and Admiral Sherman of the US Navy. The friendly atmosphere of these initial meetings gave the misleading impression that the two countries were about to come to an arrangement.

Following these talks, two US study groups went to Spain: one covering economic, the other military aspects. Chapter 9 looks at these two groups and the time they spent in Spain, while the following chapter analyses their reports as well as the resulting considerations. By this time it had become clear to both sides that the negotiations were not going to be as straightforward as it had initially seemed.

In early 1952, the US sent two negotiating teams to Spain which were to hold conferences with their Spanish counterparts for almost a year and a half. Chapter 11 looks at the progress made in these talks throughout 1952. By the end of the year it looked almost as if the agreements could be signed, but Franco's decision to withdraw concessions made by his negotiators forced the US to reconsider her approach.

In Chapter 12 this new approach is outlined. Washington initially decided to wait and see if Madrid would return to the negotiating table. Once it became clear that the Spaniards were unwilling to do so, the Americans tried to pressurize them by threatening to withhold funds already appropriated for Spain by Congress. The talks were on the verge of collapse. A compromise, however, was found and the talks resumed. How this affected the final agreements and some of the military and legal implications are summarized in Chapter 13. The final chapter takes a closer look at the agreements themselves and concludes with some developments which emerged shortly afterwards. Most of the book is based on American primary sources throughout the period. Many of the arguments developed contrast directly with those already put forward, notably by Spanish historians.

While the negotiations were going on and shortly after the agreements had been signed, a series of Ph.D. theses were written in the US on Spain's diplomatic relations with the West. These studies, while having had the benefit of the contemporary developments, nevertheless lacked the benefit of historic hindsight.

The American Arthur P. Whitaker published one of the first comprehensive studies of Spain's position in the Western defence structure. His analysis, published in the early 1960s, gives a good reflection of the negotiations from the public point of view.

Richard Rubottom and Carter J. Murphy wrote an analysis over 20 years later. While they had access to a wider range of primary material, they decided to follow the relations between Spain and the US right up to the 1980s. What is clearly pointed out in their publication is the geographic importance Spain had for the defence of Western Europe. The Pyrenees provided NATO forces with a natural defence line against a conventional attack by the Soviet Union. Even if West Germany, the Benelux countries and France had been lost in a sneak attack on Europe, NATO would still have been able to retain a strong foothold in Europe. Necessarily the depth of their analysis somehow underestimates the importance of the negotiation process itself. Spanish historians have been much more willing to comment on this.

The most thorough research conducted on the negotiations must be the one by Antonio Marquina Barrio, covering Spain in the Western defence structure up to 1986. However, his excellent investigation and broad topic leaves him little room for a final assessment of the negotiations or of the agreements. One is left guessing whether Washington's strong position forced the Spanish negotiators to compromise on several important points. Even though this is never spelled out clearly, the impression one derives from his study is that this was the case.

Florentino Portero gives a good summary of Spain's foreign policy throughout the period of isolation. Unfortunately, though, he stops in 1950, with the UN revoking her earlier recommendation of withdrawal of ambassadors from Spain.

By far the most comprehensive study of the negotiations themselves and the implications for Spain was written by Angel Viñas. He comes to the conclusion that Franco had sold out Spain's sovereignty over foreign and defence policy. Following the signing of the agreements and specifically the secret annex to the official agreements, the US could make use of the bases in case of Soviet attack without even consulting with Spain. This meant that Spain had lost her ability to remain neutral in case of conflict and thus could have been forced into a nuclear confrontation. According to this, Franco had given up a vital cornerstone of the nationalist regime and one whose importance he himself had stressed throughout the creation of the Franco myth, that is to say his great ability to avoid Spain being dragged into a world conflict. Given this development, one clearly has to question the validity of the Franco myth and of Franco's real interest in Spain as opposed to his personal position as Spain's Caudillo. In return for giving up control over foreign and defence policy, as well, though to a lesser extent, monetary and fiscal policy, Spain obtained military and economic aid. Viñas clearly feels that neither of the two made up sufficiently for the downside of the agreements. He sees that military aid came to Spain as obsolete US war material left over from the Korean War and in some cases dating back to the Second World War. He concludes that for the US it was a cheap way of getting rid of unwanted war material. On the economic side, Viñas sees that aid granted to Spain was on a much smaller scale than aid received by other European nations through the Marshall Plan. Furthermore, most of this economic aid was in fact sent for the construction of the military bases, which themselves were useless to Spain, as her air force lacked the heavy bombers which would have required these large military installations. Viñas therefore concludes that the agreements were one-sided and Spain's position throughout the negotiations had been weak. This was because Franco not only required economic aid but also needed these agreements for internal propaganda reasons, to consolidate his position and to prove that Spain under his regime had become an acceptable nation to trade with. Hence Franco's statement shortly before the conclusion of the agreements: "sign anything that they put in front of you".

Since his research, though, a series of new documents relating to the US negotiations have become available. By concentrating on these a picture emerges indicating that Washington, as well as Spain, had great military and strategic interests in signing the Madrid Agreements; hence the US willingness to compromise several times during the negotiations. This is surprising, given the findings by other investigators that Spain was forced almost by circumstances into these agreements. This analysis tries to develop a counter-argument which seeks to lay the foundation for a new discussion on the issue.

1 1945/1946: the Tripartite Statement

During the spring months of 1945, the war machinery of the Allied powers slowly ground to a halt. The victorious armies of the Americans and the British Commonwealth, with some help from French contingents, had liberated most of Western Europe. The nightmare of fascism belonged to the past. Nevertheless, the Iberian Peninsula was still dominated by a totalitarian regime. Only months before the outbreak of the Second World War, General Francisco Paulino Hermenegildo Teódulo Franco Bahamonde had consolidated his rule over Spain. However, the Spanish Civil War had drained the country of her national resources, leaving the economy in ruins. Despite having received substantial military aid from Germany and Italy during his struggle, Franco was unable to contribute to the Axis war effort. As a result, the Spanish dictator seemingly steered his country through the Second World War along a path of neutrality or non-belligerency, not because he had chosen to do so, but because Spain's economy dictated it. Franco did however continue close and cordial diplomatic as well as economic relations with Germany throughout the war. The Allies had known this during the world conflict. They knew that Spain had supplied Germany with wolfram and mercury during the war and that Spanish soldiers had fought under German command in Russia. However, they were grateful to Franco for having remained neutral during the vital period of the Allied landings in Northern Africa (Operation Torch) and they clearly realized that Spain had officially been a non-belligerent nation. Spain's past was controversial and it provided diplomats and politicians with enough material to justify either isolation from or integration into the Western defence structure.

Consequently, two contradictory versions of Spain's recent history were formulated. Those favouring isolation of the Franco regime saw it as another fascist system, created with help from the Axis and totalitarian in its structure. On the other hand, those favouring integration of Spain into the Western structure tried to prove that Franco's association with Hitler was not what it seemed and really had been a diplomatic coup for the Spanish dictator. Francoist myth-makers claimed that the Spanish Caudillo had never been willing to help Hitler in his struggle against the Allies, alleging that the military and economic support which Hitler received from Franco had been wrung out of him. In exchange the Spanish dictator was able to guarantee Spain's neutrality. The meeting at Hendaye in October 1940, which had been disappointing for both Hitler and Franco, was projected as a clever success for the Spanish dictator. Needless to say, Franco promoted this argument wholeheartedly; after all his position would have been helped by Spain's integration into the Western defence structure.

By spring 1945, the US, and not Britain, was the driving force within this defence structure. As the war had dragged on, London had lost economic and political influence all over the world, becoming more and more dependent on the US. Britain's relationship with Spain was no exception. Undoubtedly both nations had a wide range of interests in Spain. The Conservatives and the Foreign Office were inclined towards international stability wherever Britain had substantial financial investments. British interests in Spain were secure only if law, order and a sound economic environment guaranteed prosperity. For most Conservatives in Britain, social justice, freedom of speech and political rights in Spain mattered less than stability. Britain also favoured a continuation of the present regime to assure and protect her sea lanes through the Straits of Gibraltar. This overall attitude towards Spain continued despite the ascent to power of the Labour Party.

The change of government in Britain occurred during the Potsdam Conference when, on 26 July 1945, stunning news from London proclaimed a Labour victory over the Conservatives. Winston Churchill was replaced by Clement Attlee. The new Prime Minister was a Labour leader with distinctively conservative characteristics; an Oxford graduate who was evidently very fond of his three-piece suits, which he wore throughout the Potsdam Conference despite the intense summer heat during July and August 1945.

His foreign minister, Ernest Bevin, had risen from the bottom of the social ladder and had a much more traditional Labour background. Wearing thick glasses and weighing almost 250 pounds, he spoke with a thick working-class accent demonstrative of his trade-union beginnings. In theory it could have been expected that a Labour government would have implemented a harsher policy towards Spain. However, Britain's precarious economic position after the war left Bevin and Attlee little room to manoeuvre. Despite pressure from Ian Mikardo and Francis Noel-Baker in the House of Commons, and Attlee's proposal in the War Cabinet to condemn Spain, British foreign policy continued to be short-term, commercially orientated and, above all, strongly anti-Communist.

On the other side of the Atlantic, the US administration, less concerned with trade relations, was fast to criticize Spain. In a letter drafted by the State Department and dated 10 March 1945, President Franklin D. Roosevelt outlined to Norman Armour, US Ambassador in Madrid, his country's policy towards Spain. The ageing President summarized the domestic disapproval in America of the totalitarian regime in Spain. He wrote: "Having been helped to power by Fascist Italy and Nazi Germany, and having patterned itself along totalitarian lines, the present regime in Spain is naturally the subject of distrust." Even more forcefully, he wrote that "I can see no place in the community of nations for governments founded on fascist principles."[1]

As would happen in Britain only months later, the wartime leader of the nation, who had spurred on the population to increasing degrees of sacrifice in numerous and long-remembered speeches, was replaced by a quieter character.

Franklin D. Roosevelt had been part of the wealthy and influential northeastern Establishment, nephew to another President and favoured by birth, class and education. Harry S. Truman was none of these. He had been born in a tiny house, measuring some 20 by 28 feet, in a small, dusty market town called Lamar, Missouri. Throughout his early life Truman had little time for study and was forced to work hard to earn a living, as a farmer, a soldier and finally as a politician. Helped by a local political lobby, the Pendergast machine in Kansas City, he obtained a seat in the Senate and, fortuitously, saw the Vice-Presidency fall into his lap during the 1944 Democratic Convention. Roosevelt's death catapulted this quiet man into the White House on 12 April 1945. Unlike his predecessor, Truman lacked eloquence and his speeches were frequently interrupted by a brief silence, a mispronunciation or sometimes even a stammer or stutter. This farmer from Missouri had taken his place in the White House initially to continue Roosevelt's policies, both domestic and foreign.

Truman, just like Roosevelt, condemned the Franco regime in an early news conference, claiming that "None of us [the US Government] like Franco or his Government."[2] This reaction was only too natural. During the war the ostensibly cordial relations with Spain had been implemented to prevent Franco from being forced into an alliance with Germany. However, as the war ended, the President came under pressure from liberal Congressmen like Joseph Guffey, John Coffee and Hugh de Lancey to take strong measures against the Spanish dictator. It was recognized that an association with Franco was bad publicity for the US, and the Liberals hoped that Franco could be replaced with a respectable regime which would support America's policy in Europe. Unlike Britain, the US had fewer economic ties to Spain and thus had fewer concerns about short-term stability on the Iberian Peninsula. It was only to be expected that the US would put pressure on Franco. However, the US military was already considering Spain's strategic potential. As early as 19 April 1945, the Joint Chiefs of Staff commissioned a report of US defence policy towards Spain. In its final version the report stressed Spain's geographic importance, claiming that "should our most probable enemy attempt to draw the nations of Europe together into a single power structure in war, Spain would be potentially next in importance to the British Isles in thwarting any major continental power from creating an almost impregnable fortress of Europe". The study continued to argue that "in terms of land warfare in Western Europe, Spain is at least as important as Italy, if not more important, because Spain provides a [cushion] of defense space". And in terms of "naval and air warfare, Spain's strategic location gives a higher potential value as a base" for naval operations. The Pyrenees provide an ideal defence while the Peninsula dominates southwestern Europe. As a result the study claimed that "Spanish–United States military cooperation is of significant importance to the implementation of our immediate, middle-range, and long-range war plans." This analysis led to a vital policy recommendation that "from the strictly military point of view, . . . arrangements are urgently needed in spite of pressure from other nations to delay our acceptance of Spanish cooperation".[3] The importance of this report cannot be overemphasized. It summarized the military point of view for years to come.

Shortly afterwards this argument was reiterated in another study. In early November the Joint Chiefs of Staff looked at different military base systems. The Canary Islands in particular were perceived as an ideal spot for joint navy and air-force military bases. The Joint Chiefs of Staff, with little concern for the political implications, favoured Spain's complete integration throughout the coming years.

There were also other considerations for the US which favoured a gentle approach towards Spain. Due to Spain's neutrality during the war, she had been able to supply the fighting nations with raw materials which in turn led some sections of the mining industry to expand rapidly. Bitumen coal, anthracite, lignite, potassium and mercury production had all increased considerably. The US had previously imported several of these strategic raw materials for military use and was thus favourably inclined towards Spain. Furthermore, economic developments in Europe helped Spain in the medium and long term. The Western European markets had become slowly saturated by American products, while the inability of European nations to pay for these imports led to a widening of the dollar gap. Spain offered a new market for American products and as US economic interests expanded worldwide, stability in Spain became more important to American foreign policy makers.

Furthermore, there did not seem to exist a real alternative to Franco. The Joint Intelligence Committee wrote that "there is no prospect of any form of popular rising taking place in Spain . . . [and] a rising, caused by foreign intervention, if strong enough to avoid immediate suppression by the police with army backing, would almost inevitably result in the outbreak of another civil war". This on its own might still have been acceptable. However the Committee asserted that "a civil war in Spain with French and Russian intervention would also be likely to precipitate a crisis in France".[4]

This assessment limited America's policy considerably. The US not only would not intervene against Franco but eventually would press France to avoid clashes with Spain lest this lead to an unstable situation in France itself. Washington accepted the Spanish regime and was determined to avoid causing general European instability.

In its relations with Spain, the French government was more readily prepared to represent the feeling of its people and vent its disapproval of Franco. The hatred in France towards the Spanish government, dating back to the Spanish Civil War, was dramatically demonstrated during June 1945 when a French mob attacked a train travelling from Switzerland to Spain passing through Chambéry. Allegedly the train carried troops of the Blue Division, while in reality Spanish diplomatic personnel and workers were on board. In the ensuing conflict more than 150 people were injured.

Unlike the US, the French armed forces had little military interest in Spain. On the contrary, it was feared that if relations between the US and Spain improved US troops might withdraw from Central Europe in case of Soviet attack. Furthermore, the Soviet military mission in Paris, under Colonel Lapkin, organized Spanish exiles and the French Communist Party to put pressure on the French government. Above all, this agitation sought to obstruct any *rapprochement* between Britain and the US on the one hand and Spain on the other. Lieutenant Xilitzin and Captain Nobikov, both at the Soviet mission in Paris, were permanently in contact with Spanish exiles in the hope of preventing this alignment.

Spain's problem in seeking international acceptance was highlighted during the 1945 UN Conference, held between 25 April and 26 June in San Francisco. In June the Mexican delegate to the Conference, a Spanish exiled anti-fascist named Luis Quintanilla, appealed for the exclusion of Spain from the UN on the grounds that the United Charter excluded all those countries ruled by regimes established with the help of Germany or Italy. One of the reasons for this appeal was the influence of Spanish immigrants in Mexico. James C. Dunn from the US delegation, who was to become ambassador to Spain during the early 1950s, said that the US was in full agreement with Quintanilla's statement. Nevertheless John Foster Dulles, future Secretary of State under Eisenhower, was already championing the Spanish cause and tried to exclude Quintanilla's proposal on the grounds that the Spanish question was not part of the order of the day at the Conference. Dulles's attempt remained fruitless and Spain was excluded from the UN.

During the Potsdam Conference, the Soviets wanted to go one step further and proposed on 19 July 1945 that all relations with Spain, including diplomatic and economic links, should be severed. In a joint statement, issued during the Conference, the three great powers, the US, Britain and the USSR, expressed their wish that Spain should not apply for membership of the UN, given the fact that her regime was founded with the help of the Axis powers, was closely associated with the Axis and did not posses the necessary qualifications to justify membership. For the Spanish government, the delicacy of its position concerning foreign relations was obvious. To avoid more drastic measures taken against his regime, and knowing that there was little point in trying to improve relations with Moscow, Franco embarked on a policy upholding the neutrality myth. According to this, his regime stood for the defence of Christianity against Communism. He tried to distance himself from his former German links, claiming that his pro-German attitude throughout the early phase of the war had been forced upon him by Hitler. At the same time he wanted to assure the West that he had the capability of making democratic changes within his country. In his attempt to improve relations with foreign nations, Franco embarked on a conciliating policy which took the form of seven specific measures. The first was to withdraw from the occupied city of Tangier. Franco mendaciously argued that by seizing the city, he had prevented it from falling into German hands during the war.

Next, the Fuero de los Españoles (Charter of Civil Rights) was issued on 18 July 1945. In itself the Fuero failed to be accepted by the West as a genuine bill of rights. Salvador Madariaga, a former Spanish diplomat to the League of Nations and influential critic, described the Fuero thus: "The Charter of Rights is the most mendacious document ever penned. It guarantees every right which the government tramples upon daily. . . . There is not a single article of this Charter that is not in itself an insult to the nation whose daily experience gives it the lie."[5]

Two days later Franco reshuffled his government in favour of the Monarchists and Catholics and against the Fascist Party, the Falange. It was a step in the right direction. An influential Spanish general had claimed that "as long as the Falange continues, it will be impossible to have cordial relations with France".[6]

The Caudillo's fourth measure was the appointment of Alberto Martín Artajo as Foreign Minister. The Catholic Martín Artajo was generally acceptable to the West primarily because he was not a member of the Falange. Instead, the 41-year-old had a legal background, and was President of Catholic Action in Spain and a member of the Catholic Association.

Franco's next initiative was the creation of the Franco myth, which was assiduously spread by members of the media and the diplomatic corps. For example, the Spanish Ambassador in Washington told the American Secretary of State that his country's foreign policy during the war had been a result of constant pressure by the Axis on Madrid.

Another way in which Franco also hoped to create a democratic air in Spain were the municipal elections. These were initially greeted with some enthusiasm in Britain. This initial enthusiasm soon faded away, however, when the extent of governmental coercion became known.

Finally, Franco diminished the powers of the Spanish Falange, withdrawing many of their privileges. The Falange, the political party of Francoism, had been structured along lines similar to Germany's Nazi Party and Italy's Fascist Party and was by now a burden for the regime.

Despite all these changes, politicians in France continued their vehement opposition to Franco's dictatorship. Three French political parties, the Communists, Socialists and the Popular Republican Movement, together with the French Foreign Minister, Georges Bidault, appealed during December 1945 to London and Washington to end all political and economical relations with Spain. This appeal was a diplomatic blunder. Britain rejected it outright on the grounds that to head the call might provoke a second civil war. London argued that under the existing circumstances, the opposition to Franco was so disorganized that even with foreign intervention, the outcome of a struggle in Spain remained uncertain. In any event a second civil war would probably have lead to another fascist victory and disaster for the Republican and Monarchist forces. In the eyes of the British, sanctions or political isolation would end all possibilities to pressure Franco into further evolution of his regime and would adversely affect the British economy which needed Spanish foodstuffs.

However, the USSR realized that diplomatic gains could be made by seizing upon the French proposal, and from 9 January 1946 onwards officially supported the French appeal to isolate Spain. While the White House disliked Franco's regime, it was nevertheless unwilling to go as far as the French had proposed. The US favoured greater freedom of the press and the liberation of political prisoners, as well as the return of exiled politicians to Spain. However, this fell substantially short of the French proposal to terminate all relations. Furthermore, as we have seen, cordial relations with Spain became increasingly desirable as fear of a military threat by the Soviet Union grew.

A report by the Joint Committee of War Planning concluded that "the Soviet economic war potential is not now adequately developed and at least for the next ten to fifteen years, the gains to be derived internally during peace outweigh the advantage of any external objective that might be attained at the risk of war". Eventually, however, this period of peace was to come to an end. The US expected that "at the present time the USSR possesses the military means to overrun Europe". As for Europe's defence against a possible attack, the report read:

> the chaotic conditions in the western European countries, the low combat efficiency of Allied occupation troops, the proximity of Russian forces, and the communications available to the USSR make it possible for the Russians to overrun western Europe at any time. The Russian advance might be slowed down at the Pyrenees, but only temporarily.

Despite this the Joint Chiefs of Staff concluded that "the Soviets will endeavor to avoid a major conflict for the next ten or fifteen years". In the same study Spain and Tangier were listed under "areas subject to Soviet political and/or military aggression in pursuance of their immediate objectives". It was suspected by US policy makers that the USSR had an interest in establishing herself as a Great Power in the Mediterranean.[7]

A plan, which later became known as the Pincher Plan, estimated that after 70 days of struggle in Spain, Soviet troops would reach Gibraltar and close the Straits. The plan reflected the grave concern of the American armed forces over the Soviet threat and at the same time recognized Spain's geographical importance. The Joint Staff Planners issued another report during April 1946 which was concerned with military problems deriving from the Pincher Plan. It was noted that France feared any military agreements between the US and Spain on the grounds that this would allow the US to withdraw its troops to Britain and Spain in case of Soviet attack which, under the circumstances, would have caused France to fall to the USSR. Section 37 of the report by the Joint Staff Planners made French fears of an American withdrawal more than simple paranoia. It read: "it appears that should the USSR initiate an offensive in Western Europe, our occupation forces there must be immediately withdrawn from the continent of Europe or withdrawn to a defensive position in Italy or possibly Spain".[8]

The report claimed that

The withdrawal of US forces across France into Spain also may prove feasible. This, too, will be largely dependent upon political considerations. It is probable that an anti-Communistic government [in Spain] will remain in power for at least the next year or two, and if Spain is willing to desert her position as a neutral, then the withdrawal of US forces into Spain would make a material contribution to any required defense of the Pyrenees. On the other hand, the Allies would probably be committed to the defense of Spain, which might well entail a substantial diversion of resources. Retention of an anti-Communist government in Spain would materially assist in maintaining the security of the western Mediterranean.

Appendix B of the report argued that Spain "is suitable and desirable as a base for fighter and short-range aircraft in defense of friendly or interdiction of enemy lines of communication. It is not suitably located as a base for long-range bombardment aircraft in prosecution of the strategic mission." Appendix C stressed the importance of the Straits of Gibraltar, and thus Spain. It analysed the Soviet arguments for and against an attack on Spain. During an invasion of the Iberian Peninsula the US had two choices. Either support Spain with troops or let her fall to the Russian invasion. The first option, the defence of Spain, would have enabled the US to retain control over the western Mediterranean. At the same time it would have reduced the risks of a counter-attack against occupied Europe. The report ended with a priority list in case of a Soviet sneak attack on Europe. The US would hold the Cairo–Suez area first and above all. Next, it would have supported Spain's resistance against an invasion and, if this turned out to be impossible, Spain's fall had to be counterbalanced by establishing military bases in Morocco.

The French fear of being left alone by the Americans increased as relations between the US and Spain improved. While French authorities sought a guarantee that the US army would not evacuate the front line, the arrest of Cristino García Granda and nine other guerrillas in the Sierra Guadarrama offered an opportunity to force Washington into condemning Spain. Cristino García had fought on the Republican side in Asturias and Catalonia during the Spanish Civil War and had subsequently fled Spain. He then became a prominent member of the French Resistance during the German occupation. After France's liberation from the Nazis he returned illegally to Spain in April 1945 to continue his fight against fascism. Accused of murder and armed robbery, he was soon condemned to death.

On 17 February 1946, France, under pressure from the Communist labour unions and the Communists and Socialists in the National Assembly, asked Spain for clemency. The Spanish authorities countered that García was accused of terrorist acts against Spain and illegal entry into the country. His prominent past during the war mattered little to them. Disregarding the French plea, the condemned were executed shortly afterwards. In return, the French National Assembly responded: "The National Constituent Assembly has learned with shocked sorrow of the execution of Cristino García. . . . The Assembly . . . calls upon the French government to prepare to break relations with the government of General Franco." France and the Communist propaganda machinery wanted to make an issue out of the execution of these French Resistance fighters in February by demanding dramatic international action. However, these grounds were weak. While García's intentions were noble, his methods had clearly been illegal and ruthless. With the intention of isolating Spain and implicitly guaranteeing the defence of France by US troops, the French government decided not to wait for a more appropriate incident of violation of human rights. Despite being warned by the Spanish Chargé in Paris that a break of foreign relations would result in impounding of French assets, the Quai d'Orsay continued.

On 27 February, the French Foreign Minister Bidault proposed to the governments of the US, Britain and the USSR to end all diplomatic relations between Spain and UN member states. The reason to include Moscow was both cunning and bold. After the first proposal to condemn Spain it became obvious that neither Britain nor the US were terribly fond of isolating Spain, while Moscow was clearly in favour of the French proposal. With the appeal to Moscow, the Quai d'Orsay hoped to force the hand of the State Department and the Foreign Office. Bidault argued that Franco had made no changes towards democracy and continued his fascist reign. The French Foreign Minister therefore concluded that the Spanish regime threatened international peace and security. As a solution he proposed a condemnation by the four nations and a submission of the problem to the Security Council. It seemed that France had much to gain from this policy. The Security Council would either verbally condemn Spain and thus make a *rapprochement* between the US and Spain more difficult. This in turn would make a defence of France by US troops more likely. Alternatively, the Security Council would force economic sanctions against Spain. This would increase the share France received from American aid. The French government decided to close its borders and seriously reduce trade relations with Spain. Embargoes were enforced.

Support for a limitation on trade with Spain could be expected from the Division for European Affairs of the US State Department. The US had already shown some restrictions in her trade policy towards Spain. However, US economic interests in Spain made sure that the State Department would not abandon Spain completely.

Washington was not enthusiastic about Bidault's proposal. However, the US had expressed the desire to follow a common Western policy towards Spain. Either Britain or France had to compromise. In a memorandum, Harry N. Howard of the Division of International Organization Affairs wrote that the US should not discourage discussions at the UN if they arose. He did not exclude the possibility of ending diplomatic relations with Spain. Thus it seemed at first that the US might follow the French proposal in order to secure a common Western foreign policy. First, however, Washington wanted to find a compromise which would allow the continuation of trade and diplomatic relations, while also meeting French demands. It was hoped that such a compromise could be found in a public condemnation of the Spanish regime.

In fact the idea of a public statement had already received some support in the State Department after the first French appeal in January 1946. Dean Acheson, the acting Secretary of State, had already proposed a statement by France, Britain and the US expressing their dislike of Franco's fascist regime. This would have pointed towards a solution of the "internal" problem and, ideally, Franco would have been replaced by a caretaker government. Acheson knew, through the British ambassador in Washington, that Britain wanted to avoid discussions in public of the Spanish problem altogether. Whitehall sought to solve the complications through more discreet diplomatic channels.

The US Chargé to Spain argued against the State Department. He

believed that, in the long run, it was best not to make a public statement as this would limit future policy options. He favoured a slow
evolution of Francoism, bringing about eventual international acceptance. However, after the French proposal, the State Department could
no longer oppose the general idea of a common statement, nor could it
accept the French demand to end all diplomatic relations. A policy
report produced by the US Airforce Intelligence even feared the beginning of a military conflict between France and Spain.

Fortunately for Washington, the American policy makers were able
to act as mediator between France and Britain. Naturally, Britain tried
to prevent the French initiative. Sir Victor Mallet, British Ambassador
to Spain, wrote to Bevin that: "A weak Government in Spain, whether
of the Right or the Left, would pave the way for increased Soviet
influence and pressure through the Spanish Communists. The one real
merit of the present Government is that it does at least maintain order."[9]

The French proposal played into Soviet hands. While Britain and
the US might have contemplated getting rid of Franco without too
much social instability and political complications, the USSR was con-
templating exactly the opposite. Another civil war in Spain was in
Moscow's interest. Alternatively, the Kremlin wanted to discourage
lasting bonds between the West and Spain. George Kennan, then US
Chargé in the USSR, analysed the Soviet position. He claimed that the
past had created a deep hatred between Russia and Spain. He feared
that Spain offered Russia a strategic base and the possibility of ex-
panding Communism into France, Italy, Morocco and, eventually, into
Latin America.

Ambassador Mallet echoed this argument in a note to the Foreign
Office, and the British Chargé in Moscow believed that Russia was
not well informed on Spanish affairs and was only using France as a
"spearhead" to split the Western allies. After the French proposal, it
became even more obvious that Moscow was using France for its own
mischief. From all this, he deduced that the USSR was hoping for
instability, an overthrow of Franco and possibly a Communist takeover.

Once Bidault had made his proposal to London, Washington and
Moscow, the USSR was waiting impatiently for the British and American
reply. The Kremlin knew that, whichever way the situation turned out,
it would further Soviet plans. If strong measures were taken, Spain
would have been isolated and might have fallen more easily to a
Communist coup. If no statement was issued, the USSR would have
had a good chance to split the Western powers and increase its influence in France.

Franco and Martín Artajo, unwilling to compromise, were concerned by these developments. The Ambassador in Washington, Juan Francisco Cardenas, claimed that even a public statement by the four nations could not move Franco a single inch. Franco was willing to risk another civil war, even one inspired by foreign powers, but he would not peacefully relinquish his stranglehold on Spain. Expecting that the US feared a renewed struggle in Spain almost as much as Franco did, Cardenas, in a conversation with Paul Culbertson, then Chief of the Division of Western European Affairs, painted a spectre of civil war and Communism looming over Spain.

As a result of the French proposal, the three Western powers faced a dilemma. Above all they had to prove that they still stood united in their foreign policies. Yet the French proposal had pressured them into taking some sort of stance against Spain or else into admitting that a rift had developed between them. Britain was unwilling to go along with the French proposal. According to London, the French government's unilateral actions of closing the border and demanding a public statement condemning Franco had caused a crisis in foreign relations with Spain.

The US was less outspoken in this respect but tacitly agreed with the British. France, however, was unable to retreat completely as this would have led to accusations by the Communists that French foreign policy was dictated from London and Washington. Undoubtedly this would have had domestic repercussions in the already precarious political climate. Thus the three Western powers had to find a compromise which would lessen the French embarrassment without jeopardizing Anglo-American interests.

As a result, on 4 March 1946, following the French communiqué, the three Western Powers issued a joint statement condemning the Franco regime. According to this statement, the unfriendly relations with Spain were designed to bring about: "a peaceful withdrawal of Franco, the abolition of the Falange and the establishment of an interim or caretaker government under which the Spanish people may have an opportunity freely to determine the type of government they wish to have and to choose their leaders". The caretaker government would guarantee political amnesty, freedom of assembly and of expression. Once these changes had taken place, the caretaker government would have been diplomatically recognized and would receive economic assistance.[10]

Nevertheless there were no plans for direct action interfering in the internal affairs of Spain. Nor did the statement offer any solutions to Spain's problems. Franco stood to gain nothing from stepping down, and he would have alienated the political Right and the army, if he had shown any willingness to seriously reform his regime. The undoing of the Falange would have infuriated its members, making Franco's personal position untenable. The inducement of assistance for Spain mentioned no particulars and thus remained unattractive.

The statement was as important for what it said as for what it omitted. There was no threat to end diplomatic relations, nor did it mention a proposal to put the problem before the Security Council. It was an empty compromise, pleasing Britain and saving France from embarrassment.

Almost immediately after the statement, Russia tried to split the Western powers. The Soviet Chargé in Washington, Novikov, wrote to the Secretary of State that he was in full support of the French proposal to put the Spanish problem before the Security Council. By this Novikov had placed Washington in an unenviable position. If the US agreed, the problem might still come before the Security Council against US and British wishes. On the other hand, if the US disagreed, a wedge would have been driven between France and the US concerning foreign relations with Spain. For the time being Washington decided to ignore the problem.

In Spain the result of the statement was counter-productive. Franco capitalized on it by presenting it as a Communist-inspired conspiracy which demonstrated that Spain had to continue her struggle against Communism alone. The tripartite statement was one of the reasons why large, enthusiastic crowds turned to the Plaza de Oriente during the annual victory parade on 1 April 1946 demanding a speech by General Franco. This public support was one of the first signs of the success of the regime's efforts to orchestrate faith in the Caudillo's role as sentinel of the West. The nationalist feeling in Spain was skilfully manipulated and, for the time being, Madrid was almost unaffected by her foreign isolation. It is true that Spain was not a member of the UN nor of any of its numerous agencies and committees, but the economic costs of this ostracism were minor. Furthermore Franco enjoyed the wholehearted support of Salazar's dictatorship in Portugal, which argued that no civil unrest should be risked in Spain by overthrowing Franco, as Spain's resources were urgently needed in the struggle against Communism.

On 8 March 1946, Truman's Secretary of State, James F. Byrnes, wrote two notes to the US Ambassador in France, Jefferson Caffry. The Secretary of State could not see why Franco's failure to give an impression of evolution abroad should bring the Spanish problem before the UN, nor could he see how Spain endangered international peace and security. Realizing Russia's intentions, Byrnes wanted to avoid bringing the Spanish problem to the UN and, at the same time, give the French a possible escape route through which to avoid further alignment with the USSR.

The statement made on 4 March meant that the Western powers continued their coordinated policy towards Spain without harming Anglo-American interests in Spain. However, while France had backed down without losing diplomatic face, the Soviet pressure did not ease. Four days after the two notes to Caffry, Byrnes sent him another note. In it he suggested that Paris, having acted under Communist pressure, could escape further public outcry by stressing the value of the tripartite statement.

In Europe, the statement of 4 March seemed to the public to be in line with US policies. The US refrained from naming a new ambassador, granted no assistance and discouraged the private sector to invest in Spain. Furthermore, a report by the Subcommittee on Rearmament asserted that US military supplies for foreign nations were not being sent to Spain. However, on deeper analysis the statement was not in line with US policies. Washington favoured a stable government in Spain. James Byrnes vehemently opposed embargoes on oil and petrol, as this would create political and economic chaos. Nor did the US accept Bidault's attack on Spain.

Bidault argued that all the allied powers had demonstrated at Yalta and Potsdam that Spain was a threat to international security by banning her from the UN. He claimed that Article 2, Paragraph 7 of the UN Charter applied to Spain and thus made the problem one which concerned the UN. Furthermore, he maintained that a prolonged totalitarian regime in Spain could threaten the maintenance of peace and international security in the future by her continuous colonial ambitions. Seemingly, France had tried to strengthen her opposition to Spain but, by signing the tripartite statement, the Quai d'Orsay had proven that for the time being, France was willing to follow an Anglo-American policy in order to avoid confrontation with the two allies over Spain. Despite making waves, France did not want to rock the boat for fear of falling out.

The US administration in general and the Secretary of State in particular were unmoved by this new French argument. The threat of more serious border conflicts was dismissed by the American Joint Intelligence Committee, which argued that in the Spanish army "as a whole, small arms and light artillery pieces are of good quality, well maintained and in sufficient numbers. . . . The Army would . . . give a good account of itself in a defensive role." The Committee claimed that there had been no aggression by the Spanish side and the border skirmishes had been caused by French revolutionaries. As a result, the Spanish army was acting purely defensively.[11] Byrnes warned the French authorities through the US Ambassador in Paris that his country would not support France in the Security Council. Washington had been willing to follow a mutual policy towards Spain with France and Britain, even if this required a public condemnation of the Franco regime. However, Byrnes was unwilling to go any further. Thus Western foreign policy would publicly condemn the Spanish dictatorship but without having any lasting effect on the totalitarian government.

The British realized soon after the Joint Statement that their fears voiced before 4 March had been justified. The ground on which the three Western nations had made their stand was weak and after the declaration exiled Communists in France increased their attacks across the Spanish border. Britain accused France of scarcely having been able to choose "a worse wicket on which to bat". Additionally, Westminster argued that sanctions against Spain could not be enforced without Portuguese and Argentinean cooperation. As a result Britain would only withdraw her Ambassador if this brought about a solution. Clearly London was unwilling to follow the French proposal, arguing that pressure on Spain would only strengthen Franco or result in chaos.

In response to a note by the British Ambassador in Washington, outlining this point of view, the American State Department expressed its agreement and claimed that a solution in Spain had to be found in talks between the three Western nations. Given the weakness of the tripartite statement, this meant a continuation of Anglo-American policy, with France following incredulously.

The implementation of the British and American policy had been aided by Winston Churchill. On 5 March 1946, Churchill spoke in Fulton, a little town 20 miles north of Jefferson City in the rolling farmland of Missouri. In his famous speech, Churchill claimed that:

> From Stettin in the Baltic to Trieste in the Adriatic, an iron curtain has descended across the Continent. Behind that line lie all capitals of the ancient states of Central and Eastern Europe. . . . All these famous cities and the populations around them lie in what I must call the Soviet sphere, and all are subject in one form or another, not only to Soviet influence but to a very high and, in many cases, increasing measure of control from Moscow.

Churchill believed that what was needed was a "cordon sanitaire", a union of the Western democracies, against the USSR. He upheld that the US and Britain should give less importance to their own international ambitions and make a united stance against the USSR. For Spain this meant that Britain and the US should enforce a joint policy. By implication, if France wanted to join this policy and stay within the Western Alliance, she had to abandon her present stance. Public opinion and most of the American press, however, strongly opposed Churchill's *Weltanschauung*, sketching him as a warmonger, poisoning the difficult relations between the West and Russia. The journalist Walter Lippman portrayed the speech as an "almost catastrophic blunder". However, what Churchill spelled out in public was already common knowledge behind the scenes. Despite attempts by Truman to limit the diplomatic blunder, the strained East–West relations could be seen in Turkey, where the US was forced to support the Turkish government against Soviet diplomatic pressure by moving the US Navy battleship *Missouri* to Istanbul.

Away from the public, Britain and the US, worrying about the Mediterranean, held military conversations about the vulnerability of allied shipping and the impact of the fall of Gibraltar to the USSR. Concern over the Soviet Union meant that if France wanted to join a common foreign policy, she had to do so on their terms. This included Allied policies towards Spain. After some reluctance, even after the tripartite statement, the Quai d'Orsay finally conceded and slowly started reversing her attitude to Spain as far as this was possible.

It is unclear whether this was the result of America's inflexible position towards Spain or simply a realization by the Quai d'Orsay that the international climate favoured the Anglo-American position. It was becoming obvious that the international climate had made a bipolar world a reality. France, being between Scylla and Charybdis, had to choose either closer alliance with the Anglo-American bloc or a precarious international independence. The former would limit French foreign policy and result in clashes between public opinion and governmental policies. Alternatively, France could have moved away from a common Western policy. In doing so, the French government would have faced even more Communist threats.

In a volte-face, Bidault now wanted to avoid the Spanish problem coming before the Security Council. The Soviet Ambassador to France, Alexander Efremovich Bogomolov, however, continued to pressure the French foreign policy makers. Bidault turned to the US asking for suggestions on how to avoid this embarrassing situation. To achieve a cohesion of policies towards Spain, France was suggesting a closer coordination of diplomatic representations. Implicitly this meant that the Quai d'Orsay would from now on follow policies made in London and Washington. The diplomatic stage was set and the Spanish problem became a classic East–West conflict.

NOTES

1. FRUS, 1945, V, pp. 667–8.
2. *Public Papers of the Presidents of the USA: Truman*, 1945, Doc. 107.
3. NA, Civil Branch, NSC 72, Background Information, 19 April 1945, JCS "Study on United States Security and Strategic Interests in Spain".
4. NA, Military Branch, CCS 092, US Joint Chiefs of Staff, Spain (4–19–46), Sec. 1–8, 15 March 1946, Possible Developments, JIC Memo 242.
5. Whitaker, *Spain and the Defense of the West*, p. 122.
6. Fernández, *Tensiones Militares*, p. 69.
7. *APWSU*, I, p. 2/5/26.
8. *APWSU*, II, p. 17.
9. PRO, FO371, 60375, 15 February 1946, Sir V. Mallet to Mr Bevin.
10. *Decade of American Foreign Policy: Basic Documents 1941–1945*, Doc. 182.
11. NA, CCS 092, US Joint Chiefs of Staff, Spain (4–19–46), Sec. 1–8, Memo 209.

2 The UN Barks

Despite the outcry of the press, Churchill's speech reflected the point of view of many policy makers in Washington, including Averell Harriman, former ambassador in Moscow, Secretary of State Dean Acheson and Secretary of the Navy James Forrestal. Two weeks earlier George Kennan, the US Chargé-d'affaires in Moscow, sent a 8000-word message outlining Russia's *Weltanschauung*. This "long telegram", as it became known, argued that the international doctrine of Communism made a permanent peaceful coexistence between Communist and capitalist states impossible. Kennan claimed that the current Soviet regime was "only the last of a long session of cruel and wasteful Russian rulers who had relentlessly forced their country on to ever new heights of military power in order to guarantee external security for their internally weak regimes". The Chargé also claimed that Moscow was sensitive to logic and could be expected to back off if faced with strength.

The implications were clear. If the US wanted to avoid a military conflict in the near future with the Soviet bloc, she had to portray enough strength to discourage Moscow from exploiting her weaknesses. However, the press kept hammering away at the White House and the State Department for their position towards the Soviet Union. The public was not yet ready to see Russia, the ally against Nazi Germany, as an enemy in a new struggle.

While Washington was deciding on its future global foreign policy, interest groups such as the military were able to exploit the situation. This was the first post-war situation where the US military considered giving covert aid, out of the glare of publicity, to a country whose regime was objectionable to the US. For Spain in particular this meant that help was given as long as publicity could be avoided. As a result secret information was released to Spain via the US Embassy in Madrid, covering military information on types, production, and the current development stages of radar systems, including exact technical specifications.[1] In return the Defense and State Departments hoped for better military and trade relations.

While this clandestine *rapprochement* towards Spain was going on, worldwide public opinion was moving further against Franco. Canada publicly rebuffed Spain's attempt to establish diplomatic relations. During spring 1946, six Communist, four Latin American, three Commonwealth and four other states severed diplomatic relations with Spain. There was also speculation that Italy, a country with relatively cordial relations to Spain, might follow. The foreign opposition, the international atmosphere of hostility and the resulting economic isolation of Spain had their effect, and revolts against the Franco government reappeared. Workers went on strike in several cities. The strongest opposition was in Asturias, and Republican flags appeared on buildings in Gijón and Oviedo. Even some senior officers in the army, who had originally supported Franco's rule, drifted away from the dictator. General Aranda visited foreign representatives and sought political asylum in the US Embassy in Madrid. He planned to set up a new provisional government, but lacked the support of the legitimate heir to the Spanish throne, Don Juan, and the government in exile. In the end his efforts came to nothing and the ill-prepared attempt resulted in his arrest. Franco remained stubborn. His ruthless victory in the Civil War guaranteed control over the country. Internal opposition alone was not sufficient to oust Franco from power. If foreign governments wanted to get rid of him, they would have to apply stronger measures.

The first move after the tripartite statement came from the Communist states. After some encouragement from the USSR, in April 1946, Poland pleaded to the UN Security Council to include the Spanish problem in the UN agenda. One week later Poland called for an end to diplomatic relations. The Secretary-General of the UN, Trygve Lie, expressed his support for the exclusion of Spain from the UN and hoped that a change of government in Spain would bring about liberty and democracy.

After the Polish request, the Spanish problem came before the Security Council. Working for the US delegation to the UN, Alger Hiss, who became famous during the McCarthy era when convicted for perjury, drafted a paper on US policy for the UN. This was channelled through the Secretary of State to Edward Stettinius, former Secretary of State, now representing the US in the UN. In this paper, Alger Hiss claimed that it would not damage the US if the problem came before the Security Council, and hence there was no need to prevent it. Even though he strongly opposed sanctions, changes to diplomatic practices and any other serious measures, he admitted that the US would have to support any recommendation by the Council. This was a risk that the US delegates were unwilling to take.

Britain's view on this was similar to that of the US and, arguably, even more supportive of the Spanish position. Sir Alexander Cadogan, the British representative at the UN, reasoned that the Polish proposal should not come before the Security Council because Article 2, Paragraph 7 of the UN Charter specified internal affairs as being outside the UN influence and Articles 34 and 35, allowing UN action to secure peace and security, did not apply to Spain because she lacked global significance. Oscar Lange, the Polish delegate, alleged that Spain posed a threat to world peace because of her 600 000 soldiers, an independent nuclear project and a large war material industry. Lange also accused Spain of harbouring 2200 German scientists and Gestapo employees. These accusations would have led, under Article 34, to condemnation and punishment, and under Articles 35 and 41, to the termination of diplomatic relations.

Unconvinced, Sir Alexander argued that all these accusations were based on unfounded claims. It was true that Spain was uncooperative in the repatriation of Nazis. Madrid also had tried to delay the confiscation of German state property in Spain. However, these were minor complications and were a far way off the Polish accusations. In April a UN resolution finally authorized the formation of a subcommittee on Spanish affairs, following a prolonged campaign by Edward Stettinius. Despite instigating and strongly supporting the idea, the US excluded herself on the grounds that other nations had closer links with Spain. By doing so, Washington avoided embarrassing France, keeping her policy options towards Franco open, and escaped the necessity of making her policy public.

The Subcommittee was formed by 18 delegates, representing Communist as well as Democratic states, and had an Anglo-American proposal as a starting point for the discussion. Its mission was to investigate whether the Spanish problem was a domestic one, and thus outside the interest of the UN, or an international one, which threatened to cause military conflict. The discussion in the Subcommittee largely turned around two problems. Oscar Lange had condemned Spain under Article 34 of Chapter VI. However, this chapter of the UN Charter merely allowed recommendations. The Polish delegation tried, however, to enforce measures allowed under Chapter VII. Sir Alexander Cadogan went to some length to point out that in order to enforce diplomatic measures against Spain, she had to violate Chapter VII and not simply Chapter VI. The second problem concerned Spain's position *vis-à-vis* international peace. The Communist states claimed that the UN had an obligation to intervene. Western nations strongly opposed this. Colonel Hudgson, representing Australia, summarized the difficulties of the discussions: "The line between what is of international concern and what is of domestic concern is not fixed, it is mutable."

In the end, the Subcommittee's findings resulted in the Spanish problem being covered under Chapter VI, thus any diplomatic measures were from the outset limited to recommendation. It was also decided that Franco's government was not at the moment posing a threat to peace, yet it was a situation "likely to endanger the maintenance of international peace and security" in the future. Thus the Security Council was advised to recommend procedures or methods to improve the situation as under Article 36. The Subcommittee also suggested that the UN should condemn Spain and recommend ending diplomatic relations. The report was put on the Security Council agenda for 6 June 1946.

In the meantime, and in order to prevent further international pressure, Franco moved further away from the fascist state. The press, radio and theatre were placed under the Education Minister and no longer under the Falange. The fascist greeting, together with the party uniforms and decorations, were abolished. Franco also became more cooperative concerning the repatriation of Germans and the confiscation of German property in Spain. At the same time a series of strange rumours were started by Spanish diplomats about a possible Spanish–Soviet cooperation. The Spanish Foreign Minister, Martín Artajo, informed Bonsal, the US Chargé in Madrid, that the USSR was trying to improve relations with Spain. The US Air Force Intelligence reported that "Franco could be flirting with Russians" and the Secret Service reported that a Persian official had visited Barcelona to arrange a Soviet–Spanish friendship and non-aggression treaty. Allegedly, Perón was approaching the Russian Embassy in Buenos Aires to resume cordial relations with the USSR and to act as a mediator between Madrid and Moscow. Others also claimed that Admiral Moreno had left Spain for Argentina to investigate Spanish–Soviet relations. All these rumours remained unsupported by any facts or further developments.[2] Nevertheless, they caused a certain amount of uncertainty in Washington and London, where lessons of Machiavellian diplomacy were not forgotten so soon after the Second World War.

In Britain, the Foreign Office feared that Moscow might recognize Franco to strengthen commercial links with Spain. In an internal memo this concern was outlined: "we might in fact suddenly be faced with a hostile Spanish Government in close contact with Moscow" and "many of Franco's supporters in the Falangist party would at a pinch be ready to accept such a volte-face".[3] The British Chargé in Moscow, Sir Frank Roberts, rejected such an absurd possibility out of hand and a lecture by a Soviet general on "The Campaign to Liquidate the Fascist Regime in Spain" supported this view. Yet the rumours had created unease in the West. In order not to be sidelined in the unlikely event of an Hispano-Soviet *rapprochement*, the West was determined to show more support for Franco.

The Spanish authorities argued that Spain was of no concern to the UN because as a non-member state she was outside UN jurisdiction. The Spanish press claimed that the Subcommittee had been stacked heavily against Spain. Brazil was in fact the only nation on the Committee with diplomatic relations at ambassadorial level. The Spanish Foreign Minister claimed that international pressure made political evolution in Spain impossible because it had as its corollary bombings and shootings in Madrid and guerrilla struggle along the Spanish border with France. He implied that the government had to concentrate its efforts on such events, and accordingly made any serious attempts to liberalize the regime impossible.

In the meantime some Labour MPs in Britain came down heavily against Spain. Ian Noel-Baker and Leah Manning argued that ending diplomatic relations and economic sanctions would remove the current Spanish government and thus prevent a further rift between the two countries. The proposed radical break of all relations would have inevitably hurt the economy and forced unpredictable changes in Spain. London was unwilling to risk these changes and continued believing that a rupture of diplomatic relations would do more harm than good. Churchill remarked from the floor of the House of Commons that: "It will affront Spanish national pride to such an extent that there will be a general rallying of Spaniards to the government of their country and to its sovereign independence". Another Conservative, Sir Hartley Shawcross, argued that ending commercial and diplomatic relations would lead to starvation and possible civil war in Spain, as well as economic loss for Britain. Echoing Churchill, he claimed that "nothing has done more to maintain Franco in power than the fear of foreign intervention in one way or another, the threat of starvation and the danger of civil strife".

Washington too was unhappy about the way discussions had developed in the UN. In its final report the Subcommittee recommended to the General Assembly ending diplomatic relations with Spain. The US representative at the UN proposed an amendment modifying this recommendation. However the USSR vetoed the US modification and the report went unmodified to the First Committee. The Soviet Union felt uneasy about the Spanish problem going into the General Assembly because as long as it had been discussed in the Security Council, the USSR could use its veto. Once in the General Assembly this was no longer possible. Andrei Gromyko, the USSR delegate, had used his veto three times alone on 24 June 1946 merely to keep the Spanish issue in the Security Council. In the General Assembly, Moscow was forced to use more subtle methods, but could count on the support of other Communist members.

Poland continued demanding that each member of the UN should terminate diplomatic relations with Spain. Furthermore, Lange wanted to bar the fascist regime from membership in any organ or agency related to the UN. Belorussia wanted to go even further and suggested a suspension of communication by rail, sea, air, post and telegraph. Britain called the Belorussian position unrealistic and argued that economic sanctions would kindle the flames of a new civil war. Naturally London would welcome democratic elections in Spain. Nevertheless a number of policy makers, including the British ambassador in Madrid, publicly stated that in their view international pressure had actually decreased the possible success of a government composed by the democratic parties in exile.

It was clear that the UN was split over the Spanish question. The authorities in Madrid shrewdly tried to use this to their own advantage. Artajo told the British Ambassador to Spain, Sir Victor Mallet, that if the Belorussian proposal was passed, Spain would resist to the end, "and if there was no petrol Spaniards would ride on mules".[4]

An Anglo-American counter-proposal to the Polish plan was put forward. It only asked for Spain's exclusion from the UN. The two nations hoped that "Franco [would] surrender the powers of government to a provisional government". Other countries, including Canada, India, the Netherlands, Sweden and Denmark, favoured this alternative. Iceland maintained that economic sanctions could not be enforced as those countries having to enforce them (mainly Argentina and Portugal) were unwilling to do so. El Salvador and Costa Rica argued that Spain's problem was an internal affair. Other Latin American nations – Guatemala, Uruguay and Venezuela – opposed this and pointed out that foreign intervention in Spain's internal affairs during the Civil War had set a precedent which had allowed Franco to establish his power. Therefore a renewed involvement in Spain's internal affairs to remove Franco was allowed. France went even further. Together with Belgium and Norway, Paris argued that the Spanish problem was no longer an internal affair because Franco had moved colonial troops from Morocco towards the French border. As a punishment, France asked for a resolution prohibiting the purchase of Spanish food exports as long as Spaniards were going hungry. During the past Spain had to sell more food than was advisable in order to pay for vital imports. France, buying only 12 million gold pesetas of foodstuffs compared to Britain's 250 million, was naturally more inclined towards enforcing economic sanctions.

As the discussions on the Spanish problem in the General Assembly dragged on, the US Joint Chiefs of Staff issued a report on 10 July 1946 which expressed a desire to obtain base rights for the Navy and the Air Force on Spanish soil. The armed services also wanted to make use of ground facilities on the Canary Islands and obtain landing rights throughout Spain. At first glance this was a strange desire, as it ran counter to overall US defence policy. After the Second World War, the military were dismantling tactical bases worldwide to reduce costs. Consequently, the State Department contested "that this Government [US] is not now in a position to institute negotiations for military rights with the Spanish Government nor does it appear likely that such negotiations can be undertaken within the predictable future".[5] The Department was fully aware of the diplomatic complications and negative impressions such negotiations would cause, especially while the UN was still discussing the Spanish question.

Commercial interests in the US also favoured a lenient approach towards Spain. Washington had to make up its mind between relaxing trade restrictions or getting rid of Franco once and for all. The longer Washington waited, the less interested the public became. Already certain politicians spoke out in favour of cordial relations with Spain. In October, Senator Tom Connally outlined his position towards Spain, before the Political and Security Committee. According to the Senator, the US should not oppose another public condemnation of Spain nor her exclusion from the UN. However, he was strongly opposed to the severance of diplomatic relations or economic sanctions, as these might cause a civil war. According to the Senator a civil struggle without international intervention, resulting in a renewed fascist victory, would have added to Franco's power, while a struggle with international support threatened to destabilize the whole of Europe.

For three days, the First Committee of the UN discussed the Polish and American proposals extensively as well as eight possible amendments. Finally it passed a new proposal to the Subcommittee. This proposal condemned Spain and excluded her from the UN and its agencies. It unequivocally proclaimed that Franco was in power due to the help of the Axis and had supported them during the war. As a consequence it recommended an immediate recall of all ambassadors and ministers and, in the near future, the Security Council was to take

such measures as deemed necessary to improve the situation. On 8
December, the Subcommittee agreed to this resolution with a vote of
11 to 5, with 2 abstentions. A small change in Part 2 of the Anglo-
American proposal was made, and it was recommended to "take indi-
vidually the same attitude they have taken collectively and refuse to
maintain diplomatic relations with the present Spanish regime". The
next day, 9 December, the Subcommittee's proposal returned to the
First Committee, which agreed upon a condemnation of the regime
(no dissension) and decided to bar Spain from UN agencies (vote 32–5
with 8 abstentions). The proposed diplomatic breach with Spain was
defeated (22–22 with 6 abstentions) and so was the French foodstuffs
proposal (10–32 with 6 abstentions). Instead a Belgian compromise,
which included barring Spain and condemning the Franco regime, was
struck (27–7–16) and was, according to UN regulations, put on the
agenda of the General Assembly.

Initially the US opposed the Belgian compromise and disagreed with
the right of the Security Council to take further action. Yet upon getting the news of the vote in the First Committee on the Belgian compromise, Alger Hiss, then Director of Special Political Affairs, phoned
two members of the US delegation, John C. Ross and Durward V.
Sandifer, informing them that he and Acheson had agreed to vote in
favour of the Belgian compromise. Hiss instructed the two delegates
not to push for an American amendment as this would have attracted
unnecessary publicity. US disagreement with possible future actions
by the Security Council was not to be expressed unless the resolution
was considered paragraph by paragraph. Furthermore, he instructed them
not to press for a vote by paragraphs, but to vote for the proposal in
its entirety. The next day the US delegation was specifically instructed
to vote in favour of the paragraph giving the Security Council the
right to take further action against Spain, even if a vote by paragraphs
took place. Spain hoped in vain that the US would vote against the
recommendation. Finally the Spanish problem was back on the agenda
 of the General Assembly. On 12 December 1946, the Belgian proposal, already passed in the Political and Security Committee, was ratified
by the UN as a whole (34–6 with 13 abstentions). No member of the
Security Council voted against the recommendation, and thus future
action by the Council members seemed likely.

As the vote was taken on the entire Belgian proposal rather then by
paragraphs, the Acting Secretary of State could inform the Chargé in
Spain that if a vote by paragraphs had taken place, the US would have
voted against possible measures in the future by the Security Council.

This was not true: the delegation had been instructed on 11 December not to vote against this paragraph in order to achieve unanimity in the Assembly. However, claiming that the US would have voted against it gave America more room for political manoeuvre. Should the Security Council decide to take severe action, America could veto it, saying that it had disagreed with this part of the recommendation from the very beginning but had voted in favour for the sake of unanimity. The text of the final resolution condemned the regime, excluded Spain from the UN and its agencies, branded her as fascist, and noted her aid to the Axis during the war. It threatened further measures by the Security Council and, most important of all, the resolution called for "immediate recall from Madrid of Ambassadors and Ministers plenipotentiary accredited there".

A good deal of propaganda surrounded this last point, as large parts of the public were under the false impression that recalling the ambassador was tantamount to ending diplomatic relations. This was far from the truth. An ambassador, representing his country's foreign policy, has the right to negotiate with the chief of state. In Spain ambassadors were to be replaced by Chargés-d'affaires as heads of missions. Any messages from the Chargé to the chief of state had to go through the foreign secretary. Thus withdrawal of ambassadors meant slower communication between the two countries. Apart from this, and the prestige value, relations continued unchanged. Diplomatic relations as such never ended. The US and Britain had recognized the Franco regime since 1939 and continued to do so after 1946.

Clearly the December resolution had little effect. Britain, El Salvador, The Netherlands, Italy and Liberia withdrew their ambassadors. Thirty other nations had no diplomatic relations anyway and 19 others, including the US, had no ambassador in Spain to begin with. Argentina, in defiance of the UN, even appointed an ambassador who claimed that "it is a glory to have relations with Spain". Barely two years later the Dominican Republic, Egypt, El Salvador, Paraguay and Peru resumed normal relations with Spain and she was able to sign a Treaty of Friendship with the Philippines in September 1947.

In Spain itself, the anti-Franco international feeling was dismissed by the state-controlled propaganda as a "consequence of the false climate created through the slanderous campaign of the expatriated reds and their like abroad". Concerning the UN argument that the current Spanish government was forced upon Spain, the Spanish Minister for Foreign Affairs claimed that "the Spanish people know that the regime implanted on 28 July 1936 [*sic*] was not imposed through violence". It is difficult to explain the three years after 18 July 1936 if one believes that the Franco regime was imposed without force.

In a conversation on 2 January between Artajo and Bonsal, the Spaniard argued that the UN resolution was a setback for Spain's evolution, including political concessions to the UK and the US. He claimed to favour evolution in Spain but disagreed with the way in which Spain was used by the West to get concessions out of the Communist states.

Artajo assured Sir Victor Mallet on his departure on 22 December 1946 that Spain would continue its liberal evolution. Franco himself explained Spain's unstable international position as a result of Communist agitators of the vote in the UN committee, in a speech on Plaza de Oriente:

> What is happening in the UN should not baffle Spaniards. When a wave of communist terror ravages through Europe, and the violence, crimes and persecutions of the same order as many of you have experienced or suffered, preside over the lives of twelve nations, then it should not baffle us that the children of Giral and la Pasionaria influenced in continuation by the newspapers of the time and, secured by the system of organized censorship, found tolerance in the medium and support by the official representatives of those wretched nations. However, it is one thing how some delegates express themselves, yet the sober aspiration of the nations is different.

At the cabinet meeting following the UN vote, Franco over-confidently proclaimed that the UN was fatally wounded. Despite the international developments throughout 1947, which showed considerable bias towards Spain, the resolution continued in place for several years and, naturally, so did the UN.

NOTES

1. WNRC, Army Intelligence, Project Decimal File, Spain, 1946, 7 June 1946.
2. WNRC, Records of the Army Staff, G-2 Intelligence, Spain, 11 June 1946.
3. PRO, FO371, 60441A, 4 July 1946, Hoyer Miller to various.
4. WPIS, 20 November 1946, No. 369.
5. NA, Military Branch, ABC Decimal Files relating to Spain (6–Nov–43), 5 August 1946, State–War–Navy Coordinating Committee.

3 Return to Spain

The British economic position had continued to deteriorate after the Second World War. Industrial production was roughly at the same level as in 1939, but unlike before the war, Britain now had a large trade deficit, mainly created through trade with the US. A dollar gap developed and, naturally, Britain was looking for trade outside the dollar area to avoid further widening of this gap. Within the British trade system, Spain was no exception. Britain's trade deficit with Spain had increased by £4.3 million. Under these conditions, and despite having withdrawn its ambassador from Spain, Britain was interested in a continuation of close commercial relations while enforcing military trade embargoes on Spain only loosely. Aircraft engines were being transported to Madrid for civilian or possibly military use. Britain was certainly not the only country to trade military equipment with Spain, and the constant threat that America, Sweden or Italy rather than Britain would gain lucrative military export contracts meant that no nation wanted to step up pressure on Spain.

Whitehall strongly opposed any enforcement of economic sanctions for fear of losing contracts to other nations. Britain also had to import potash fertilizers from Spain to cover 50 per cent of domestic needs. Almost 100 per cent of pyrite fertilizer imports came from Spain. At the same time sanctions on iron ore would have severely hit Britain's building and metal industry. While Spain could have sold these products to other European nations, Britain could not have imported them from elsewhere. Policy makers in London concluded that no sanctions could have been implemented against Spain without a serious blow to Britain's economy.

In order to facilitate the trade between the two countries, a trade agreement was signed on 28 March 1947. This gave a mutual trade credit to both countries over the next two years, with a ceiling of £2 million or the equivalent in pesetas. The exchange rate, £1 to 44 pesetas, greatly favoured Spain. Thus, despite the condemnation of Spain by the UN resolution and Britain's interest in re-establishing a monarchy in Spain, the two countries continued to have close commercial relations.

While Britain was hoping to re-establish a monarchy in Spain, some policy makers in the US briefly showed interest in a possible coup by

33

the army against Franco. The State Department was in contact with General Juan Beigbeder Attienza about the possible success of such a plan. It is likely that Beigbeder's hopes were supported by the realization within the Spanish Army that Spain was unable to produce heavy war material without external help, and would therefore be unable to defend herself for more than two to three weeks after a full-scale invasion by the USSR. Under these circumstances, several members of the armed forces felt that it was necessary to come to some arrangement with the West over the defence of Spain's territory.

Juan Beigbeder Atienza, an old associate of Franco who had helped secure the support of the Moroccans during the 1936 rising, and Tomás Peyre, a moderate Republican, went to see Bonsal, US Chargé in Spain, on 1 February 1947. The two Spaniards hoped to receive aid from the US during an uprising against Franco. General Beigbeder claimed that during the following days a coup had a chance to succeed, but he estimated that about half of the conspirators would be arrested in the period of preparation and underground work. Thus the conspirators would be weak and would need immediate support from London and Washington. From the very beginning the success of such an endeavour was questionable and the US would have been foolish to support the plan on such treacherous grounds.

Bonsal dispatched his opinion to the Secretary of State concerning the proposed coup. He made it clear that he did not favour a recognition of the new government before a successful removal of Franco. Only after a successful coup would the US recognize the new regime, resume full diplomatic relations, appoint an ambassador, grant economic aid and advocate her admission to the UN.

The reluctance to support a coup by the Embassy was due to military as well as economic reasons. The Embassy was informed, through several unofficial contacts with Spanish officers in the army, that the Spanish armed forces were already committed to the West in the event of war with the USSR. Hence, there was little incentive for the US to change its current policy. Furthermore, an unstable situation in Spain would have endangered commercial interests and might even have resulted in an increase of Communist influence. In early 1947 the Joint Intelligence Committee reconfirmed its recommendation made a year earlier, that the US would send aid to Spain if the economic situation deteriorated to such an extent as to cause another civil war which might endanger the stability of Italy and France. This was unacceptable to the US. Paradoxically, the worse Spain's economy performed, the more support Spaniards could expect from Washington. Just as in 1946, US interest in stability overruled any attempts to remove Franco.

Apart from the threat of civil war in Spain, other reasons favoured a more friendly approach. In February, due to lack of air-traffic control, a DC-4 crashed near Avila, killing all 11 passengers and crew on board. A permanent radio station at Barajas could have prevented the disaster, but Spain lacked the financial means to provide this. If civilian air travel in Spain was to be made safe, somebody would have to pay for the necessary installations. Furthermore, by improving Spain's civilian air transport, the US could make sure that military airfields in Spain would be available for military purposes if the need arose.

However, the US also had to take public opinion into consideration. In Washington, Salvador de Madariaga, an exiled Spanish diplomat, argued during a conversation with State Department officials that Franco was a public relations disaster for Spain as well as for the West. He claimed that Franco's image prohibited economic and military aid from being sent to Spain and made her integration into the Western defence system impossible. Madariaga claimed that embargoes on oil and cotton were in the interest of the West, because they would eventually force Franco to step down. Madariaga's argument, that Franco's regime prevented America from fully supporting Spain's economy and taking full advantage of her strategic position, was accepted by the State Department. However, overall Washington preferred the known evil of Franco to the unknown surprises a coup might bring.

Dean Acheson, then Acting Secretary of State, echoing Madariaga, asserted that the Communists were actually gaining from Franco's survival in two respects. Firstly, Franco's survival could cause such a strong opposition as to lead to a new civil war. Secondly, relations with Franco provided the USSR with propaganda material against the US. While this was true, there is no doubt that Russia would have preferred a coup, economic unrest or a new prolonged civil war which would prepare Spain for a Communist takeover.

In April 1947, Washington policy makers once more raised the question of how to react to a new conspiracy against Franco. Unwilling to put all its eggs in the same basket, the US urged London to develop a joint policy towards a possible new Spanish government emerging from a coup. The State Department proposed that after a coup, the West should establish friendly political and economic relations during the interim period and later grant political and economic aid. Washington was unwilling to support a new government without British support.

In the meantime, Franco rebuffed British interests in restoring the monarchy through Don Juan by granting himself the right to appoint a monarch for Spain through the Law of Succession. Article 1 of this law declared that "Spain as a political unit is a Catholic and social State which in accordance with its traditions becomes a kingdom". Article 3 dashed the hopes of many monarchists: the king must be "a person of royal blood, having been proposed by the Regency Council and the Government together and accepted by two-thirds of the Cortes".

The Regency Council included the Cardinal Primate, the Chief of the General Staff, the President of the Council, the President of the Institute of Spain and one counsellor from each of the chief vocational groups in the Cortes. Overall, it was clear that the power to appoint the king lay in Franco's hands. Almost immediately, Don Juan declared the Bill void because there had been no consultation with him, the legitimate heir to the throne, nor had there been conversations with the legislature, the Cortes. Others, like the Duke of Alba, Count Rodezno and Don Salvador de Madariaga, also argued against the Bill. Franco explained, in the newspaper *Arriba* on 29 April 1947, that the "Bill of Succession is not concerned with a restoration but with a new installation" of a monarchy. Put bluntly, Don Juan had lost his legitimate right to inherit the Spanish crown from his father. The Regency Council and the government would appoint the monarch and the Cortes would approve their choice. Franco made it clear that if Don Juan ever received the crown, he would get it through the grace of Franco and not through his father Alfonso XIII.

The Law of Succession had obvious advantages for Franco. In Spain it split the monarchists between those accepting and those rejecting the law, allowing Franco to play off one side against the other. Countries interested in Spain undoubtedly realized that Franco's Law of Succession had changed little, apart from strengthening the dictator's hand.

The law dashed British hopes of a restoration of the monarchy in the near future and made her even more reluctant to support a military coup. Under these circumstances it was not surprising that Britain informed the US that she was unwilling to follow a joint policy against Franco. While the UK was reluctant to risk its cordial relations with Spain, she nevertheless advised the US to go ahead.

Britain hoped for the establishment of a monarchy through Franco and argued that ending trade relations was disadvantageous for all. Pyrite imports was one example that was analysed. If pyrites could no longer be imported from Spain, steel production in Britain would decrease and more Swedish ore of a lower grade would have to be bought. This would mean more consumption of coal to melt the lower-grade ore.

Concerning a possible coup, Ernest Bevin considered the American proposal to be too dangerous, as leaks by the conspirators could seriously embarrass London and worsen strained relations with Franco. It seemed to him that the economy in Spain was improving and people were starting to accept the regime. Furthermore, the Foreign Minister claimed that the proposed policy would mean internal intervention in Spain's affairs and would give the USSR the opportunity to intervene in other parts of the world. Instead, Bevin wanted to avoid complications concerning Spain and join others in a common policy to prevent further action by the Security Council against Spain. For the time being he wanted to continue talks between Washington and London. Britain's refusal to join the US in a common policy against Franco ended Washington's interest in a provisional government replacing Franco. However, both nations agreed that Franco was a long-term threat causing economic hardship which might eventually lead to civil unrest. After their discussion both Britain and America agreed that no action against Franco should be taken for the time being. Nor were the two countries to issue a public statement against international action, as they feared that Franco would use such a statement for propaganda reasons, claiming that his regime had finally become acceptable.

Washington and London were to continue their old policies towards Spain and encourage Franco to make further liberal changes, without pressurizing him. In the meantime in Spain, the Law of Succession had been passed and was politically strengthened by a referendum on 6 July. The question posed to the Spanish people was: "Do you ratify the law which makes Generalissimo Francisco Franco Chief of State of the Spanish Kingdom and establishes the machinery by which his successor will be chosen?" It gave the appearance that Spain had become a monarchy without a king and that Franco would soon choose a successor. Yet in no way did it obligate Franco. Again, Britain claimed illegitimacy of the Bill and the referendum. Only Spaniards over 21 years of age, non-convicts and those not held by the tribunals were allowed to vote. Thus, London estimated, 2 million Spaniards lost their political rights.

The official results of the referendum claimed that 92.9 per cent of the votes cast were affirmative. No physical threat was needed at the referendum, because identification had to be produced in order to vote; this being enough to deter most opposition. It is very likely that the real turnout, claimed to be over 90 per cent, was exaggerated. Above all in the cities, people did refrain from voting. An estimate of only 40 per cent voted in the electoral region of Bilbao, 26 per cent in San Sebastian, 40 per cent in Navarra and 27 per cent in La Coruña. Strong evidence also suggests that Burgos had returned the voting forms, signed, but with the results blank, so they could be filled in later, two days before the actual referendum.

Despite all this, the referendum had undoubtedly further weakened the position of Don Juan and his supporters. Franco was confident enough to ask the US for cooperation. Spain wanted military ties with the West under an "anti-Communist" headline. In an interview, Franco told C. L. Salzberger from the *New York Times* that he wanted to be part of an anti-Communist alliance and enter direct and bilateral agreements with Western nations. So far, Washington had done little to discourage closer relations between the two countries. After the 1946 UN resolution, the US did not appoint an ambassador to Spain, but cordial relations continued. Early in 1947, Paul T. Culbertson was appointed Chargé-d'affaires, replacing Bonsal. Culbertson was a lawyer from Pennsylvania and had been an official in the State Department since 1924. He had served as Chief of Western Europe Division of the State Department from 1944 to 1947. This post was only one step below the Assistant Secretary of State and he had good reason to expect a post as ambassador somewhere. However, at the time, the Chargé-d'affaires in Spain was also the head of mission. The post undoubtedly required diplomatic finesse, which could be found in Culbertson. Over the coming years he had to combine the different American interests in Spain into a coherent policy towards Franco's government, without attracting criticism from other nations.

While the State Department was formulating its policy towards Franco, the Joint Chiefs of Staff became more interested in the country. The Joint Strategic Survey Committee informed the Chiefs that Spain was the twelfth most important nation to receive aid because of her significance to US national security. The report read: "Italy and Spain are of primary importance in connection with control of the Mediterranean sea lanes, shortest route to the oil and processing facilities of the Middle East" and "assistance should be given if possible". The report also stressed the military importance of Spain's geographical position thus: "the United States desires base rights, considered essential to her security from Portugal, Ecuador, France and Spain. Of these, base rights from Portugal and Spain are the most essential."[1] At the same time, it was obvious to the Joint Strategic Survey Committee that military assistance to the present Spanish government opposed current US policy. Despite this the report deemed it desirable to initiate or prepare programmes for US military assistance to Mediterranean countries, including Spain. These programmes were to cover military supplies, equipment and technical advice, above all tactical air-force and limited naval equipment. Naturally, air-force and navy interests were going to be the driving force behind a *rapprochement* with Spain.

More important than the military perception of Spain were policy changes by the US administration. Clearly the relations between East and West deteriorated. In 1946 the Greek Civil War was resumed and the Soviet Union caused problems in Persia and Turkey. Furthermore, political opposition was removed, sometimes ruthlessly, by the Communists in Eastern Europe. Meetings by the foreign ministers of the war allies during 1946–47 ended without an improvement of relations. In 1947 the situation deteriorated further and conflicts between East and West became more and more frequent. Europe's economic stability was also called into question.

Britain's financial position was deteriorating rapidly. In 1946/47 Europe experienced one of the worst winters on record. Winter wheat was destroyed by the cold in France. Prague's electricity was disconnected for three hours every day. Ice caused the closure of the Kiel Canal in Germany. Britain, however, suffered more than any other country in Europe from the weather. Snowdrifts blocked roads and railways. Schools and factories had to close down. *The Times* warned that the cold threatened the coal supply, and London offices were being lit by candles to save electricity. The economic knock-on effect meant that Britain had to cut back on her armed forces and overseas commitments. On 21 February 1947 the British Ambassador, Lord Inverchapel, delivered a "blue paper" to the State Department. This paper made it clear that Britain was no longer in a position to provide military and economic support to Greece and Turkey. It was estimated that 40 000 troops would be pulled out of Greece and economic aid would cease by 31 March. Lincoln MacVeagh, the American Ambassador in Athens and later in Madrid, had for some time warned the State Department that Britain was pulling out troops from Greece. Fearing that the Communists would take advantage of this situation, he dispatched a note on 12 February urging the consideration of American aid to Greece. In the autumn of 1946, Truman had expressed his commitment to Greece through his ambassador and had promised economic aid to maintain democracy and the independence of the Greek government.

The situation in Turkey was almost as desperate. Three days after the "blue paper" had been received, Truman met with Marshall and Acheson and decided to come to Greece's rescue as early as possible. However, the global situation called for more than a simple aid bill. The US had to make a serious long-term commitment to Europe if she did not want to see herself sidelined by Russia. It was time for a new American doctrine concerning foreign policy. During a cabinet meeting on 7 March the level of commitment was discussed, and as a result a new foreign policy came about.

The Truman Doctrine, proclaimed on 12 March 1947 in a special message on Greece and Turkey in the House Chamber before a joint session of Congress, called for containment of the socialist and Communist advance and guaranteed American financial and economic aid to all countries which were threatened by Communist external powers or internal minorities. Truman, dressed in a dark suit and reading from an open notebook, asked Congress for $250 million for Greece (59 per cent military aid) and $150 million for Turkey (100 per cent military aid). Congress was initially to approve a total of $500 million in aid for Truman's containment policy. Then the President concluded: "If we falter in our leadership, we may endanger the peace of the world, and we shall surely endanger the welfare of this nation."[2]

On 22 April 1947 the Senate approved the aid to Turkey and Greece and on 9 May the House followed. The Truman Doctrine was to guide American foreign policy for over 20 years and is of paramount importance when looking at twentieth-century US foreign policy. On 5 June 1947, the brainchild of George F. Kennan, Senator Hoyt S. Vandenberg, John F. Dulles and George C. Marshall was born. The Marshall Plan was the practical result of the Truman Doctrine.

This radical change of US foreign policy meant that Washington now sought an acceptable compromise with Franco. The Truman Doctrine provided enough support for this new approach. Again, the State Department tried to move Britain towards a common policy on Spain and argued that the Truman Doctrine "would indicate that we are prepared to shift our policy in regard to Franco and support any non-communist regime in Spain, including his own". However, predicaments remained at all levels. The State Department advised the service attachés in Spain not to request audiences, nor to receive decorations from Spain, as this might have been exploited by the totalitarian regime for propaganda purposes.

The Truman Doctrine was welcomed above all by the military planners. After its proclamation, the military were confident enough to push for a new policy towards Spain. In August 1947, the Joint War Plans Committee (JWPC) issued a study entitled "The Soviet Threat against the Iberian Peninsula and the Means Required to Meet It", or simply, "Drumbeat".

The report noted that ten days after the beginning of aggression in

Spain, the invaders would reach a line from Avila to Valencia. It was expected that heavy fighting would be going on around Madrid and that within 45 days the Soviets would have conquered all of Spain apart from the area south of Lisbon and Cartagena. This meant that the USSR would have closed the Allied lines of communication along the Mediterranean and denied an Allied foothold in Europe.

In order to defend Spain, the study recommended granting economic aid to improve her infrastructure and military strength, target the enemy's lines of communication, defend the Pyrenees with a total of 34 divisions and finally defend the southern tip of the Peninsula.

Politically, it was not expected that Spain would join the USSR but in case of Spain's neutrality, the study proposed to assemble forces in Spanish Morocco, French Morocco, the Azores, the UK and, if deemed necessary, in Spain herself. Obviously this might have led to conflict with the Spanish authorities. The report concluded that from the military point of view, the US should furnish economic aid to Spain to strengthen her capacity for military resistance and, implicitly, to secure her cooperation in the event of war.

In a meeting of the State Department, on 7 August 1947, it was argued that early economic and military aid to Spain would hold the USSR for an extra three to four days at the Pyrenees and allow enough time to rush help to Spain. It was becoming clear that political problems linked with this aid no longer outweighed the military advantages. Surprisingly, in a State Department meeting it was asserted that the UN resolution, which was barely a year old, was no obstacle to this new policy.

Two weeks later the JWPC issued "Guidance for Mobilization Planning as Affected by Loss of the Mediterranean Line of Communications". In this study Spain was considered valuable for several reasons. Above all her geographic position meant that she was a valuable asset for strategic air operations. On the other hand, if Spain was conquered by the Soviet Union, the whole of North Africa was open to Soviet war plans. By successfully defending Spain, the US would retain the flanks, tie down Soviet troops and increase its military options. Finally, Spain would provide a useful base from which to aid European guerrillas.

The JWPC asserted that if Spain fell and troops had already been committed to the Middle East, a disastrous situation would arise as contact with these troops could be lost. To prevent this, forces were to be deployed in Spain during the conflict. The report recommended that after three months of hostilities, seven Infantry Divisions should be stationed in Spain.[3]

Another governmental study in October on the Mediterranean stressed that the US policy was to "encourage Spain's anti-Communist attitude by all practicable means including her induction to the family of Western powers".[4]

In Spain, the Franco government did not yet realize the full magnitude of this new attitude by the US military planners. However, the change of policy by the US towards Greece and Turkey meant that the Mediterranean was gaining in importance. In a conversation in October, José Erice, Director of Foreign Policy of the Spanish Foreign Office, told Culbertson that in the event of conflict Spain would join the West against the USSR. The Spaniard estimated that without American intervention, the Soviet Union could overrun Western Europe, including Spain, within three months. He continued, saying that his country could help little as it lacked a modern army or air force. Without serious aid, the US could not make full use of Spain as a base. Erice had made Spain's willingness to cooperate with the US clear and the implications were obvious. If the West wanted to use Spain's potential as a military base, aid to improve military facilities had to be granted without delay. The US decided to alter its policy towards Spain. This shift was expressed in PPS/12 by the Policy Planning Staff (PPS) on 24 October 1947. PPS/12 was laying the foundation for the very similar NSC 3 decision taken in December. The PPS assessed that American policy so far had been a political and military failure. In the economic sphere Washington had withheld assistance, governmental credits and had held purchase of Spanish goods to a minimum. This had worsened Spanish–American trade relations and Spain's economic situation. The PPS now believed that Franco would not depart peacefully and the army had shown no serious signs of wanting to topple his regime. The only opposition to the Caudillo was political, and even these forces were fundamentally and irreconcilably split between Republicans, socialists and Monarchists. Concerning the United Nations, the US delegates were instructed to minimize the discussions on Spain. The delegates were to vote against economic sanctions, diplomatic rupture or other proposals conceivably hurting Spain. The study concluded that the net result of the American policy so far had been to strengthen Franco, to impede Spanish economic recovery and to be forced to operate in an unfriendly atmosphere in Spain in case of international conflict. Thus, the PPS wrote: "the Staff believes that, in the National interest, the time has come for a modification of our policy towards Spain". The report continued, asserting that "it is the recommendation of the Policy Planning Staff that instead of openly opposing the Franco regime, we should work from now on toward a normalization of US–Spanish relations, both political and economic".

It was recommended to quietly end various commercial controls and drop restrictions on private trade. Furthermore, it was advocated that Spain's industrial and commercial resources had to be developed urgently. Yet the report surreptitiously pretended that this normalization was not going to strengthen Franco's regime in Spain. Needless to say, any normalization or improvement of relations between Spain and the US would strengthen Franco's grip on power. Concerns about Franco's position were merely an afterthought of the PPS. Normalization was to go ahead, no matter what the impact on Spain was.[5]

Other parts of the State Department generally disagreed because of political implications. Robert A. Lovett, then Acting Secretary of State, claimed that normalization with Spain was still not fully possible due to Franco. He argued that the State Department would still prefer an evolutionary change in Spain to either stagnation or a threat of civil war. Lovett's justification was strengthened by strategic information on Spain. It was obvious that Spain's army was unable to defend her against the USSR. Another report argued that a coalition war between Spain and the US was very unlikely, as certain characteristics in Spain were missing, and it was assumed that Franco would only fight if his position was hopeless, otherwise he would attempt to remain neutral.

Political considerations and a new military study temporarily reversed a desire for close military relations with Spain. On 8 November 1947, the Joint Strategic Plans Group issued the "Broiler" report which looked at a possible conflict with the USSR in the near future. It read: "outweighing all other considerations would be the Soviet desire to concentrate on the seizure and neutralization of the United Kingdom and the seizure or neutralization of the Cairo–Suez area. Hence, at this time it seems improbable that the Soviets would risk the expenditure of men and material against the Iberian Peninsula."[6]

In this new report, it was estimated that an attack on Spain would start 30 days later than had been expected previously. This would decrease the necessity of granting economic aid to Spain. The report also said that "should the Soviets elect to seize Spain, the magnitude of the US forces required to hold Spain . . . is far beyond US capabilities to supply. Hence, the possible loss of Spain must be accepted as a calculated risk." As American resources could not be sent to Spain once an armed conflict had broken out in Europe, economic aid given before a war became all the more important. Similar to the "Drumbeat" study, "Broiler" argued that in order to deter a Soviet invasion of Spain, the US would have to give Spain as much economic aid as early as possible. This was in fact a confirmation of option one outlined in "Drumbeat". The study did not envisage any military aid being sent to Spain.

"Broiler" considered several ways in which to get aid to Spain. Given Spain's position, one was for Franco to apply directly under the Marshall Plan for aid on the grounds that Communist guerrilla fighters and a possible Soviet invasion threatened his government. Nevertheless, political implications made this approach less than ideal, as the Marshall Plan for Europe was to be administered by the European nations themselves and some of them, above all France, were unlikely to welcome Spain with open arms.

Britain, considering her own commercial benefit from American aid for Spain, argued diametrically. The British Foreign Minister, Bevin, strongly disagreed with American hesitation to extend economic aid to Spain, and through the US Ambassador in London, Douglass, he informed Washington of his scepticism. He argued that a voluntary resignation by Franco was impossible and, given his refusal to resign, any exclusion of Spain from a recovery programme would lead to economic disaster in Spain, and thus threaten British and other European trade with Spain and therefore their recovery. According to this, Spain's exclusion from the Marshall Plan was undermining the very purpose of the Plan.

Unsurprisingly, the Spanish Foreign Office parroted this argument, stating on 15 November 1947 that Spain's exclusion

> subtracts from the American [Marshall] plan a vital piece which would make a conclusion of the pursued objectives difficult. It does not seem logical that the mentioned plan could have made omission of the surplus of exports of Spanish products and Industry which traditionally filled the necessities of the European continent. . . . For a task of urgent reconstruction of the devastated territories, such as the one to be realized within the next five years 1947–1951 in Europe, the general economic establishment of Spain with a production capacity which now only reaches reduced effective production, is an already prepared element which results absolutely essential.[7]

Despite the support from Britain, Madrid's hopes to receive $50 million for agriculture, $190 million to maintain basic industry, $211 million for transport and $600 million for imports was mere wishful thinking. As late as 4 January 1948, Artajo claimed that if the Great powers, as is expected, conserve the good political sense and effectively want to put into play all possible methods for the reconstruction of Europe, being benefited at the same time of an important market, they will soon give Spain facilities for her purchase of primary material and machinery, which will allow her to increase her production and contribute with her surplus to a re-establishment of equilibrium in Europe.[8]

It was true that Spain could aid other European economies in their recovery once she had received substantial aid, but so could most other European countries, and none of them carried the political baggage Spain did.

While the US was discussing new policies towards Spain, Britain contacted exiled Spanish politicians. A meeting between Bevin and Prieto took place in London on 23 September 1947. Prieto, a right-wing socialist, hoped to establish an alternative to Franco by creating a centre-right government in cooperation with Monarchists. However, very little of practical value emerged from this meeting, and any hopes of peacefully removing Franco disappeared.

The alternative was to force Franco into liberalizing his regime, and this had to be done through the UN. Five Latin American countries reminded the General Secretary that more than six months had passed since the December resolution and the Security Council still had not appointed an alternative regime or suggested any other way to deal with Franco. Poland went even further, and wanted the General Assembly to recommend concrete steps to remove Franco, all of which fell just short of direct intervention. Unsurprisingly, the Communist countries supported the Polish proposal. At the same time the USSR propaganda machine made Spain an issue, claiming that the US wanted bases on the Balearic and Canary Islands. The USSR asserted that this showed US imperialistic ambitions as well as Anglo-American pressure on small, defenceless states. The USSR was no longer seeking to overthrow the Spanish regime but preferred its current existence for propaganda reasons. The Communist bloc could comfortably point towards the improvement of relations between the West and Spain and claim that it proved Western imperialism. The USSR had ceded Spain to the Western sphere of influence in return for propaganda material. Discussions in the UN were well suited for these attacks on the West.

On 12 November 1947, the First Committee in the UN passed a recommendation to the General Assembly. In this recommendation seven Latin American countries, the US and six others opposed a reaffirmation of the December resolution. On 17 November 1947 a Compromise Application was accepted by 36 to 5 with 12 abstentions. It outlined the steps taken since 1946 and expressed confidence in the Security Council to take action towards Spain whenever appropriate.

This result posed a legal dilemma. As the recommendation did not reaffirm the 1946 resolution in its entirety, it became questionable whether the 1946 resolution was still in force. This gave more room for diplomatic manoeuvring. Iceland took advantage of this and promptly resumed full diplomatic relations with Spain.

As the year came to an end the relations between the US and Spain visibly improved. Spain was visited by numerous Republican representatives, including Karl E. Mundt (South Dakota), Lawrance M. Smith (Wisconsin) and Walter H. Judd (Minnesota). In the US administration, the PPS, headed by George F. Kennan, influenced the National Security Council in matters concerning Spain. Forrester recalls a conversation with Kennan over lunch, during which the latter said that US policy needed adjustment with respect to Spain and Japan. In the first instance, Kennan felt that the US should direct its representatives at the UN not to join in any further attempt to discredit the present government of Spain. He continued, claiming that the Mediterranean could not be considered without considering Spain and the question of transit through the Straits of Gibraltar.[9]

Kennan saw three geopolitical interests which the USSR might have had in Spain. Firstly, Spain flanked France and Italy, two countries on the verge of Communism. He feared that if Spain fell to a Communist revolution, all of Europe was threatened. Secondly, Spain was the key to North Africa. A defeat by Spain might precede closer arrangements with the Soviet bloc and hence threaten oil production in the Mediterranean and the Persian Gulf. Thirdly, Kennan saw Spain as the springboard to Latin America and to the American sphere of influence. Thus, for the American diplomat, the loss of Spain would pose a triple threat to US national security: a loss of control in Europe, a threat to vital raw materials and eventually a threat to America. He asserted that:

> Soviet policy has thus been a) to do all in its power to render impossible achievement of any permanent modus vivendi between Western powers and Franco . . . b) to utilize every possible channel for mobilizing Western opinion against Franco in the hopes that Western governments will have to yield to pressure and take strong action to bring about the downfall of the Franco regime.

He concluded that the UN policy had actually strengthened Franco. Under the circumstances, he wanted to integrate Spain into the Western community.

There is little doubt that by 1948 the Franco regime had a solid backing from potentially dangerous agitators. The army was supportive and the police and security forces were well taken care of. The internal opposition against Franco was ineffective and the exiled government of the Republic was disorganized. The ostracism, if it was aimed at the removal of Franco, had failed.

Now, the US made arrangements to start a new policy towards Spain. On 5 December 1947 "NSC 3 United States Policy Towards Spain", based on PPS/12, was issued. It argued that the net result of the present policy, governed by the UN resolution, had been to strengthen Franco, impede economic recovery and create an unfriendly atmosphere with Spain. NSC 3 confirmed that "it is the recommendation of the Policy Planning Staff that instead of openly opposing the Franco regime, we should work from now on toward a normalization of US–Spanish relations, both political and economic". There was, however, no public announcement of the new view as this would undoubtedly have led to Spanish propaganda and a public outcry in the US. However, the changes were genuine and significant: a relaxation of the US restrictive economic policy and an elimination of official restrictive measures. It was hoped that this would encourage private trade and financial assistance. From now on, Spain was to develop her resources and play a normal part in world trade. The US decided to oppose any UN resolutions against Spain and to approve any resolutions favouring Spain.[10]

Unsurprisingly, the Joint Chiefs of Staff expressed their agreement with the military aspects of NSC 3. After all, they had provided the foundation of this policy in their military studies conducted throughout 1947. However, the American Chargé in Spain, Culbertson, still believed that indirect pressure by the US and Britain could slowly liberalize the Franco regime. The bad economic situation, Culbertson advised, should be exploited through economic assistance to obtain modification and liberalization. Abrupt changes, on the other hand, would be counter-productive and might put him and the State Department in a difficult and untenable position in Spain. However, despite his foresight, the Chargé could not escape the extremely enigmatic situation, and ultimately his fears came true and his position was irreparably undermined.

NOTES

1. FRUS, 1947, I, p. 736.
2. McCullough, *Truman*, p. 548.
3. *APWSU*, 5, Guidance, pp. 27–39.
4. NA, P-2, The Mediterranean and the Near East, 1947.
5. NA, CCS 092, US Joint Chiefs of Staff; PPS; 12 FRUS, 1947, III, p. 1091.
6. *APWSU*, V, pp. 26–7.
7. Viñas, *Guerra, Dinero, Dictadura*, p. 266.
8. *Ibid.*, p. 269.
9. Mills, *Forrestal Diaries*, p. 328.
10. NA, NSC 3, December 1947.

4 Year of Change

The political situation of 1947 meant that the US armed services became more interested in Spain. The Navy in particular had two good reasons to hope for gains from closer relations. First, with a permanent base in Spain, costs could be reduced by cheaper repairs, refuelling and general maintenance near the theatre of operations. Secondly, the fact that naval forces in the Mediterranean were placed under an independent command, the Sixth Fleet, favoured having headquarters nearby. The Navy was to become the most ardent supporter of bases in Spain.

The Joint Strategic Plans Group took the decision to modify its earlier studies on 11 February 1948. The result consisted of a combination of the two previous studies "Broiler" and "Drumbeat". Two scenarios were analysed. View A assumed that due to logistical problems, the Red Army would not attack Spain. View B argued that Russia would invade the Iberian Peninsula.

The undertaking of this study implied that a Soviet invasion of Spain had once more become a real threat. This study, named "Bushwhacker", argued that the US would not be able to defend Europe before at least 1952 and thus, if Europe was faced with a Soviet invasion, the US would have to withdraw its troops to Britain. Scarce resources meant that the US was expected to be unable to send military aid to Spain in the event of a European conflict breaking out. This meant that any economic aid granted before such an attack would become even more important, as it would prepare Spain and possibly deter a Soviet invasion altogether.

Unsurprisingly, Kennan, co-creator of the Marshall Plan, wanted Spain to be part of this aid programme. The State Department expressed its partial agreement with Kennan's point of view and called for a normalization of relations towards Spain. As a result Spain was to be taken off the "E List", which meant that export controls on Spain were terminated and normal trade relations resumed. Furthermore, the State Department considered Spain's inclusion in the European Recovery Programme (ERP) possible as long as the 16 European countries which administered the fund agreed. However, it was clear to the State Department that close and cordial relations had to wait for further democratization in Spain and a cooling down of US and Western European

49

public opinion against the Franco regime. Until then, direct governmental grants could not be considered.

On 2 February 1948, Culbertson had a meeting with Artajo and Erice
concerning an article published in the newspaper *Arriba* claiming that
the West had finally recognized its error in relation to the vote in the
UN. The Chargé maintained that such propaganda did not help to improve relations. He continued to stress the State Department's argument that governmental credits would only follow an evolution by
Franco's regime towards democracy. With regard to the ERP, Spain's
inclusion depended entirely on the other 16 nations which administered the funds. Naturally, their attitude was based on Spain's democratization process. Finally, Culbertson pointed out that future relations
between the two countries were still governed by the UN resolution.
Artajo contended that the *Arriba* article was only meant to help Spain
get into the Marshall Plan. Yet as the conversation continued, Culbertson
noticed that Erice and Artajo showed no sign of understanding Spain's
international image as a fascist police state where crimes against the
authorities were handled by harsh military tribunals. On the commercial side, Artajo explained that Spain had great difficulties in obtaining
international credits due to the persistent interference by the INI (Instituto
Nacional de Industria) in private enterprise, creating an undesirable air
of insecurity. Artajo stated that if Spain evolved too soon and introduced democracy too early, serious unrest would break out.[1]

Despite these differences between the Chargé and Artajo, there had
been a transparent change of the American position. Instead of trying
to remove Franco through force, governmental grants were promised
for an evolution towards democracy. However, instead of making these
changes, Spain tried to get into the ERP with the help of the US. If
this were to have become known, the nations within the Programme
would have naturally voiced diplomatic complaints.

After the US Information Service (USIS), a US cultural organization, had informed London that there were no impediments to Spain
being included in the ERP, Britain began to fear that Spain would
obtain funds by bypassing London and Paris. The Foreign Office required a reassurance from the US that the administration of the Marshall
Plan lay in European hands. The British Embassy in Washington contacted the Assistant Chief of the Division of Western European Affairs, Outerbridge Horsey. Horsey confirmed that there were no impediments
to Spain's entry into the ERP from the American side, but also reassured the British that it all depended on the approval of the 16 nations. Britain was satisfied.

It was clear that Spain had to improve foreign relations with Europe to get into the ERP. This is precisely what the Foreign Ministry in Madrid attempted. The Treaty of Friendship between Portugal and Spain was renewed and Portugal promptly invited Spain into the Programme. Yet Dr José Caeiro de Mata, the Portuguese Foreign Minister, was opposed by the other 15 nations. Not willing to risk his own precarious situation as Foreign Minister of a fascist state, he backed down.

Apart from Portugal, Spain gained support from the Latin American countries. During the Ninth International Conference of American States in Bogotá a resolution was passed which upheld that "the establishment or maintenance of diplomatic relations with a government does not imply any judgment upon the domestic policy of that country". This was obviously directed against the UN resolution of 1946 and aimed at improving relations with Spain.

Even France was willing to improve relations with Spain, and decided to reopen the border to allow the export of industrial machinery from France to Spain.

The UK, France and the US also settled a long-standing dispute with Spain concerning German property and the liquidation of balances and payments between Spain and Germany.

In an attempt to exploit these developments and in order to gain credits from the US, José Félix Lequerica, former ambassador to Vichy France, was to go to Washington as an inspector and counsellor to the Spanish Embassy. However, due to the diplomatic implications, this became a controversial issue. In a conversation between Culbertson and Erice in the Palace of Santa Cruz on 23 January 1948, the Chargé advised that Lequerica should delay his trip until April, when Congress would have finished discussing the Marshall Plan. This would avoid any unnecessary embarrassment between the two governments and subsequent speculation by the press that the US wanted funds flowing to Spain under the Marshall Plan. Culbertson made it clear that he was prepared to grant Lequerica a visa whenever he demanded one, but that he preferred the visit to be delayed until the ERP debates were over. Obviously it had been Spain's intentions to link Lequerica's trip to the US with the Programme. Under the circumstances, Artajo decided that it was wiser to give in, and agreed to a postponement of Lequerica's departure.

This discussion over Lequerica's arrival in Washington reflected the position of the two countries. The US had come to the conclusion that Spain would be excluded from the Marshall Plan due to political opposition from Europe, while Spain had still hoped that the US might gain access for her into the aid Programme against Europe's antagonism. Instead, from now on, Spain's integration into the Programme was to depend entirely on the talks held by the European nations. Nicolás Franco, as ambassador to Portugal, was trying to procure Salazar's support in these discussions. The Spanish Foreign Ministry informed Culbertson that Holland, Portugal, Switzerland, Greece and Turkey all favoured Spain's inclusion.

Had this been correct, Spain would still have had an opportunity to obtain some aid. Legally, there were no impediments to justify Spain's inclusion in the ERP. The Foreign Assistance Act, regulating the Programme, allowed the extension of aid to all countries which were members of the Committee of European Economic Cooperation formed in Paris in September 1947, and to any country in Europe, provided such country adhered to a joint programme for the economic recovery of Europe.

In relation to Spain, it could have been argued that her economy was indispensable to accomplish the aims of the Act. However, few countries in Europe accepted this view. In the US, Charles E. Bohlen, Counselor of the State Department, argued that Spain was not part of the programmes as she had not been invited to Paris when the ERP was initiated. As a result, it was really up to the 16 nations who had taken part in Paris to let her in. The State Department would not push the issue, even though it would welcome Spain's inclusion.

Lewis W. Douglas, Ambassador to Great Britain, supported Bohlen. He argued that it had not been Washington's decision to exclude Spain from the Paris meeting but Bevin's and Bidault's. The Ambassador supported his argument by claiming that the UN resolution could be interpreted in such a way as to exclude Spain. For Douglas, as for Bohlen, everything depended on the other European countries. The American diplomat in London said: "There are two sides of the coin. One is assistance which we are prepared to give these nations and the other side is the extent to which the participating countries extend an invitation." Douglas claimed that "it was their club. We do not choose the membership."[2]

Congress had mixed feelings. Several Senators believed that, as the issue involved American money, the US had a right to decide where it would go. However, the State Department was in a fortunate position. In talks with Spain, it could blame Europe for her exclusion, while relations with the ERP countries would not be put under strain.

In Madrid, the situation was clarified to Artajo at another meeting with Culbertson on 8 March 1948. Culbertson expressed the view of the State Department that Spain should be included but explained that it could not admit so publicly. Artajo mentioned the forthcoming discussions in Paris, which might still have resulted in Spain's incorporation into the ERP. Culbertson politely sidestepped this issue. Artajo insinuated his interest in bilateral agreements between their two nations. The Spanish Minister claimed that Spain had really more interest in grants from the US than in the Marshall Plan. In an earlier conversation Culbertson had explained that the impediment for such a governmental grant lay partly in the intervention by the INI in the market. Knowing this, Artajo now claimed that the INI was only a crisis measure, which would be removed as early as possible, so that nothing stood in the way of American grants to Spain. Culbertson did not rule out governmental grants, but he thought that it would be easier for Spain to obtain private credits and credits from the Export–Import Bank.[3]

This interview between Artajo and Culbertson was important. Madrid had avoided US damnation by promising to abandon governmental economic intervention to begin the liberalization of her economy. In return, Madrid hoped for economic aid. After the conversation Artajo noted that "the North American opinion has difficulty in understanding the Spanish position. In this sense it is convenient to start remembering that it is not reasonable to mix the internal problems of each country with the international relations."[4]

The following day Culbertson sent a telegram to George Marshall, Secretary of State, describing the meeting with Artajo. The Secretary's reply came two weeks later. America's policy was unmoved by Artajo's arguments. No credits were to be extended, nor was Europe going to be pressured into accepting Spain in the ERP.

After receiving Marshall's letter, Culbertson concluded that Spain really wanted to be part of the ERP, despite Artajo's claim that Spain preferred bilateral relations with the US. The Chargé believed that Spain had only turned away from the Programme because Madrid knew that France and Britain would never allow the totalitarian regime admission. The American diplomat speculated that Spain would blame the US and Britain for not being included; the former because it had refused to put pressure on Europe; the latter because it acted out of selfishness. However, according to Culbertson's opinion, Spain was strategically too important for the US to ignore in this way.

From the State Department's point of view, Spain was not a great loss to the West, and diplomatically, it was much easier to have limited relations with the totalitarian regime. The military point of view was different. Shortly after the Artajo–Culbertson conversation, the military inquired into the progress of diplomatic relations with Spain. James Forrestal, Secretary of Defense, telephoned Norman Armour, Secretary for Political Affairs and former Ambassador to Spain. The Defense Secretary, worried about the military situation, wanted to know if relations were improving. Norman Armour informed Forrestal of the economic and diplomatic complications, asserting that commercial relations were not improving due to the strict control imposed on Spain by the INI over foreign trade.

While the State Department in Washington was downplaying the military potential of Spain, the Embassy in Madrid was not. Culbertson believed that military considerations should overrule diplomatic ones. He believed that Spain's military strength had to be improved urgently with US aid. In addition he argued that Spain's economic isolation was slowing down Western recovery. Culbertson therefore suggested that normal relations should be resumed as early as possible. He wanted to accelerate the integration of Spain into the ERP and suggested that Washington should stress the economic advantages of Spain's integration for Europe's recovery.

Culbertson's point of view was supported and probably influenced by the deteriorating East–West relations. On 20 March the USSR walked out of the Allied Control Council, the body officially charged with governing Germany. Reports of Red Army troop movements and comments by Communists in Berlin increased fears that a Russian military move against Berlin was imminent. Civil servants in the State Department speculated that the fall of Berlin would start an avalanche of Communist takeovers in Europe. Under these circumstances, a military conflict in Europe could not be ruled out. In such a case Spain's resources and her military support had to be secured.

Shortly after the concern over Berlin, a meeting between representatives of the State Department and the US Air Force took place. Major-General Samuel E. Anderson, USAF, claimed that the Joint Chiefs of Staff had discussed the use of three airfields in Spain which should be constructed and equipped for the heaviest US bombers. The State Department pointed out that the public would be appalled if the US offered military help to Spain, but saw no objections to the financing and equipping of airfields for civil aviation. Anderson accepted this line of thought and informed the Joint Chiefs of Staff that securing base rights at the moment was politically inadvisable, as was exporting military aircraft but, from his point of view, there were no objections to a civil aviation programme as suggested by the State Department.

Secretary of Defense Forrestal sent two officers to Winthrop Williams Aldrich, Chairman of the Board of the Chase National Bank of New York, to discuss financial loans for the improvement of Spanish air-fields. In this initial meeting Aldrich showed great enthusiasm for the idea. Promptly, another meeting between a Colonel of the Spanish Air Force, a representative of the civilian airline Iberia and the Chase National Bank was organized. During these talks it became clear that the Span-iards hoped to obtain credits without granting securities in return. The Bank insisted on gold coverage for the loan. An agreement could not be reached and the meeting broke up without compromise.

The State and Defense Departments continued to encourage private loans but made it clear that they were unwilling to intervene. The Bank, realizing the Departments' concern, sought possible solutions. Their representative in Washington, Mr Schermerhorn, got in contact with the two Departments on 22 June and suggested that the loans would be granted if the State or Defense Departments guaranteed them on national security grounds.

Hickerson, representing the State Department, passed the responsi-bility on to the Defense Department, arguing that such guarantees should be extended only if the Department of Defense thought that they were needed to promote safety in international aviation. Forrestal, represen-ting the Defense Department, was put under pressure. The whole idea of guaranteeing credits to Spain for civil aviation was a disguise for the improvement of Spanish airfields for future military use. However, public opinion would have been appalled if this became known. Unwilling to risk a public backlash, Forrestal refused to issue the necessary guarantee and, for the time being, the idea was shelved.

On the other side of the Atlantic, British military strategists also became increasingly interested in Spain. On 16 April 1948, in a meet-ing of the Chiefs of Staff, Lieutenant-General Templer stressed Spain's strategic importance for the defence of the maritime lines of commu-nication and the military value of her armed forces. Despite realizing the difficulty of the link between military advantages and political com-plications, he encouraged the idea of a general agreement with Spain. The Joint Planning Staff acknowledged that Spain's exclusion from security pacts would lessen the effective defence of the Atlantic and the Mediterranean. The diplomatic problem was noted, but a *modus vivendi* with the Spanish military authorities was strongly desired.

As a result of the meeting a study was commissioned and a month later, on 26 May 1948, the Joint Planning Staff concluded that Britain's minimum strategic requirement on the Iberian Peninsula was successful resistance to any aggression launched by the Soviet Union. To achieve this, the Joint Planning Staff asserted that Madrid had to be assisted in training and organizing her armed forces. Furthermore, the West had to fund substantial military equipment. The study acknowledged the diplomatic implications and, despite the desire to assist, concluded that any policy of direct support for the fascist regime had to be ruled out. The Chiefs of Staff were dissatisfied with this conclusion and Major-General Ward asked for a new approach. After further discussions, the Chiefs of Staff concluded that Spain was of first importance if the Rhine line was overrun by Soviet troops. It was deemed vital that Spain's support in the event of war had to be guaranteed and appropriate steps had to be taken.

In addition to strategic military considerations, the UK was concerned about flight security to and from Gibraltar. To make air travel in Spain safe, loans for modern air-traffic control equipment had to be granted. However, these looked alarmingly like military credits and thus were kept to a minimum and restricted to the private sector. Following the earlier collapse of talks concerning these credits, the authorities in Madrid backed down and decided to put up gold securities.

In the meantime the debate in Congress about the ERP had finished and Spain was allowed to send Lequerica to Washington. He was able to gain strong support in Congress, organizing interest groups into an effective Spanish Lobby.

In this task, Lequerica was aided by Charles Patrick Clark, a member of several Congressional committees and government agencies with some influence with the Truman government.

As 1948 was an election year in the US, Lequerica joined the pre-election lobbying. In Congress, five interest groups came together, united by their pro-Spanish inclinations. The groups were Catholics, Anti-Communists, Republicans, trade-orientated Congressmen and finally, the military. The lobby that emerged was very influential, as the interest groups were bipartisan, supra-sectional, supra-economic and supra-religious in appearance, and hence not clearly identifiable as a lobby.

The Catholic lobby was composed of men like Pat McCarran, Joseph McCarthy and Alvin E. O'Konsky, and especially Dr Joseph F. Thorning. They identified with Spain because of their deep-rooted Catholic beliefs. Education by the Church, crucifixes at schools and universities and a strong link between the government and the Church were well-known aspects of the Franco regime.

The Anti-Communist lobby grew alongside McCarthyism, the Cold War and subsequent political scandals such as Alger Hiss's conviction for perjury, the executions of the Rosenbergs and Oppenheimer's withdrawal of security clearance. The most outspoken Republicans in the lobby were Senators McCarthy, Taft, Clark and Zablocki. Later these were supported by Senators McKellar, Brewster and Bridges.

The economic lobby can be broken down into three groups: cotton, wheat, and oil interests. Spain required cotton for its textile industry in Catalonia, at the same time as the Southern states were looking for new cotton markets to sell their surplus products. The two interests fitted like hand in glove. At the same time Spain still required wheat imports. The harvest of 1947 was particularly unsatisfactory. Thus Spain opened up the possibility to satisfy the overproduction of wheat in the Northwestern states. Finally, the oil companies saw the financial advantage of oil refining in Spain. Congressmen from these three areas, i.e. the Southern cotton states, the Northwestern wheat states and the oil-producing states, pushed for better commercial relations with Spain.

The last component of the Spanish Lobby were military experts including Admiral Richard L. Conolly. They saw Spain as a vital country for future bases, because Italy and France only provided treacherous grounds due to their unstable political situations. Stanton Griffis, who became Ambassador to Spain, supported this view. He told Forrestal over breakfast, on 26 May 1948, that he found it difficult to understand how the US could talk about the control of the Mediterranean at one end and ignore Spain at the same time.[5]

The actions of the Spanish Lobby did not go unnoticed by the American public and many were appalled. Harold L. Ickes, Secretary of the Interior under Roosevelt and Truman, accused Lequerica of having organized a celebration dinner in honour of the Japanese surprise attack against the US at Pearl Harbor, and of trying to manipulate American politics when he was lobbying for Dewey at the Republican Nomination Convention in June 1948. Yet his strongest accusation concerned the Spaniard's role during his appointment to Vichy France, when Lequerica allegedly instructed members of the Embassy not even to shake hands with North Americans. Ickes ended a series of articles published in the New Republic and bearing such provocative titles as "Heil Lequerica" and "Von Lequerica" with the following suggestion: "upon Lequerica's visits to the State Department, he should be greeted by Señor Don Dr. Pat McCarran y Shea and an honor guard with a Fascist salute and a 'Heil, von Lequerica!'"[6]

Lequerica did little to improve his image when, in 1952, the American journalist Drew Pearson, who had written hostile articles about Lequerica for some years, revealed him as the head of the Spanish

Lobby. Lequerica, losing his nerve, punched Drew Pearson in the face, and was successfully sued for assault.

Lequerica was not the only one of the Spanish Embassy staff in Washington to be verbally abused by the American press. Pablo Merry de Val, the counsellor of the Spanish Embassy, was accused by Ickes of going from party to party, socializing with Senators, Representatives and the social elite of Washington, always trying to further the Spanish cause.

Ickes also attacked Propper de Callejón, who had been First Secretary in Vichy France. Propper then became Consul in Rabat and French Morocco at the time of Operation Torch. He was a good friend of Lequerica's and was not trusted by the Allied authorities. The Free French even labelled him *persona non grata* and refused him as counsellor. Yet now, after the war, he came to Washington to assist Lequerica. Ickes wrote: "What is not good enough for Paris is good enough for Washington."

Unimpressed by such criticism, the State Department lifted all embargoes on Spain, ended all quotas and re-established free trade between the two countries.

Lequerica was using his supporters in the US successfully. In March 1948, Myron C. Taylor, the Presidential Representative at the Vatican, paid a visit to Franco at the Pardo Palace. By pure coincidence a proposal to include Spain in the ERP was put forward shortly afterwards by Representative Alvin E. O'Konsky, an ardent Catholic supporter of the Spanish Lobby. It was accepted by the House of Representatives with an overwhelming majority of almost three to one.

The unfortunate timing of the meeting between Myron Taylor and Franco, and the vote in the House, created the impression that the amendment had presidential approval. This was not true. The vote in the House was the result of growing Communist influence, such as the threat of a victory in the coming Italian election of the extreme Left. The Foreign Assistance Act of 1948, which included the proposal to grant funds to Spain, was also passed by the House.

The decision of the House to include Spain in the Programme forced the Senate, under presidential pressure to use a veto, to call for a Joint Congressional Conference Committee, which promptly eliminated the clause relating to Spain.

However, one nation to offer help was Argentina. On 9 April 1948 the two countries signed a four-year agreement, the Franco–Perón Protocol, concerning financial and economic matters. Spain's credit limit was increased and, in return, Argentina was allowed to buy Spanish goods, gain interests in Spanish industries and receive a free-trade area in Cádiz.

The agreement convinced many Latin American countries that the UN December resolution was not working and that it handicapped their trade and commerce relations with Spain. To encourage cooperation, Brazil, together with six other nations, decided to send a navy delegation to the Spanish Navy's 700th anniversary exercises.

Portugal also supported Franco. At the Paris Conference in 1948, Dr José Caeiro de Mata, the Portuguese Foreign Minister, argued that if the Marshall Plan was to include Germany, an aggressor state, then Spain "of 28 million people with great agricultural and mineral resources and commanding positions in the Atlantic and Mediterranean" had to be included as well. It was becoming clear that certain countries in the Western sphere were unhappy about the UN resolution.

In order to prevent Communist propaganda, the Western nations in the Security Council on 25 June 1948 bluntly refused to debate a Russian proposal on the Spanish dilemma. Washington decided that it was best to avoid publicity altogether and the Secretary of State commented that "what reason and endeavor cannot bring about, often time will". Others, however, were unwilling to wait.

Latin American countries presented a proposal to the UN which supported Spain and split the US delegation in the General Assembly. Truman and Acheson were ready to go along but the New Dealers Eleanor Roosevelt and Benjamin V. Cohen, as well as John F. Dulles, were inclined towards neutrality. The rest of the delegation wanted to support the new proposal.

It was clear that ostracism had failed. After the 1947 resolution fell short of the two-thirds majority, four Latin American states appointed ambassadors to Spain. In 1946 two-thirds of the member states had voted against Spain, in 1947 only a majority voted against her and, as it turned out, in 1948 a majority voted in favour of Spain.

Many countries still opposed the Franco regime in public. Ernest Bevin expressed his opposition towards Spain, saying that moral and material values of our Western civilization forced the exclusion of Franco's Spain from Western cooperatives such as the OEEC. However, as international relations between East and West deteriorated, Britain's position with regard to Spain came under pressure.

The crisis in Czechoslovakia caused by Communist infiltration was resolved by a *coup d'état* in February 1948. From then until the 1990s, the country was ruled by the extreme Left. The loss of Czechoslovakia – one of the most advanced industrial states in eastern Europe – to

Communism induced the Pentagon towards a policy of military bases to guarantee state security of Western nations. The US still had its base structure of the world war in place and could use this to provide stability. Relations with Spain and the US representatives in Madrid were naturally affected by this.

By now Paul Culbertson was well established in Spain. He was invited as a state guest to go goat hunting in the Picos de Europa during the month of September. His brother William C. Culbertson, a prominent lawyer in the US, was doing legal work for the Spanish Embassy. On 13 June 1948, Paul Culbertson drew up a long list of economic changes required in Spain. These covered topics such as exchange rates, treatment of foreign capital, and state control over industry. It was a long time before Spain could meet these demands. Economically, Spain continued to suffer from inflation, and many Spanish businessmen claimed that foreign credits would be poured into a bottomless pit because of government intervention.

In a policy statement, the State Department asserted that it favoured a full integration of Spain and an overall normalization of relations. The statement claimed that the primary objective of US policy towards Spain at this time was the reintegration of Spain, politically, economically and militarily, into the free Western European community of nations, through the progressive normalization of Spanish relations with those countries and with the US.

Politically, US policy was still governed by the UN resolutions, implying that Spain would only be included in the ERP if she gained international respectability. The statement concluded:

> we believe, therefore, that the most desirable course of action for the present is to avoid international pressure on Spain and to continue our efforts to emphasize the need for political liberalization. . . . We can concurrently encourage private trade with Spain and private investment on a purely business basis, and we can develop informal contact between Spanish and US military authorities, provided in all cases our political line is made clear.[7]

Even though political considerations made it difficult to grant direct military aid, civil aviation aid was a discreet channel for improving airfields in Spain. The Secretary of Defense, Forrestal, continued encouraging US companies to grant credits to Spain for the improvement of airports, and the Secretary of the Army, Kenneth C. Royall, advised the National Security Council on 20 May 1948 that a plan for the defence of Europe should be flexible enough to include Spain.

There was a real threat, as expressed by John D. Hickerson, that Spain might get the impression that the Pentagon and the State Department were speaking with different voices and thus allowing Spain to sit back and wait for military necessities to overrule diplomatic considerations. To avoid this, the service attachés in Madrid were specifically instructed to give an impression of harmony with their civilian colleagues.

There was a certain amount of pressure on Spain herself. The Spanish General Staff knew perfectly well that the armed forces could not defend the Pyrenees against a Soviet invasion, and hence Spain's defence line was not the Pyrenees but the Rhine. This was, of course, music to the ears of American military planners. In a conversation with Colonel Dasher, General Vigón asked the US Military Attaché for aid, above all anti-tank weapons. Vigón stressed that the military value of the Spanish Army was being wasted, as Spain could not contribute to the Western defence system without military support. Vigón assured Dasher that in return he wanted to send troops north of the Pyrenees and allow the US Army to purchase cheap raw materials.[8]

These were good reasons for the Pentagon to desire closer relations. Forrestal inquired in a letter to Marshall on 30 October 1948 how he assessed the international situation. He did so hoping to increase the Defense Department's allocation from $15 billion to $17.5 billion. Marshall's reply, drafted by Under-Secretary Lovett, claimed that not much had changed, but that nevertheless it was crucial to rearm Western Europe. Marshall might have opposed the ban on ambassadors, but he did not favour sending aid to Spain because of the political complications this might have caused with other countries.

Despite political restraints, during September and October 1948, a number of influential American politicians, businessmen and officers visited Spain. Senator Chan Gurney, movie tycoon Eric Johnston, Democratic Leader and Coca-Cola manager James A. Farley and the Presidential Representative to the Vatican, Myron Taylor, as well as Rear-Admiral Roscoe H. Hillenkoetter, who replaced Vandenberg as Director of the CIA, were among those visiting Spain.

Nevertheless, as long as Spain's government interfered in the economy, foreign banks and multinationals remained cautious about making large investments. Despite this, foreign commerce, above all military-related, flourished. Portugal exported 25 000 kg of military optical equipment. Greek entrepreneurs were selling substantial amounts of ammunition to Spain. Britain started to sell aircraft-testing machinery and Rolls-Royce aircraft engines. A Dutch company sold Spain military engines. Spain bought five River class frigates from Britain and ICI exported

19.5 tons of dinitrophenol which, mixed with shellite, was used in HE (high explosive) shells. 175 tons of gelatine dynamite were bought by Spain and discussions concerning two corvettes, 60–80 planes and loans for state-owned Iberia were in progress. Companies in Europe were increasingly asking for a review of the export ban so that they could win export contracts.

While businessmen saw financial opportunities in Spain, politicians in Europe still opposed close cooperation. Paul Henry Spaak, the Belgian Prime Minister, voiced his opposition to closer relations and Robert Schuman, French Minister for Foreign Affairs, stressed that Spain should remain excluded from the Western Union defence organization.

It was clear that Western defence was no longer directed against a German threat but against a Soviet invasion. The Pact of Dunkirk of 1947 between France and Britain against a German aggression was expanded in 1948 into the Treaty of Brussels. The Benelux states joined. Eventually, in 1949, under Truman's guidance, the Vandenberg Resolution was passed to form NATO.

The three Foreign Ministers Marshall, Schuman and Bevin, from the US, France and Britain respectively, held a meeting in order to try to coordinate their policies towards Spain. Marshall claimed that it was crucial to consider Spain's importance for Europe in the political and economic sphere. The French and British ministers stated that the people in their countries opposed relations with Spain and that they would try to play down the Spanish question in the UN on Spain.

On 9 October 1948, General Marshall held a press conference during which he stated that he no longer favoured the ban on the appointment of ambassadors to Spain, nor could he initiate its removal.

Spain had to cooperate with the US if she wanted Washington to put pressure on France and Britain. In November, Erice told the American Embassy that economic aid could be exchanged for military bases on the Canary and Balearic Islands and on Spain's mainland.

US Senator Chan Gurney, chairman of the Congressional Commission on the Armed Forces, had a private audience with Franco during a visit to Spain in September. On his return he described relations between the US and Europe, including Spain, as positive. He went even further, claiming that all those who resisted Communism had to understand that it was in their interest to bring Spain into the UN.

In a meeting on 5 October 1948 between Chan Gurney, Forrestal and the other three Secretaries of the Armed Forces (Royall, Sullivan and Symington), Gurney asked for "complete re-establishment of all relations between Spain and the United States".[9]

Spain had already come a long way. Many countries all over the world had signed trade agreements with her. On 23 June 1948, a sterling payment agreement between the UK and Spain was concluded. This facilitated money transfers between the two countries. Within the UN, Spain's position also had improved. The Sixth Committee of the General Assembly in the UN had decided that Spain should be included in the International Convention on Economic Statistics. This was done in direct contravention to the UN resolution of 1946.

Spain's international reputation had improved without any substantial liberal reforms. Municipal elections in Spain in 1948 were clearly undemocratic. The only party to stand in these elections was the Falange. It was claimed that more than 75 per cent of eligible voters turned up, electing Falangist representatives in 80 per cent of all cases. The accuracy of these numbers must be called into question.

In 1947 youths of the Catholic Action had damaged Protestant places of worship in Madrid. Three Protestant chapels were closed by the authorities, accused of propaganda activities. Between 1947 and 1949 another ten Protestant churches were closed, one of them even having its furniture seized permanently. Protestant church magazines, recreative gatherings and benevolent societies were banned for "attack[s] on the spiritual unity of the nation". Several local Catholic priests stole furniture from Protestant churches and went unpunished. Even worse, in June 1948 in the province of Jaen, a group of 30 to 35 young men belonging to Catholic Action and the Falange stormed a Protestant church, shouting "Viva la Virgen", and started beating up the congregation and destroying the interior. The Spanish authorities promised an investigation, but little came of it.

Throughout all this, there was no alternative to Franco. The Monarchists were outmanoeuvered when Franco held a meeting with Don Juan on 25 August 1948, during which it was agreed that Juan Carlos, son of Don Juan, should go to Spain for his education. With this Franco had succeeded in splitting the Monarchists. Socialists, representatives of the trade union (Unión General de Trabajadores, or UGT), members of the Confederación del Trabajo, or CNT, and the Izquierda Cataluña hoped in vain for support from France, Britain and the US.

However, the split between Monarchists and Republicans became inevitable when Don Juan publicly agreed to send his son Juan Carlos to Spain. In return Franco granted political amnesty to the Monarchists. The Monarchist paper, *ABC*, was granted limited press freedom.

Satisfied with the way things were turning out, Franco exposed his thoughts on international affairs in an interview with the *Newsweek* reporter Edward Weintal. The dictator said that before any agreements between the US and Spain could be accepted, the Spanish people themselves had to desire them. The Caudillo blamed the British for the problems between Spain and the US. As for the question of liberalization within his own country, the Generalissimo argued that each country was different and thus needed a different regime. According to him the Spanish domestic climate, which had been brought about by international condemnation, prevented liberalization of his regime. Implicitly, the West could not complain about a situation brought about by their own foreign policies.

NOTES

1. FRUS, 1948, III, p. 1020.
2. Selected Hearings Executive Session Foreign Relations Senate, 12 February 1948.
3. FRUS, 1948, III, p. 1026.
4. Viñas, *Guerra, Dinero, Dictadura*, p. 277.
5. Mills, *Forrestal Diaries*, p. 445.
6. *New Republic*, vols 121, 124, 125.
7. FRUS, 1948, III, p. 1041.
8. WNRC, Army Intelligence, Project Decimal File, Spain, July 1948.
9. Lowi, "Bases in Spain", p. 676.

5 A Secret Policy

The fear of a world conflict which had led to the creation of the North Atlantic Treaty Organization greatly influenced future relations between the US and Spain. On 8 March 1949, the Senate reanalysed Spain's strategic value. Senator Connally claimed that Spain was a much more important country than Italy. Senator Fulbright acknowledged that from a military point of view, Spain offered the best base of all in Europe.

During 1948, the USAF and the RAF had reached an agreement on the joint use of bases in Britain. The geographical position of Great Britain allowed the USAF to disperse bases outside the reach of the Red Army, while remaining within striking distance. James Forrestal, Secretary of Defense, claimed that over-concentration of military bases courted hot war. Naturally, further dispersion of bases would have been strategically beneficial. The lack of other suitable bases along the Mediterranean put the stability of Middle East countries at peril. Thus it was concluded that strategic bases were needed in either French Morocco or Spain.

Worldwide, and specifically in the Mediterranean, the US Navy aimed for strategic bases and mooring rights, which would minimize costs and political difficulties created by the dependence on British bases. The Sixth Fleet had to operate from Gibraltar, Malta and Suez. This arrangement created political problems with the Royal Navy and increased maintenance costs which a naval base in Spain might have reduced. Therefore it was only too natural that the US Navy favoured good relations with Spain. Admiral Richard L. Conolly, the Commander of the Naval Forces in the Eastern Atlantic and the Mediterranean, requested to pay a courtesy call on Spanish ports. Nevertheless the State Department, fearing unnecessary propaganda by the Spanish authorities, delayed this visit until September.

Major-General William H. Turner, from the USAF, secretly visited Madrid in order to make sure that Spain would not blow these military exchanges out of proportion, and thus irrevocably damage US prestige in Europe. After the successful conclusion of Turner's trip, the State Department was authorized to go ahead with Conolly's visit. From 3 to 8 September 1949, a US naval squadron under the Admiral and some British ships visited El Ferrol. Shortly afterwards, the Admiral visited Franco in Madrid. This visit was to test both Franco's reaction and public opinion in Europe. The result was satisfying for the US as Franco did not use the visit for propaganda purposes, nor did it cause diplomatic complications with other European countries. The Department of Defense was now prepared to push harder. After his visit Admiral Conolly told the House Armed Service Committee that the strategic importance of the Iberian Peninsula was uniquely evident. During the same month several members of the Armed Services Committee went to Madrid. Even the new Secretary of Defense, Louis Johnson, contemplated visiting Spain, indicating strong military interest.

It was obvious that the military planners in Washington had accepted the disadvantages of the Franco regime. The very nature of NATO gave Spain hope of escaping isolation once and for all. The fact that Portugal had been included strengthened this belief. On radio Franco compared NATO without Spain to an omelette without eggs. Yet most member states in Europe did not want her to be part of the Organization.

London recognized that the US and Latin American countries had a growing desire to bring Spain into the Western sphere. Even France decided to improve relations with Spain. French radio stopped referring to Spain as totalitarian and stopped hand-outs and free broadcasting time to Spanish Republicans. Paris, by falling out with London over commercial policies to Spain and relaxing trade restrictions, had gained commercial advantages, securing the sale of 86 Jumo aero-engines ahead of the British company Vickers–Armstrong. The strained relations between Britain and Spain meant that the UK was losing profitable contracts in Spain.

In the UK, the Chiefs of Staff improved the treatment of Spanish service attachés. Ignacio Martel, the Spanish Naval Attaché in London, expressed his desire to take off in a plane from a British aircraft carrier. The Foreign Office feared that by granting his request too quickly, it might invite more serious pleas. Yet not to do so would counter the decision by the military planners in Britain to improve relations. Thus a compromise was reached and instead of going to the carrier, Commander Martel received information about Britain's post-war organization of civil defence.

In the US, Senator Pat McCarren and Alvin E. O'Konsky favoured a rejection of the previous UN recommendation and advocated the release of funds from the Marshall Plan to the whole of the Iberian Peninsula.

Before the Spanish problem re-emerged in the UN, the State Department wanted to know the attitude of other NATO members in this matter. Whatever happened, Washington wanted NATO to form a united front in talks on the Spanish question. Concerning the stance of NATO, two problems had to be analysed; first, the member states' attitude towards Spain's participation in special UN agencies and, secondly, their position towards full membership of Spain in the UN.

London and Paris wanted to avoid the whole topic. The two European nations would have tolerated a US abstention vote concerning the resumption of full diplomatic relations and might even have supported Spain's participation in special agencies. What mattered most to them was that the US made it clear that Spain would not become a member of the European Recovery Programme. Belgium would have supported the US in a move to resume full diplomatic relations and would have welcomed Spain in the UN. The Netherlands, Norway, Sweden and Denmark would probably have abstained in both cases because of recent pressure by the US on these countries, but would not be pleased.

After the study, the State Department concluded that it had underestimated the Spanish problem in Western Europe and the Department recommended that Washington should continue its secret policy to improve relations with Spain, stressing the Communist threat. However, US prestige within NATO was not to be endangered for Spain's sake.

In the meantime, Culbertson brought mixed news from Madrid. He observed that all Spain needed to be accepted by the West were superficial political changes. Franco might, for example, grant limited amnesty, modify the censorship of the press or reduce the power of the police force. The Chargé also realized that Franco gave little importance to Spain's image with other Western European nations. The Spanish dictator was convinced that he would not gain anything from liberalizing his regime as long as the nations in Western Europe were ruled by socialist governments. The American Embassy in Madrid speculated that Franco's aims were to reverse the December resolution and to reach bilateral agreements with the US.

If what Culbertson wrote was right, only pressure by Washington might have forced Franco to make changes. It had to be put bluntly before him that if he made liberal changes, his country would obtain economic aid and military support, and the US would resume full diplomatic relations.

It was discussed how the US delegation to the UN should reconcile these positions. The study of the Policy Planning Staff made in October 1947 had called for a normalization of relations with Spain. During January 1948, the President and the National Security Council (NSC) had approved this policy. Thus no further pressure was to be applied to

Spain. The US delegation to the UN was therefore instructed to support any views opposing the 1946 resolution. Nevertheless, to avoid complications with America's European allies, the delegation was not to initiate any policy favouring Spain and was instructed to decrease the importance of the Spanish problem.

These instructions split the US delegation in two. Eleanor Roosevelt said that even anti-Communist groups in Western Europe would criticize the US for bowing to military interests. Benjamin V. Cohen, another New Dealer, and John F. Dulles agreed with her. Nevertheless, Dr Philip C. Jessup argued that the US was not yielding to military pressure but to the simple fact that the 1946 resolution had been ineffective. In the end the argument of the State Department prevailed. The delegation had to play down the Spanish Question. If a vote became unavoidable, the US should vote in favour of Spain's inclusion into special agencies and in favour of the return of ambassadors.

Charles Bohlen, Counselor of the State Department, argued that the US had no sympathy for Franco but that Washington was unwilling to encourage another civil war, and allowed Spain to file for credits through the Export–Import Bank for the first time since the end of the war.

Soon thereafter, pressure by European nations caused a new change in US instructions to the delegation. On 20 April 1949, Acheson informed the delegation that from now on they should abstain in any vote concerning the resumption of full diplomatic relations or on amendments to the 1946 resolution.

Secretary Acheson announced publicly that the US would abstain from a vote in the UN in order to leave the decision to other countries with stronger links to Spain. He explained that the US was torn between resuming full diplomatic relations and the undesired gesture of goodwill which would follow the appointment of an ambassador. This statement was welcomed by European allies but caused Spain's diplomats to turn away from the State Department towards relations with the Service Chiefs. In a conversation with an Italian businessman, Franco claimed that relations with Truman were much less important than contacts with the American General Staff.

By reversing the instructions to the US delegates Acheson had not only alienated Spanish authorities but also came under pressure at home. Senators McCarran and McKellar asked Acheson why the US, despite the governmental decision from 1947, still had no friendly relations with Spain, to which the Secretary replied that US policy was still governed by the UN recommendation. McCarran countered that he had never voted in favour of a UN which would enslave US foreign policy.

Acheson acknowledged Spain's importance and that it had been US policy to reintegrate her into the Western community. To McCarran's question whether Spain was essential for the full success of NATO, the Secretary replied that she was important, though not indispensable.

During May 1949, when the First Committee was discussing the Spanish Question for a third time, a new Polish proposal was put forward. In this document Poland accused Britain and the US of improving relations with Spain. It recommended ceasing all exports of arms and strategic material and instructed nations to refrain from signing agreements or treaties with Spain. Obviously it ran counter to the instruction and interests of the US and other Western nations. A counterproposal by Bolivia, Brazil, Colombia and Peru was handed in. This proposal outlined the failure of the 1946 resolution and aimed to give member states full freedom of action as regarded their relations with Spain. On 11 and 16 May the two proposals came up for a vote in the General Assembly. Both failed to obtain the necessary majority. The vote on the Latin American proposal was 26:16.

Despite receiving more votes in favour than against, the outcome failed to obtain the necessary 50 per cent of all possible votes as well as the two-thirds majority of all votes cast. Thus it was turned down. However, Spain's supporters in the UN had grown in number. In 1946 only six nations had voted for Spain. The year 1947 saw an increase to sixteen; now, three years after the December resolution, twenty-six states supported her.

The economic situation in Spain remained dire. Despite improved commercial relations with European nations and increased trade, Spain's economy had not improved notably and the country faced another serious crisis during 1949. The British Vice-Consul in Melilla assured the Foreign Office that in the area of Málaga and Torremolinos the economic conditions had not been worse since 1932. Lack of rainfall also meant that not enough electricity was produced. Barcelona had only six hours of power per week and the textile mills in Catalonia had to introduce a two-day working week. The rail system continued in disarray. Sometimes, on crowded routes, travellers had to crawl through windows to get aboard and the transport fares consisted of the official price plus black-market costs. The black market also drove up the prices of basic foodstuffs. The Rastro, the famous Madrid flea market, was full of stolen and smuggled goods. The dire economic situation led to a fall in exports and balance of payment deficits, and finally to the collapse of the Franco–Perón Protocol. Under this protocol Spain had received a total of 11 billion pesetas and had returned only 300 million in goods. As the gap grew, authorities in Buenos Aires became more discontent. Finally, Argentina decided to end exports to Spain and Spain faced a food shortage. In order to feed the country, Franco required at least an extra 500 000 tons of wheat. The payment for these imports was financed through a $25 million loan of the Chase National Bank, backed with gold deposits.

The situation was so desperate that the US Embassy in Spain feared that the Spanish economy was about to collapse. The drought from September to January had been a staggering 40 per cent below the average rainfall. Culbertson recommended that the Export–Import Bank should negotiate loans and that US trade with and investment in Spain should be encouraged.

Since January, the State Department had had its economic policy towards Spain under review. Following Culbertson's description of Spain's economy, Willard Thorp, the Assistant Secretary of State for Economic Affairs, sent a memorandum to Under-Secretary of State Webb in which he recommended normalizing relations with Spain. He wanted the US Embassy in Spain to inform the Spanish authorities that the Department no longer objected to the filing of applications with the Export–Import Bank for credits or direct loans to Spanish agencies or enterprises. On 11 April, Truman approved Thorp's memorandum. Two days later, Acheson sent instructions to Culbertson. He wrote that the economic situation in Spain could be improved with the assistance of the Export–Import Bank. Even though the Bank would consider Spanish applications on the same financial grounds as those from other countries, there remained many impediments before any credits could be considered financially sound. However, it did not take long for Spain to apply for credits.

On 17 May, Andrés Moreno, Chairman of the Banco Hispano-Americano, talked to representatives of the Export–Import Bank, explaining that Spain needed a total of $1.5 billion for basic foodstuffs and capital investments. The Bank rejected this on the grounds that Spain lacked the ability to repay such an amount. Spain's food supply was about to collapse. In desperation, Andrés Moreno had four more meetings in May with senior managers from the Export–Import Bank. This time he asked for $200 to $300 million and pleaded for a mission to Spain by the Bank. The Bank believed such a mission to be premature and thought that considerable investigations had to be conducted beforehand. On the other hand, the Bank encouraged credit applications for cotton.

Another possibility for Spain to obtain funds was via the Marshall

Plan. However, a paper by the State Department explained why Spain was not a member of this aid programme. It argued that European countries opposed closer Spanish–American relations because of internal public pressure. As long as Spain was not a member of the Western European defence arrangements, the US could not openly enter bilateral agreements as this would undermine the rest of Europe. The conclusion of the report was that Spain's political, economic and military integration into Western Europe was desired but that changes in Spain had to precede this.

That same summer, Culbertson decided to leave Madrid in early August 1949 to join the Spanish elite in the holiday resort of San Sebastian. There he expected to be in closer contact with the administration, which traditionally left the capital during the hot summer months.

He had become enchanted with Spain. His reports turned more pro-Spanish as time went by. In a memorandum dated 22 June 1949, he claimed that democracy in Spain was only possible in the far future because Spaniards had always been very individualistic. He claimed that the present Spanish regime was no worse than its predecessors and condemned the current American economic policy towards Spain. As for Franco's evolution, the Chargé argued that Franco took no measures of an evolutionary character, and without evolution he feared that revolution was possible.

Culbertson's report had little effect in the US. In a conversation between Bevin and Acheson, the British Foreign Minister expressed the same view as his American counterpart, and Truman stated in a press conference on 2 June 1949 that he would not favour a loan by the Export–Import Bank to Spain. Shortly afterwards Acheson stated his opposition to any Export–Import loans. The very next day the President described Spanish–American relations as not friendly. Before loans from the Export–Import Bank were to flow to Spain, certain monetary changes in Spain had to take place.

Senator McCarren continued his efforts in Congress to obtain funds for Spain. Former Secretary for the Interior Harold L. Ickes wrote that McCarran was trying to "raid the United States Treasury on behalf of Generalissimo Franco". For Ickes, McCarran had disgraced the US Congress and called him an "undesirable member of Senate" and "socially retarded". A proposed $50 million loan to Franco, Ickes claimed, was to maintain the Spanish "trigger-happy" soldiers in luxury. In early April, McCarran's amendment to the Foreign Aid Appropriation Bill was defeated in the Senate.

Undeterred, Madrid continued its efforts to secure financial aid. The

Conde de Marsal, a wealthy and influential businessman from Madrid with close ties to the government, contacted the State Department. He planned to submit four or five credit applications for projects totalling between $50 and $60 million. The American Director of the Office of Western European Affairs reiterated that there existed trade and exchange-rate problems which made approval difficult. The Conde de Marsal replied that Spain would prefer funds directly from the US rather than via the Marshall Plan. He justified government intervention in the economy, claiming that economic hardship had forced these policies upon Spain.

In the US, the Spanish Lobby increased its activity. In April 1950 the Spanish government contracted the very respectable law firm Cummings, Stanley, Truilt and Cross as its American counsel. The Lobby contacted directors from ITT and oil companies. As a result, the California Texas Oil Company negotiated with the Empresa Nacional Calvo Sotelo, an offspring of the INI, on a refineries project near Cartagena.

The head of the Lobby, Lequerica, had initially concentrated on improving relations with the Republican Party and therefore, after the re-election of Truman, was sidelined by the Democratic government. With no alternative, he concentrated his efforts on Congress. The State Department wanted him to leave the country but he was already too well dug in. James J. Murphy, a Democratic Representative from New York, visited Spain and called Franco a "very lovely and lovable character". The Democratic Senator Chavez from New Mexico declared that Spain should receive military and economic aid to improve the defence of Western Europe. Joseph L. Pfeifer, a Democrat from New York, told the press that Spanish–American relations were "a matter not simply for the United States to settle. It is in the last analysis a question for Spain and the Spanish people to settle." Thomas Gordon and Clement Zablocki, both Democrats from Illinois and Wisconsin respectively, supported Pfeifer's statement. Senator Owen Brewster pointed towards Spain's role during Operation Torch and outlined a report by Max Klein, a prominent member of the Chamber of Commerce in Spain, on religious freedom, as proof of Franco's relatively liberal government.

James Richards, the Chairman of the House Foreign Affairs Committee, visited Spain together with other Representatives, including Mr Keogh, a supporter of the Spanish and Catholic cause in Congress. The two became unfortunate victims of a robbery of $5000 while travelling on a train from Barcelona to Zaragoza. Embarrassingly for the two, the thief also decided to take all their trousers, leaving them with little to wear during the meetings in Zaragoza. Despite this unfortunate experience, James Richards had become an ardent supporter of Spain, and upon his return pointed out that certain countries receiving aid from the US were just as totalitarian in nature as Franco's regime. All this enthusiasm about Spain gave McCarran hope of pushing through a new $50 million loan programme for Spain under the Economic Cooperation Act.

McCarran's efforts were complicated by the fact that the President took the ultimate decision on whether a nation would qualify for aid under the European Cooperation Administration.

On the Spanish question in the UN, the Spanish Lobby strongly opposed the abstention vote in May 1949. A booklet published by the Madrid Diplomatic Office in 1949 called for a rectification of the UN's 1946 resolution. It stressed Spain's opposition to Communism and pointed out that Spanish Francoism, unlike fascism or Nazism, was based on Church and Army as well as Party. The authors of the booklet wrote that Spain's neutral position during the war had been decisive for the Allies. It was a blunt propaganda publication trying to justify Spain's selfish actions of the past.

Naturally, such a document did not convince in Washington. Dr Lloyd V. Berkner, Special Assistant to the Secretary of State and Chairman of the Foreign Assistance Correlation Committee, re-explained the decision to exclude Spain from the military assistance programmes. He claimed that despite strong trade links, Spain was not an integral part of the North Atlantic Pact.

Acheson was informed by the Chargé in Madrid that US policy towards Spain had to change. Culbertson stated that Franco was not going to step down due to the economic situation. As for the armed services, Culbertson thought that they would be willing to stage a revolt if they believed that a restoration would come about, but fear of the unknown held them back. The Chargé believed that only strong support by the US for the government in exile and other opposition groups would break the deadlock. Culbertson concluded that only a change of the December resolution and favourable relations with Franco could bring about democratic changes.

International events supported this interpretation. The fall of China to Communism in September 1949 increased the urgency of coming to an agreement with Spain. At the same time as the political question of Spain was coming under reconsideration in Washington, the US military continued their quest for Spain's integration. In a report on military aid, Spain was listed in the third most important category (out of seven). It had become as important as Denmark, Norway, Portugal and Sweden. Yet the programme also said that aid could only be granted to Spain if the political orientation of Western Europe changed.

On the political side, Mr John Kee, chairman of the House Foreign Affairs Committee, expressed his criticism of the December resolution, claiming that the withdrawal of ambassadors had not weakened Franco's regime. Senator Hickenlooper supported him, arguing that Spain was a strategically important country, more important even than Yugoslavia.

Acheson argued strongly against this, stating that Franco would not be a loyal and true ally. For the Secretary of State US policy could not change without a notable change in Spain as well as a change of public opinion in favour of Franco. However, Acheson held on to a policy which was no longer popular nor realistic. American businessmen were already selling military items to Spain, taking handsome profits by doing so. In March the State Department authorized the export of 42 military planes. In October a merchant named Ceasare Sabatucci filed for a permit worth $400 000 for US surplus airplane engines which he wanted to sell on to the Spanish army for more than $700 000. Military exports to Spain were in no way limited to the US. The Dutch company Philips was selling radar fire-control equipment to Spain. While Britain refused to sell 200 Merlin engines, France seized the opportunity and supplied them with 200 Jumo engines, and Germany added another 150 BMW 132As. The US sold 200 US Jeeps which Franco proudly presented in military parades. France even assisted Spain in building nine destroyers at El Ferrol. By the beginning of 1950 trade restrictions with Spain were easily bypassed.

Trade relations generally improved. Raw cotton export volumes to Spain are a good indicator of relations between the US and Spain. In 1945, Spain imported 66 per cent of its cotton from the US. During 1946 relations between the two countries worsened and by the end of the year only 44 per cent of Spain's raw cotton came from the US. At the end of 1946, the UN had passed its resolution condemning Spain and American trade fell dramatically. In 1947 Spain imported less than 2 per cent of its raw cotton from the US, while Brazil made up more than 40 per cent. After 1947, relations improved, and so did the cotton trade. In 1948, the US had regained 8 per cent of cotton imports to Spain. In 1949 the trend continued, and the US now made up 31 per cent of Spain's cotton imports. One year later the US had regained its first position, making up 52 per cent of all of raw cotton imports.

Commercial relations between Spain and other European nations also improved. By 1948 Britain had seen her 16 per cent (1932) market share of the Spanish automobile sector drop to only 1.2 per cent. Yet in 1950 this had increased to 35 per cent. In 1948, France had imported goods worth 19 million pesetas and exported to Spain 64 million pesetas. One year later this trade had increased to imports of 129 million pesetas and exports worth 132 million pesetas. Italian-owned Fiat constructed a factory near Barcelona after the Spanish government had increased foreign permitted capital participation. International air travel also increased. British Airways and Pan Am commenced flying to Barcelona three times weekly from London and New York, respectively. Air passengers increased from an average monthly 20 500 in 1949 to 27 000 in April 1950.

As the year 1949 came to an end, Secretary Acheson was receiving more and more reports urging him to reconsider his position towards Spain. In the US, many Congressmen encouraged Acheson to take action. Congressmen Buchanan (Pennsylvania), Chatham (North Carolina), Colmer (Mississippi), Green (Pennsylvania), Poage (Texas) and Richards (South Carolina) all supported Spain. The Secretary was advised on this point by his counsellor, Kennan, who told him that the Spanish problem had been exaggerated and change was possible.

Finally, on 18 January 1950, the Secretary of State wrote to Connally, the Chairman of the Senate Committee on Foreign Relations, that the US would abstain in the Political Committee or vote in favour of the resolution "in the interests of harmony and of obtaining the closest possible approach to unanimity in the General Assembly on the Spanish problem". He continued, saying that the withdrawal of ambassadors from Spain as a means of political pressure was a mistaken departure from the established principle that the exchange of ambassadors was usually without political significance. For the US, the prestige of the UN was more important than the ban on ambassadors. Opposition to Spain in the UN had decreased dramatically and it was time for a change. As a justification the Secretary pointed towards the 9th International Conference of American States in Bogotá, which had passed a resolution stating that the establishment or maintenance of diplomatic relations with a government did not imply any judgement upon the domestic policy of that government. Acheson concluded that the US should continue to try to get Spain to change and to integrate her into the West where she belonged, but full relations were nevertheless to be resumed. The new policy towards Spain would open up new possibilities for American business. Government credits would be granted for specific and economically justifiable projects only.

Acheson's letter was to become the official stance of the administration. Spain was still to be excluded from the Mutual Defense Assistance Program because the programme was administered through the European nations which felt that Spain's integration would weaken the collective effort to safeguard and strengthen democracy in Europe. Given European feelings, Washington concluded that to approach Spain would worsen her relations with the rest of Europe and a military bilateral agreement between Spain and the US would inevitably increase French fears of an American withdrawal behind the Pyrenees. As a result, relations between the US and Spain could only be improved if this did not upset relations with European allies.

While some Congressmen welcomed this new approach, others, like La Follette, expressed deep concern. The American press, while generally accepting the necessity to change the UN 1946 resolution, was almost evenly split in their feelings towards Spain. Out of a total of 33 US editorials only six, including the *New York Times* and the *Daily Worker*, openly disagreed with Acheson's position. Eleven wrote that change was necessary, but still made it clear that they did not like the Spanish regime. Seven wrote that a change of the UN resolution, while necessary, should not result in cordial relations with Spain. The *Herald Tribune* and eight other editorials went further, stating that relations with Spain should be cordial and the UN resolution had to be reversed.

London and Paris were concerned about the changes of the US policy towards Spain, but on 20 January Britain declared its unwillingness to vote against the December resolution, and France followed suit. Already, one month earlier, the British Foreign Office had reviewed its policy and had written that "as a general principle it is the view of the United Kingdom Government that accreditation of an Ambassador to a foreign government implies neither approval nor disapproval of that government".[1]

London was well informed about Acheson's letter to Connally. For the Foreign Office, this letter only confirmed that the US saw no alternative to Franco, and that Spain was part of Western Europe should not be permanently isolated from normal relations. New discussions in the UN concerning the Spanish problem had to be held.

In February the UN General Secretary, Trygve Lie, admitted that he had been wrong on the stance against Spain. He now believed that it was better to discuss the issue rather than to ignore it. However, the General Secretary still opposed Spain's integration into the political system of the West. For him such a step was only possible if certain political changes took place in Spain.

Nevertheless, Acheson's letter to Connally gave hope to Spain and new attempts were made to obtain credit facilities. Mariano Yturralde, Director-General for Economic Affairs of the Spanish Foreign Office, contacted Herbert E. Gaston, Chairman and President of the Board of Directors of the Export–Import Bank. The Spaniard was trying to obtain credits for fertilizer plants and for phosphate, lead and zinc mining machinery.

While the feasibility of these credits was being discussed, new military considerations favoured improved relations between Spain and the US. A National Security Council report (document NSC 68), drafted by Paul Nitze under the direction of Dean Acheson and with help from the Defense Department, called for a more aggressive foreign policy with respect to the use of conventional forces against the USSR. This implied that West Germany had to be incorporated into NATO, which at the same time had to secure its southern flank. Spain's importance was highlighted again and it was stated that her geographical position meant that she was a vital part for the control of the main oil supply lines. NSC 68 established that the USSR could conquer Europe within just days of the outbreak of a conflict. On 7 April 1950, the paper was delivered to the President and on 25 April it was discussed in a NSC meeting at the White House.

The coming problems in Korea and the first successful explosion of a nuclear bomb by the Soviet Union made a change of policy necessary. Soviet nuclear capability, which had not been expected to be achieved before 1954, rendered security plans before NSC 68 obsolete. The fact that the US had lost her monopoly meant that her nuclear threat no longer balanced the threat posed by the Red Army in Europe. Once the USSR had built up its nuclear stockpile and delivery systems, the risk of a conventional war would again become reality. As a result, new strategic plans for the use of conventional forces had to be worked out.

For Spain in particular this was good news. All over Western Europe she was gaining in importance for military planners. The Chiefs of Staff from most NATO countries agreed on the necessity of military bases in Spain. Portugal in particular remained adamant in getting Spain into the Western European structure. Now military consideration in Europe and the US drew closer together.

General Bradley, Chairman of the Joint Chiefs of Staff, argued that not enough importance was given to security and strategic aspects. He claimed that France and the Low Countries were unable to defend themselves against the USSR, thus Spain had to be secured as an ally. Bradley wrote that if a major war occurred before the Western powers had the capability of successfully defending France and the Low Countries, Spain became the last foothold in Continental Europe. For military logistics, Spain held the key between the Atlantic and the Mediterranean. As a result of these considerations, the Joint Chiefs of Staff called for either bilateral agreements or the integration of Spain into NATO and the Western Union Treaty. It was recognized that Spain on its own was incapable of any effective offensive action or even of defending herself against a Soviet attack, due to obsolete war material, insufficient modern training and, generally, the archaic military concepts employed by the Spanish armed forces. In order to access Spain's military requirements, the US Military Attaché in Madrid received a very detailed questionnaire from Washington. The information was to be used to establish Spain's military needs.

On 4 May 1950, the US military authorities in Germany allowed German technical specialists to go to Spain to help out in the production of fine steels, high explosives and synthetic gasoline. Shortly afterwards a number of US Navy ships visited Palma de Majorca. Political considerations complicated these approaches by the armed forces, and shortly afterwards the Department of the Navy decided that for political reasons no further naval visits to Spain should be planned for the balance of the year. Nevertheless, the military was convinced that from a national security point of view, Spain was as important to the US as many other countries in the North Atlantic Pact.

These military considerations undoubtedly put pressure on the State Department to come to an agreement with its European allies. Dunham, from the State Department, recommended that Acheson should attempt to find a compromise with France and Britain during his forthcoming visit to London. Throughout these talks it became obvious that the US State Department had given in to military interests. Dunham argued that the political and economic situation in Spain, caused not by Franco but by isolation, required the rule of a strong and centralized regime. He claimed that Franco was tolerated and no political change would take place without a military conflict or a serious deterioration of the economic climate. Dunham speculated that if the Spanish economy worsened further, riots and conflicts could not be ruled out. He expressed his fears that a Communist takeover of Spain would spell disaster for all of Europe. The British Foreign Office noted that Dunham had been under pressure from the Pentagon to improve relations with Spain and to get London to approve such a policy.

Political considerations by the State Department in Washington had clearly given way to pressure by the military. The State Department's representative in Madrid argued that the US should study the Spanish problem from a practical, even selfish, point of view. For Culbertson the policy to eliminate Franco was unrealistic, and evolution was the only possible way to bring about changes in Spain.

On 6 June 1950, General Bradley was asked, by Senator Vandenberg, in an Executive Session of the Senate Foreign Relations Committee, if he believed that the President should have the possibility of increasing the number of those in receipt of the Mutual Defense Assistance Program. The General answered that it was up to the Committee to decide on that issue, but also pointed out that without aid Spain would be unable to hold out for very long if attacked by Soviet troops. General Bradley supported the strategic concept for the defence of the North Atlantic area and recognized that the reason why Spain was excluded was because it would be discouraging to France.

Two days later, the Secretary of Defense issued NSC 72, which argued that because France could now be defended against a Soviet attack, the US and allies should take proper steps to ensure that Spain would be an ally in the event of war. The paper outlined the military advantages of Spain and recommended that the State Department should assure Spain's military cooperation and overcome possible objections by France and Britain.

At first glance this seemed strange. If France could be defended by NATO troops, the importance of Spain as a last foothold in Europe was greatly diminished. However, this removed an important stumbling-block to agreements with Spain. Fear and suspicion in other NATO countries about a withdrawal of US troops from central Europe were no longer of great importance.

Any bilateral agreement with Spain required sufficient US funds to attract interest in Madrid. This question was promptly raised in Congress. On 19 June 1950, the Senate discussed the Amendment to the Mutual Defense Assistance Program which was to give the President the right to provide military assistance to any other European nation whose increased ability to defend contributed to the preservation of the peace and security of the North Atlantic area. Still concerned about political complications with its European allies, the State Department in Washington wanted to limit the President's power and decrease the likelihood of a *rapprochement* with Spain in two ways. First, military assistance should only be granted to other free European nations. Second, the President should only do so after consultation with the governments of other nations.

The second amendment was passed but it was made clear that the

President was to consult and consult only before making his own decision. Discussions on the first proposal were more complicated. The expression "free" included Finland, Sweden and Switzerland but would have excluded Spain and Yugoslavia. "Non-Communist" was dismissed because it clearly excluded Yugoslavia. In the end there seemed only one possibility left: to allow the President to make the final decision. The Senate decided to do this and supported the Department of Defense against the State Department. The only impediment to granting economic aid to Spain was the President's personal opinion and, for the time being, Truman remained unenthusiastic about his stocky Spanish counterpart.

NOTES

1. PRO, FO371, 89500, 20 December 1949, UK Policy towards Spain.

6 Korea and New Concerns

On 21 June 1950, George F. Kennan told Mr Cannon, a Counselor to the State Department, that he was certain the USSR would not invade Spain out of fear that this would stretch their supply lines to the limit. If this was the case, Spain had little interest in joining the West. Kennan claimed that political concessions made to Spain would bring no military gratitude, only a new excess of Falangist arrogance. This reluctance to approach Spain by policy planners in Washington was swept away that very same month. Only four days later the Korean War broke out. Under the leadership of Kim-Il-Sung, the troops of North Korea overran the sparsely defended border of South Korea and dashed towards the capital, Seoul. Some politicians in Washington had already wanted to change American foreign policy but lacked popular support. The military budget had been increased in 1949 to $15.9 billion but NSC 68, a decision on national security, demanded an increase to as much as $50 billion. So far Congress had been reluctant to support this. Korea changed all that.

Naturally, Spain was affected by this. Senator Harry Cain from the Armed Forces Committee held friendly conversations with Franco and Artajo in Madrid. He wanted to ensure their support in case of war. Slowly, political considerations were ignored. However, the State Department still upheld that Spain was considered by many important elements to be alien to the NATO principle, and any action by the US to bring about her participation would weaken rather than strengthen the collective effort.

The Secretary of Defense, Louis Johnson, countered that France and the Low Countries were unable to defend themselves against an attack by the USSR; thus Spain had to be won over as an ally. He believed that Spain had to be integrated in NATO or bilateral agreements had to be signed. Acheson pointed out that this argument was based on the theory that the NATO countries could not defend themselves successfully, but that the whole NATO planning had been based on the assumption that no conflict would occur before 1954 and that NATO was meant to prevent and not win a war.

Many in his own department disagreed. In May a paper on Spanish policy by William Dunham and James Wilson argued that in the light of the intensification of the Cold War, the potential military importance

81

of Spain had increased to such a degree that the security interests of the US and NATO members required that a programme be put into effect in order to provide at least for indirect Spanish cooperation within the Western European strategic pattern. Only in December 1950, after China's involvement in Korea threatened UN defeat, was this paper allowed to be forwarded from the State Department to the National Security Council.

The US Army had already concluded that, due to the wide disparity between requirements for forces and the Western European plans for providing them, it was wholly unrealistic to expect success in the initial defence of Western Europe. The memorandum continued, recommending that NATO powers should avail themselves of the military potentials of Spain and Western Germany. This was against French political interests, which strongly opposed a German rearmament and an American–Spanish military agreement.

Political feelings of NATO countries had to be tested. In a conversation between the US Army Attaché and the British Military Attaché in Spain it became clear that the British War Office favoured military cooperation with Spain but that the Labour government did not, nor did the French authorities. It seemed unlikely that Anglo-American military cooperation with Spain could emerge.

In the meantime pressure to improve relations with Spain in Washington increased. The Korean crisis and McCarthyism created a political atmosphere under which it was difficult to oppose anti-Communism.

On 27 July the Mutual Defense Assistance Act assuring aid to Europe was signed. Four days later Secretary of Defense Louis Johnson wrote a memorandum to Truman, making it clear that under the Mutual Defense Assistance Act a total of 10 per cent of the funds to countries in Europe could be spent in other European nations as long as three conditions were met. First, the right could be exercised only in the event of a development seriously affecting the security of the North Atlantic area. Secondly, the strategic location of the nation must make it of direct importance to the defence of the North Atlantic area. Finally, the money should only be spent after consultation with the governments of the other nations in the North Atlantic Treaty. Ultimately the decision lay with the President, who had to consider that the increased ability of such a nation to defend itself would contribute to the preservation of the peace and security of the North Atlantic area and was vital to the security of the US. This opened the possibility of granting money to Spain.

Another possible source of funds for Spain was the Export–Import

Bank. The Bank decided in July 1950 that Spain could receive credits for agricultural and fertilizer projects. A third source of financial support came from Congress. For the third time, McCarran and Owen Brewster proposed a $100 million credit to Spain. McCarran, who received the "Grand Cross of the Order Of Isabella the Catholic" for his efforts to improve Spanish–American relations, had organized a secret meeting in his office at the Senate Building, which included several military officers of high standing. This was done to discuss the possibility of forcing Congress to appropriate funds for Spain.

McCarran's third attempt was planned more carefully than the previous ones. The administration was "directed" to lend money to Spain. Notes had to be issued and turned over to the Treasury. In return the Treasury would issue cash, which was handed over to the Export–Import Bank for delivery to Spain. The Bank would only handle the mechanical details while the European Cooperation Administration would administer the loans. With this system, McCarran had provided the most difficult step, the creation of funds. All the Export–Import Bank had to do was put the existing money to work in Spain. This last action had to be approved by the President. McCarran had no control over this final step but had good reason to believe that the government would approve.

The procedure to apply for a loan under this scheme required a Spanish company to seek and obtain an endorsement from the Spanish government through the Ministry of Commerce and Industry. This would be transmitted to the Foreign Minister and then passed on to the Export–Import Bank. The Bank would make its decision and pass all applications, together with the decision, to the European Cooperation Administration. One of the problems was that neither the Bank nor the European Cooperation Administration saw all applications for credits, as the Spanish Ministry had first choice. This complicated the whole issue. The Spanish Ministry was headed by Suanzes, creator of the INI. As a result one could expect that many applications would be turned down, not on economic grounds, but due to a lack of connections at the Ministry.

Despite this shortcoming, the Senate approved the credit by 65 to 15 on 1 August 1950, thus dealing a blow to the administration, and the House approved a reduced credit of $62.5 million. Against Truman's will, Spain became the only country to receive credits from the European Cooperation Administration without signing an agreement with the US.

Acheson and Truman both expressed their disapproval. However, as it was attached to the first General Appropriation Bill and thus had to be accepted or rejected in full, Truman's options were limited. A rejection by the President would have sent a misleading message to the US's Allies, implying that the US government was no longer willing to bear the costs of defending Europe. Given the strong anti-Communist feeling, Truman was forced to sign the General Appropriation Bill once it had passed Congress.

Only a few Congressmen opposed McCarran's proposal. Representative Howard W. Smith from Virginia said that the loan was an almost ridiculous situation where an attempt was made to write foreign policy on the floor of the House of Representatives.

However, when Truman signed the Bill, he pointed out that he was now authorized to grant aid to Spain but that he was in no way obliged to do so. The same day he said that money would be loaned to Spain whenever mutually advantageous arrangements could be made and whenever such loans would serve the interest of the US in the conduct of foreign relations. It was going to be a quid pro quo, where a deal would be struck only if political scepticism by Western Europe could be accommodated.

However, at the American Embassy in Madrid things looked different. Culbertson, after hearing the news from Washington, informed the State Department that since the President and the Secretary of State had clearly announced the administration's opposition to the credit, the Congress had, by its action, rather effectively taken out of US hands the conduct of one of the most important political factors in relations with Spain. As for his personal position, Culbertson argued that Congress had made him a first-class liar. The Chargé had been telling Spain that evolution had to precede credits. Now that credits had been made available, changes could no longer be expected.

Shortly before, the Portuguese dictator publicly expressed his desire to integrate Spain into NATO. He stated that the peninsular collaboration was basic for Atlantic solidarity and that the geographic frontier of Portugal was the Pyrenees. If Spain had to remain outside NATO, Salazar hoped that the US would at least grant military assistance.

Despite Portugal's interest, the campaign for Spain's inclusion in NATO had to wait until complications with Germany had been dealt with. Compared to Spain, Germany had far more military potential, yet for obvious reasons many feared her re-militarization. The Joint Chiefs of Staff agreed that General Bradley should approach the Secretary of Defense, with the idea of obtaining his concurrence to withholding action on Spain's integration into NATO until the West German situation was cleared up.

Acheson wanted to delay talks for very different reasons. He believed that the Spanish army was not well equipped, nor well trained, and was unable to fight off a Soviet invasion. He was also sure that Franco would not fight for anything except his country. The State Department conducted a study of Spain's strategic importance to the West and came up with a conclusion challenging the military point of view. It argued that a dollar spent in Spain would yield a smaller economic return than anywhere else in Western Europe. It continued to claim that without aid, Spain's military contribution was negligible. Infrastructure projects such as the railways had made no progress since the war. Spain had fewer locomotives, freight and passenger cars than in 1945. The State Department considered that Spain's only contribution could come from its natural mineral resources. Spain possessed one of the world's most important mercury, pyrites and potash deposits.

A similar report on Spain argued that any unilateral US effort to include Spain in its overall plans would be strongly resisted by Spaniards. This would result in a considerable loss of public support for Western European integration and would jeopardize the successful achievement of US policies. It was clear that the State Department favoured Germany's integration into the Western defence structure over Spain's.

After these studies by the State Department and because of his personal opposition, Truman spoke out against issuing loans to Spain. McCarran was fuming. He claimed that the President was acting unconstitutionally and against a clearly expressed directive from Congress. The President was not acting unconstitutionally at all. While he was obliged to make the necessary funds available, he was under no obligation to actually extend them to Spain. By his stance, Truman retained an important bargaining chip.

Shortly before Christmas, the Spanish Embassy in Washington made its first attempt to obtain money under the newly appropriate funds. Serrano Suñer, former Foreign Minister of Spain, and the Marqués de Nerva, the Commercial Attaché, contacted the State Department to discuss a loan. The loan was to be covered by the Export–Import Bank, but did not fall under McCarran's appropriated funds. For this particular credit the Bank wanted 3.5 per cent interest over 20 years, while the Spaniards argued for 2.5 per cent over 25 years. While the Bank was willing to finance cotton, tractors and fertilizer imports, Serrano Suñer wanted credits for corn, wheat and petrol imports. He knew that apart from the $62.5 million of appropriated funds, other credit applications by Spain to the Export–Import Bank were possible. What mattered most were the conditions attached to these credits. Time was on Spain's side.

This was also true in the UN. Spain's ban from Specialized Agencies of the UN had adverse consequences for the UN. The Intergovernmental Maritime Consultative Organization (IMCO) could not guarantee the safety of Spain's ships; thus passengers travelling on them were under greater danger. The World Health Organization (WHO) had found it more difficult to control the spread of major diseases while Spain was excluded and there was a lower health standard on ships and planes travelling to and from Spain. The International Civil Aviation Organization (ICAO) could not force Madrid to sign the Chicago Convention and therefore Spain's standards of air-traffic control and aircraft maintenance were lower than in other countries.

Eventually, the Dominican Republic requested that the Spanish problem be put on the agenda of the UN Committee on Politics and Security. Peru and Bolivia supported the request and drafted a joint resolution recommending the revocation of the 1946 resolution. In short succession El Salvador and the Dominican Republic drafted two proposals along similar lines. The US, unwilling to initiate discussions, had been urging these countries forward.

Portugal needed no convincing. The Foreign Minister, Dr Paolo Cunha, urged the North Atlantic Council to include Spain in NATO for strategic reasons. Denmark and the Netherlands were also supporters of Spain's cause. Belgium and Luxembourg wanted to cooperate with France and Britain. It therefore became paramount for the US to gain British and French support.

The French Ambassador in London made it clear that he wanted France to abstain in the coming vote, but for him it was of utmost importance that the three Western allies cooperated. As London was wavering under US pressure, not giving a clear signal, Paris finally decided to support the American cause and vote in Spain's favour.

In July the UK decided to abstain on a vote, but further US pressure and criticism by Latin American and other European nations made London reconsider its stance.

The British Chargé in Spain drafted a 16-page letter arguing that Britain should abandon her old policy and end the 1946 resolution. In London, the Foreign Office was divided on the issue. Some supported the Chargé; others argued that the British public would disagree with such a *rapprochement*. However, even trade unions like the National Union of Manufacturers encouraged better relations with Spain.

On 6 September 1950 the issue was discussed by the British Cabinet. After long arguments, it was decided that the UK delegation to the UN should abstain in the vote and that there was to be no change of general policy towards Spain.

Since the Foreign Office had initiated serious conversations concerning the Spanish Question, France had decided to abandon her policy to vote in favour of Spain. However, once the British Cabinet decided to abstain, and despite US pressure, the Quai d'Orsay reversed its decision again and the French Ambassador in London informed the Foreign Office that his nation would also abstain.

After a wave of draft proposals from Latin American countries, a joint draft recommending the revocation of the 1946 resolution was issued. This was passed to the Political Committee on 27 October 1950. During the following three days it became clear that there was overwhelming support for Spain. During the first day 13 nations spoke in favour of Spain. Poland, opposing a review of the resolution, avoided defeat only by adjourning the vote for several meetings. In the end only three Latin American states, the three Soviet delegates, three Eastern European states and Israel (a total of ten states) made their opposition to the draft proposal known. Twenty-eight other nations supported the draft.

On 31 October 1950 the UN Political Committee, in its fifth meeting, decided to hold the final vote. The result was 37 to 10 in favour and was passed to the General Assembly. On 4 November 1950, after a vote on each paragraph and finally on its entirety, the UN General Assembly, with a vote of 38 to 10 with 12 abstentions, adopted the draft passed by the First Committee.

Two days later, the Spanish newspaper *ABC* wrote that this was Spain's final victory in the last battle of the Civil War. Artajo made the most out of the reversal of the 1946 resolution. In a speech to the Cortes in December he claimed that since 1945 Spain had been a victim of Communist propaganda. According to him, the Western powers had naively tried to appease the Soviet Union by sacrificing Spain. He gloated that the West had finally realized that his country had been right all along, the Soviet Union was a threat and appeasement had to stop.

The truth was far more complex. In 1946, the UN had made the mistake of attaching diplomatic relations to a moral issue. This had linked the two, subsequently making it difficult to separate them.

The outcome was a result of Arab and Latin American countries changing their point of view between 1946 and 1950. In 1946/47, the Arab League was neutral towards Spain but by 1949 and 1950 they had reversed into a pro-Franco stance. This was in return for Spanish support against the creation of a Jewish state in Palestine. In 1946 only six Latin American countries voted for Spain; four years later sixteen supported her. They justified their reversal on two grounds. First, diplomatic relations did not mean an *ipso-facto* acceptance of the regime and secondly, they were deeply upset with the economic gains by Argentina which had continued ambassadorial relations.

The vote by the US in favour of Spain made the administration vulnerable to attacks from the left. President Truman, influenced by documents revealing Nazi investments of $200 million in Spain, stated that it would be a "long, long time" before his country would resume full diplomatic relations with Spain. This greatly confused policy makers as it implied that the President, despite his nation's vote in the UN, did not favour the abolition of the 1946 resolution. Truman's statement was a diplomatic blunder.

The State Department had a more realistic approach, and already in May 1950 had considered several candidates for the post of Ambassador to Spain. Possible candidates were also brought to Truman's attention. These included H. Freeman Matthews, Deputy Under-Secretary of State, Hersgel V. Johnson, Ambassador to Brazil, John C. Wiley, Ambassador to Iran, Mark Ethridge, a prominent publisher with experience at the UN and finally Robert M. LaFollette, former Senator. Truman knew that these candidates had been considered.

Culbertson in Madrid was particularly upset with Truman's "long, long time" statement. It came as a blow because it looked as if a split of policies between the White House and the State Department had occurred. The official US position in Spain and on Spanish affairs at the UN had been undermined. It seemed that the State Department was eager to normalize relations with Spain while Truman was not. Nevertheless, behind the scenes Truman realized that his statement had been a diplomatic mistake and on 13 November, the President was again considering who to appoint as Ambassador to Spain. Slightly more than a week later the question was settled in favour of Stanton Griffis.

Trying to lessen the embarrassment of Truman's statement, the State Department did not inform London of its final decision and Homer Byington, Director of the Office for Western European Affairs, told the Foreign Office that the two front-runners were Stanton Griffis and possibly George Garret, Ambassador in Dublin.

Only a couple of days later, Propper de Callejón from the Spanish Embassy inquired if Griffis was going to be appointed Ambassador to Spain. Byington, despite having been told of Griffis's appointment, informed Propper that no instructions had been given to him from the White House and thus he was unable to confirm the rumour.

Griffis, born in Boston in 1887, was a New York investment banker, who had served in the past as Ambassador to Egypt, Portugal and

Argentina. He also headed the 1948 UN Relief for Palestine Refugee Committee. He seemed well suited for the job as he had links with Argentina and the Arab world.

After his official appointment, Griffis cunningly decided to take a holiday to decrease the President's continuing embarrassment caused by his claim that a long delay would precede the resumption of full diplomatic relations. When the idea of a holiday was suggested, Truman told Griffis: "That's a great idea and exactly what I want. I don't want you to go for the present – so soon after what I said a few weeks ago. I have been a little overruled and worn down by the [State] Department."[1]

When Griffis finally presented his credentials at the Pardo Palace, Franco made the most of the occasion. A gilded carriage drawn by six white horses and escorted by the Moorish Guards was provided to the Ambassador.

Britain and France were also in no hurry to appoint an ambassador to Spain. Even though the British Ambassador, Sir John Balfour, was an admirer of the Portuguese dictator Salazar and had supported British neutrality during the Spanish Civil War, the Foreign Office remained cautious. When the British Chiefs of Staff urged the Foreign Office to relax restrictions on activities of the Spanish service attachés and to resume naval visits to Spain, the Foreign Office rejected both suggestions on the grounds that the timing was inopportune. The Office argued that the new Ambassador to Spain had to be appointed and present his credentials to Franco, before policy changes could take place. Madrid was also in no hurry to improve relations with London. An article in *Arriba* accused British officials of forging Spanish currency. Furthermore, during December 1950, Franco encouraged the campaign by the Falange against British Gibraltar. Given these circumstances, the Foreign Office considered delaying the appointment of Sir John Balfour, but the realization that this would do little more than worsen relations, and the fact that Falangist agitation soon stopped made London abandon the plan.

The Foreign Office was hoping that Franco would elevate the Duke of San Lucar, former Spanish Chargé to London, to the post of Ambassador. Franco, however, appointed a member of the Falange, Fernando Castiella, who had also won an Iron Cross while fighting in the Blue Division. In 1941 he had written a book entitled *Spanish Demands* in which he claimed colonial territories from Britain and France. The Foreign Office bluntly refused to accept him as Ambassador. Instead Miguel Primo de Rivera, brother of the founder of the Falange, was appointed, a decision only slightly less controversial.

Relations with the US moved in a more favourable direction. The Security Council policy decision, NSC 72/1, had revised US policy towards Spain. The State Department analysed the implications of this document. It was recognized that Spain was of strategic and military importance. However, for the time being the State Department considered Spain's participation in the Mutual Defense Assistance Program and/or NATO impossible. Spain had to improve her relations with Europe first. However, her military potential was to be developed as soon as possible by granting military equipment in return for air and naval bases. It was also hoped that, as the situation in Korea deteriorated, Congress would become more willing to increase its commitment to Spain and maybe even favour her admission to NATO.

Under these circumstances more information about Spain's strategic potential and military requirements had to be gathered. In September the Spanish Brigadier-General Aguirre and one officer of each of the three military services flew to Frankfurt to attend manoeuvres by the US Army. At the same time information was collected about the logistical needs of the Spanish Army. In October a study of Spain's topography was requested. Existing studies were almost ten years old and of limited value for strategic planning at operational and tactical level. The study, expected to take between 18 and 24 months, was to concentrate on specific areas of the Iberian Peninsula. It was considered of great importance to the US Defense Department.

All this was done in the knowledge that Germany's integration and re-militarization had priority over Spain's. The State Department was waiting until this issue had been dealt with. On 13 December 1950, the Director of the Joint Staff was reminded that "by previous action, the Joint Chiefs of Staff had stated that the question of German rearmament should be given priority and that the question of including Spain in the defense of Europe should not be pushed until the German question had been settled". Nevertheless, as the Chiefs of Staff had accepted a policy proposal relating to Germany's rearmament, it seemed to them time to "take up the paper on our policy toward Spain".[2]

NOTES

1. Lowi, "Bases in Spain", p. 691.
2. NA, Military Branch, CCS 092, US Joint Chiefs of Staff, Spain (4–19–46).

7 Convictions of Military Men

On the other side of the globe, US soldiers in Korea met disaster when the Chinese poured thousands of troops into a gap left by the Americans. In two weeks the Communists regained almost all of North Korea and defeat could no longer be ruled out. In the free world, governments feared more aggressive Communist policies.

As the Korean conflict deepened, the British mission in Madrid predicted that Washington would improve military relations with Spain. The British Chargé, Hankey, assumed that an American review of Spanish port facilities by the US Naval Attaché was the beginning of a change of policy. This was not at all welcomed by European nations, and particularly not by France, Greece, nor Italy.

As the British correctly feared, the US was reviewing its policy towards Spain. On 12 January the Joint Chiefs of Staff sent a memorandum to the Secretary of Defense, concerning NSC 71/1. It argued that Spain did not want to join NATO because France was unable to defend herself. As this strategic aspect was changing and a stance in Europe against the Red Army became a possibility, Spain was expected to change her position and not hesitate in joining NATO. The memorandum continued, claiming that Spain's participation in NATO did not *per se* mean a withdrawal behind the Pyrenees. Rather it meant using Spain's resources for the overall defence. However, for the time being, the Joint Chiefs of Staff lacked information on Spain's military capabilities to allocate her a defence task. As a result the Department of Defense asked the State Department to channel its diplomatic activities towards obtaining this information. Military association between NATO and Spain, or at the very least between the US and Spain, was to be effected as soon as the German participation question was settled.

Three days later the Secretary of State outlined the new policy towards Spain. In this justification, NSC 72/2, the Secretary of State considered Spain to be of geographical importance and thus part of the defence of Western Europe. America's ultimate aim was to get Spain into the Mutual Defense Assistance Program and NATO. Acheson claimed that the longer they waited to approach Madrid, the more the US had to pay for Spain's integration. He asserted that it was indeed possible to eliminate the political disadvantages of Spain's incorporation into Europe. In order to use military bases in Spain, a long list of infrastructural improvements had to be made. NSC 72 had encouraged closer political ties with Spain. In order to achieve this, NSC 72/2 argued that the US should develop the military potential of Spain's strategic geographical position for the common defence of the NATO area. It was clear that eventually, the US would approach Spain for long-range bomber bases and for naval facilities. In the meantime, technical advice was to be given. The Secretary stressed that the American authorities should emphasize in all discussions concerning Spain that the aim was not to liberate but to defend Europe. To do so, one required bases in Spain for which the US would allow the sale of military equipment, air-navigational aids and other electronic equipment. However, under the Mutual Defense Assistance Program and the European Recovery Program, NATO countries still held priority over Spain. The Secretary recommended that the US should make a complete survey of Spain's requirements and capabilities. In order to avoid international complications, Spain had to improve relations with other NATO countries, above all with France and Britain.[1]

On 18 January 1951, Acheson outlined why US policy had changed. He claimed that Spain had to be part of the Western European structure and as Franco's position was strong there was no alternative but to talk to his government.

The State Department, still worrying about political implications, wanted to know how Europe would react to the new approach to Spain. Portugal still favoured Spain's participation in NATO. The Netherlands had shown increasing interest in Spain and in December a Dutch naval squadron, including a carrier, visited Valencia. The British government remained unhappy with the developments but as the Labour Party was no longer united on this topic, Attlee wanted to avoid discussions in the Commons altogether. A purely bilateral agreement between the US and Spain, excluding Britain, was very unattractive to the Foreign Office as it would indicate that the US was getting Spain into NATO against the consent of Western Europe. The British Embassy in Madrid was aware of the American military plans in Spain and concluded that the US was looking after her own interests and not those of Europe. The British Chargé in Spain, discouraging US plans, claimed that Spain's army could only be mobilized with difficulty and transportation/supply lines to the Pyrenees ran along roads and railways which would not be able to deal with the increased traffic in the event of war.

France too was opposed to the new US policy to Spain. Apart from some Gaullist elements which favoured full NATO membership, most of the National Assembly deputies and Bidault personally still disliked Franco and opposed Spain's integration into NATO.

Back in Washington, despite the disagreements with France and Britain, the Joint Chiefs of Staff and the Pentagon welcomed NSC 72/2. The Joint Chiefs of Staff proposed small changes to two points; one in the analysis, the other in the conclusion of NSC 72/2. The Joint Chiefs of Staff informed the Executive Secretary of the NSC that the US should propose the acceptance of Spain as a member of NATO and if this was not possible, US military planners should enter talks with Spain directly. The Chairman of the Joint Chiefs of Staff, General Bradley, agreed with NSC 72/2's main conclusions. He too believed that Spain's exclusion threatened Europe's security and, given the right military guarantees, Spain might make her armed forces available for the defence of Europe.

On 29 January, the Secretary of Defense issued his reply, NSC 72/3. According to George C. Marshall, NSC 72/2 overcame the political complications expressed in NSC 72/1. He wanted to make clear that the military potential of Spain's geographical position had to be developed "urgently" rather than be delayed due to political considerations. He asserted that negotiations concerning bomber, fighter and naval operational bases should not wait until plans for these bases were complete. Therefore the US should not approach Spain "eventually" but should do so without delay and with the expectation of gaining a military commitment. The Defense Secretary further rejected the idea of simply permitting "the sale of military equipment". He wanted to "provide" military assistance to Spain. He agreed that negotiations were to be conducted through the Embassy, but not exclusively so. He recommended that the negotiations be conducted through close cooperation between officials of the Departments of State and Defense. Finally, NSC 72/3 tried to amend NSC 72/2 by stressing the importance of an "early" achievement of the ultimate objective – getting Spain into NATO.

The Secretary of State reacted positively to these proposals. Yet he argued that military assistance to Spain should only be granted in accordance with the final aim of US policy towards Spain. This meant that military assistance should only be granted once Spain had contributed forces to the defence of Europe. This assistance was seen as a strong bargaining position and was not to be given away before agreements had been signed. In respect to the enforcement of policy through close cooperation between the two Departments, the Secretary of State wanted the Department of Defense and the Joint Chiefs of Staff to agree at a later date on a single mission to Spain. The reason for this was to present an undivided negotiation front, thus eliminating any attempts by Spanish officials to split the US negotiations team into factions.

On 1 February, the National Security Council senior staff finished their discussion on the controversy between NSC 72/2 and NSC 72/3. The first six points of NSC 72/2, which formed the justification of the new policy, were dropped altogether and NSC 72/3 prevailed. The resulting document (NSC 72/4) did not allow the simple provision of "military assistance to Spain" but made this aid subject to consistency with other objectives. These were introduced into NSC 72/4 by the Secretary of State and implied that

> any MDAP assistance given to Spain should be given under such terms and conditions as to advance and not retard Spanish participation in NATO. The Spanish Government would doubtless prefer a purely bilateral relation with the United States under which Spain received United States aid and the United States received certain rights from Spain without involving Spain in any obligations for the defense of Western Europe. This result should be avoided and aid should be given only if we are satisfied that by so doing we are advancing Spain closer to participation in NATO.[2]

This had replaced the claim that the contribution of Spanish troops to the integrated defence forces should be presented as a necessary step to Spanish admission to NATO and as a basis for the establishment of military assistance under the Mutual Defense Assistance Program. The same day NSC 72/4 was approved and became government policy. This document was divided into two sections. Section one was concerned with the immediate objectives of US policy towards Spain and section two with the ultimate objectives. Section one called for urgent development of Spain's military and strategic potential for the common defence of NATO and thus made clear that Spain was not to be defended on her own but was part of a common defence of Europe. It urged the US to approach Spain for long-range bomber, fighter and naval bases in return for military assistance and technical advice. It also suggested that the US should assist Spain in improving her relations towards other NATO countries and hoped that after discussions with France and Britain, the US could form a common policy of Western nations towards Spain. Section two listed two ultimate objectives governing all negotiations. Spain was to be included in NATO as early as possible and secondly, the US should, if possible, avoid bilateral agreements with Spain.

Shortly afterwards, the State Department granted more funds to the USIS, representing American culture in Spain. At the same time instructions were sent to the USIS to induce people and authorities in Spain to promote US policies and to reduce Spain's isolation from international institutions like NATO, the OEEC and the UN.

On 6 February 1951, Acheson informed the designated Ambassador to Spain, Stanton Griffis, of his delicate mission. Griffis had been confirmed in office on 1 February and was planning to arrive in Spain on 20 February. He was to stay at Ramón de la Cruz 5, with the Embassy close by on the Paseo de la Castellana. Griffis, arriving in Cádiz by boat with two large limousines, was welcomed by an American Export Lobby which had organized a reception buffet for some 100 VIPs. However, more than 1000 turned up to greet the Ambassador. The resulting shortage of food and drink was not the best start to show American generosity.

Concerning talks with Franco, Griffis was instructed to point out that propaganda attacks on international institutions like NATO, the OEEC and the UN had worsened relations between Spain and Europe and that Washington disliked these vehemently. The Ambassador was to use this opportunity to outline certain economic and financial restrictions. Griffis also had to make clear that if Franco wanted to improve relations with the US, he could only do so by improving relations with Europe. The American was to make it clear that the US was committed to NATO countries first and Spain second.

In a meeting between the State Department, the Pentagon and the Joint Chiefs of Staff, officials from the State Department asked for the Pentagon to work out further instructions for Ambassador Griffis. Before this could be done Britain and France were informed of some of the instructions given to Griffis. Four days later the State Department asked for their feedback. Sir Oliver Franks, British Ambassador in Washington, found the change of policy regrettable. He feared that Franco would use them for propaganda reasons and more importantly, to drive a wedge between the Anglo-French and American policy towards Madrid. The American Ambassador in London, Gifford, met with George P. Young, head of the Western Department of the British Foreign Office, who argued along similar lines. Sir John Balfour in Madrid also feared that the Spanish Ministry would play off Britain against the US. He already knew Griffis personally and was concerned that with Griffis's sanguine temperament he would find it difficult to remain passive for long.

The Franco regime started to take a firmer stance against Britain and problems concerning British Gibraltar. At the same time the Spanish press was publishing anti-British articles. *Arriba* supported Argentina's claim for the Falklands and Guatemala's claim for British Honduras.

The US Ambassador in London assumed that if the US acquired bases in Spain then the ultimate objective to include Spain in a common defence of the West would become an impossibility. He believed that Spain would avoid multilateral agreements if she could enter bilateral arrangements and thus bypass opposition in France and Britain, making a common policy towards Spain impossible.

In March, Dunham met with the Counsellor of the British Embassy in Washington and the Ambassador. The Counsellor preferred that the US should not enter into talks with Spain over a possible inclusion into NATO, as this would slow down agreements on Germany's remilitarization. Sir Oliver Franks told Dunham that he believed that Griffis should not contact Franco at all before further consultation between Britain and the US had taken place. Dunham was unwilling to give in and could only assure the British that Griffis had been instructed not to touch on Spain's relations with NATO before the US had consulted with Britain.

The British position was the result of complicated political considerations. Public opinion and scarce economic resources in Britain meant that London would have been sidelined in a *rapprochement* to Spain. Gibraltar's strategic importance would have decreased if the US gained naval bases in southern Spain. Pravda even suggested that Gibraltar was to be transferred to the US. London was not interested in a collective *rapprochement* to Spain. The Foreign Office knew that Britain, unlike the US, would benefit little from economic or military agreements with Spain. Thus it was advisable to hinder such a development. In an attempt to get Washington to reverse its policy, London lobbied against Spain. During the coming months, the Italian Chargé in London received confidential information through the Foreign Office concerning US–Spanish relations. Italy in return supported Britain in this matter. The Foreign Office also discouraged Portugal from raising the Spanish issue in NATO meetings, claiming that the military built up in Western Europe had priority over Spain's. In the OEEC Britain argued that Spain's membership was undesirable because, owing to the generally low level of resources, the contribution which Spain might have made would have been limited. London argued that for Spain to join the

OEEC would mean a reversal of her monetary and fiscal policies, something which the Foreign Office considered unlikely.

Given previous French opposition to the Franco regime, it is strange that the Quai d'Orsay was more positive towards talks between Griffis and Franco than the Foreign Office. The truth was that French concerns about Spain were concentrated in the French National Assembly while the Government and the Ministries cared little. As a result, a vote by the French Foreign Affairs Committee of the National Assembly opposing the appointment of an ambassador had been overturned by the French government. M. Bernard Haridon was promoted from the post of Chargé to Ambassador and Jean Marc Boeger, a senior officer at the French Foreign Ministry, informed the American Ambassador that Griffis should go ahead with talks with Franco.

When Britain realized that France did not object to these talks, London back-pedalled and suggested that discussions between the three nations should take place as soon as possible.

While this was going on, Secretary of State Acheson told the Senate Foreign Relations Committee and the House Military Affairs Committee on 16 February 1951, "the importance of the association of Spain in the defense of Western Europe I think is clear. I think it is also clear that relations of this country, and I hope of other countries, with Spain are now entering a new phase." For the Secretary there seemed to be little doubt about Spain's strategic value. Military necessities had overruled previous political concerns.[3]

If Acheson was implying that Spain should receive military aid, many would have been opposed. Rearming Spain meant fewer resources for France and Germany. Yet in Europe, France was the backbone of Western defence. The Rhine, and not the Pyrenees, was to be the final defensive line, and thus resources for Spain were better employed for ten new German divisions.

There was another military consideration which covered neither strategy nor logistic distribution of war material. The Defense Department analysed their dependency on certain raw material imports. In order to meet the full mobilization requirements, the National Stockpiling Program was set up. Internal production in the US, Mexico and Spain were the sole sources for four strategic raw materials. Celestite imports from Spain were needed for signal flares, tracer ammunition and filler for paints, rubber and plastics. Fluorspar acid was required to built ceramics, flux (a substance mixed with metal to promote fusion) and hydrofluoric. Fluorspar was demanded for flux to manufacture steel, cast iron and ferro alloys. Finally and most important of all, Spain was required for mercury imports needed to produce explosives and electric apparatuses.

The State Department knew that Spain's production of raw materials could be boosted by American capital investment. Lead production could have been increased by almost 100 000 tons with an investment of only slightly more than $4 million. Similar results could have been seen with investment in the tungsten, pyrites and zinc production.

Nevertheless, due to the strong reaction of the British diplomats, Washington decided to instruct Griffis not to talk to Franco about detailed military issues. He was also told to avoid any comment on Spain's relations with NATO and bilateral agreements with the US. Before more detailed instructions could be given to Griffis, the State Department again consulted with London and Paris.

In the meantime, on 7 March the Griffis–Franco talks received the go-ahead. At the same time Washington wanted to make sure that the damage done to Anglo-American relations was minimized by holding further talks with British diplomats. The same day, during a dinner in London, Miss Willis, a young and inexperienced diplomat working at the US Embassy, stressed the importance of utilizing Spain's military potential and confessed that Washington's immediate objective was the acquisition and utilization of air and naval bases in Spain. She even revealed that the US would enter bilateral talks with Spain while continuing to consult with France and Britain. After dinner Theodore Achilles, in charge of the Western European Division and more experienced than Miss Willis, had to reassure the Foreign Office representatives that he was concerned about the Griffis–Franco talks and Spanish–American relations in general.

Developments in Madrid did not encourage the British Foreign Office any more than the dinner in London. John Balfour met his American counterpart and for over an hour Stanton Griffis outlined Spain's importance to Western Europe. Instead of reassuring Ambassador Balfour, Griffis created the impression that he was in fact challenging part of his own instructions from Washington when he spoke freely about Spain's relations with NATO and bilateral agreements with the US. The two ambassadors were obviously not getting on. Balfour had previously commented on his fears about Griffis's sanguine character endangering the delicate situation of Spain's position in foreign relations. Now he added that Griffis had shown himself to be even more impervious to reasoning than he had feared earlier. Some days later Balfour was again outraged by the American's "naive persistence", and he described Griffis as a tired man who would find it difficult to stay the course. Even

Washington was getting concerned about Griffis's over-enthusiasm and tried to stop him from further complicating the issue.

Under instructions from Washington to improve relations and despite opposition from London, Franco and Griffis held their first official talks on 14 March. Franco did most of the talking while the American Ambassador listened patiently. The Caudillo guaranteed concessions concerning religion, something which was vital for Truman. Griffis briefly mentioned his government's desire to cooperate with Spain, if possible, to use Spanish air and naval facilities. Franco was pleased about this and elaborated his thoughts at great length. Expressing his disbelief that France could be defended, he thought that America's best option was to grant aid directly to Portugal and Spain. The Caudillo said that he was willing to join the US on terms similar to those of NATO. Even without such an agreement, he said that Spain would be willing to send troops north of the Pyrenees after they had been properly armed and trained.

As for US bases in Spain, Franco told Griffis that it was possible as long as these were mutual bases and, in the event of war, remained under Spain's command. He also expressed his interest in a bilateral agreement. The Caudillo left Griffis with the belief that he could be guided along any lines the Americans wished for as long as aid to Spain was in proportion to aid given to other countries.

On 16 March, Homer M. Byington from the State Department informed the Counsellor to the British Embassy about the developments during the conversation between Franco and Griffis. On the same day the French authorities were informed. What the Americans decided to omit was the part of the conversation which concerned possible bases. Slightly later, other embassies and representatives at NATO were informed. Yet in all cases the US carefully avoided talking about military bases. The reason for this omission is clear. The State Department wanted to keep up the appearance that a bilateral military settlement between Spain and the US had not even been considered.

On the same day as Britain and France were updated, the State Department requested advice from the Department of Defense on how to proceed with the talks without upsetting France or Britain. Together, the two Departments were to work out the tactics to successfully implement NSC 72/4.

Unfortunately, four days after the talks between Franco and Griffis and two days after Britain and France had been informed a summary of the conversations was somehow leaked to the Associated Press and received publicity world-wide. It had been America's attempt to avoid this. Britain and France had no choice but to express their regret on the unilateral approach by the US towards Spain.

In pace with the military talks, economic relations between the US and Spain improved. In February 1951 Spain received the right to the first $12.2 million under the $62.5 million credit. The credit was used to buy 60 000 bales of cotton and its conditions were favourable to Spain, carrying interest of only 2.75 per cent.

There was an exchange of air-force officers to discuss a deal on ten aircraft. In April several USAF Thunderjets left Germany for flight demonstrations in Seville and Madrid. After these demonstrations, a representative of the Spanish company Ramón Escario informed the British company De Havilland that he had serious doubts about doing business with the British company. Straight away Ambassador Balfour encouraged a flight show by De Havilland Comets.

In his over-enthusiasm, Ambassador Griffis put further strain on Anglo-American relations. During an after-dinner speech at the American Chamber of Commerce in Barcelona, he advocated technical and financial assistance for Spain in return for relaxation of restrictions on foreign capital. He publicly stressed Spain's strategic importance, a topic which had great appeal to the domestic press. In another talk to the American Chamber of Commerce, this time in Madrid, Griffis requested help from Spanish companies not so much for the benefit of Spain as for the benefit of the US government itself. He even urged the firms represented at the meeting to bring pressure on Congress and on President Truman so that relations between Madrid and Washington would improve. Griffis was not even deterred when a journalist in a press conference in Barcelona caught him in a series of political blunders concerning Eastern Europe. This did not make Griffis a popular man in the State Department.

Unlike Griffis, the State Department wanted to be subtle in pressuring France and Britain into improving relations with Spain. Griffis's approach not only created a bad atmosphere between the three Western Allies but also increased military demands from Spain and made economic concessions less likely.

The State Department knew that Spain's economy was too regulated to attract substantial private investments. A report, dated 1 February 1951, to the House of Representatives was very pessimistic about Spain's economic outlook. It argued that the INI was pushing out private enterprises. In April, Griffis sent his impression of Spain's economic situation to Washington. He argued that the economy could put an end to Franco only if the army was willing to oust the dictator, which he considered highly unlikely. Militarily, Griffis claimed that Spain was unable to defend herself because she lacked modern military equipment. Thus, he concluded, military aid was urgently required.

The US Army was convinced that Spanish military capabilities were so promising that they could be improved more rapidly than capabilities in any other European country and at no greater cost. Senator McCarthy supported this view, claiming that the defence of Europe should be revised so as to provide for utilization of the military resources of West Germany, Spain, Turkey and Greece.

This analysis was not supported entirely by the military. On 13 April the International Security Affairs Committee argued that the military capacity of Spain would require the support of the Spanish people, which might be difficult to obtain if it appeared that US interest in Spain extended only to the military establishment and disregarded the welfare of the Spanish people themselves.

The Committee recommended speeding up the $62.5 million programme by issuing the notes to the European Cooperation Administration for purchase by the Secretary of the Treasury and thus make credits more available. It also argued that in order to implement NSC 72/4, further economic aid was required. Yet the document itself was not specific on the exact amount. The Fiscal Year (FY) 1952 included no budget allocations for Spain apart from the possibility of using part of the $850 million credit for Europe. Furthermore, the $62.5 million credit would expire on 30 June unless the European Cooperation Administration was extended into FY 1952, and by now only $17 million had been approved. Unless the money was extended for one year, there existed a real possibility that there would be no credits available for Spain. The International Security Affairs Committee argued that military improvements depended heavily on Spanish infrastructure, and funds had to be created so that the government could draw upon them whenever necessary. In conclusion, the Committee reported that the $62.5 million credit should be extended into the FY 1952 and Congress should raise other funds. When presented with this report in April, Truman gave his approval.

The Joint Chiefs of Staff concluded in another study that, despite opposition from France and Britain, measures should be initiated to make Spain a military ally. The US Army argued that Spain's armed forces had many experienced soldiers and its troops were not divided by Marxist theories. Its only disadvantage was that it lacked modern weapons. At the same time the Army wanted to discuss the use of Spanish resources at the Standing Group of NATO, thus widening talks to include France and Britain. The Navy and Air Force argued that if the problem came before the Standing Group, complications would arise and bilateral agreements could no longer be signed with Spain. The two services argued that NSC 72/4 called for negotiations between the two countries which at the moment could only be done directly with Spain. The Army believed that cooperation with Madrid was only possible after France and Britain had recognized Spain's usefulness. The disagreements between the three services is not surprising. The Navy and Air Force gained substantially from a deal with Spain while the Army feared complications in military cooperation within NATO.

In the meantime improvements to Spain's infrastructure were vital and credits had to be made available. In order to facilitate these, the Chairman of the Export–Import Bank, Gaston, wrote to the American Embassy in Spain clarifying the form of acceptance of credit applications under the $62.5 million credit. The Bank favoured applications for the mining and agriculture sectors. According to Gaston most applications had failed because they were not made for specific programmes. By April 1951 only five credits adding up to $17.2 million had been approved. Other credit applications had been rejected due to the size, lack of alternative funds, and because they had no economic justification. Griffis argued that the reason why few credits had been extended under the Export–Import Bank was due to the slow approval process in the US.

In order to improve military relations, the Joint Chiefs of Staff recommended sending Admiral Carney, Commander-in-Chief of the USNF Eastern Atlantic and Mediterranean to Spain in order to obtain US flight, stop and transit rights. Carney was also to ask for access to and use of military bases in Spain, Spanish Morocco and Spain's islands. These bases were useful to control the Straits of Gibraltar and for anti-submarine warfare. His official brief would have been to conduct initial military discussions of an exploratory nature.

However, complaints by Britain and France over the new US policy convinced the State Department that further talks with its European allies had to be held before Admiral Carney could visit Spain. Again the Department of Defense disagreed.

The Foreign Office in Britain was very much opposed to the new approach by the US to Spain but the British Joint Planning Staff, part of the Chiefs of Staff, were favourably inclined. Similarly to the US plans, the British study recognized Spain's strategic value. It was claimed that Germany's rearmament made a change of policy towards Spain possible. If a bilateral agreement between the US and Spain was signed, the British Joint Planning Staff hoped that France and Britain would also be able to enter secret contracts with Spain. It was feared that a bilateral agreement would reduce the US military commitment to the rest of Europe, and weaken NATO's defence concept in general.

The Joint Planning Staff saw two alternatives – either to abandon any military association with Spain or to accede to the idea of bilateral agreements. So far Washington had not been willing to give in to European concern and there was no indication that it might do so in the future. Thus London risked being sidelined. It was clear that the Americans were decided on reaching a military understanding with General Franco. It seemed useless to oppose the American drive. Thus the Joint Planning Staff recommended to associate Britain with the agreement so as to obtain the maximum advantages. However, the Foreign Office chose not to follow the military recommendations and decided instead to continue its opposition.

As feared by the British military, the US cared little about Europe's concerns. On 23 April, a directive went to Admiral Carney instructing him to conduct initial military discussions with Spain, to form the basis for future military cooperation.

The Admiral was informed that US military requirements were long-term rights in Spain to base and rotate air groups. The Navy sought anchorage rights in several ports. Arrangements for his trip were being made through the Senior Military Attaché in Madrid and the American Ambassador to Spain was kept informed of developments.

Two weeks later the service attachés in Spain organized aerial photographs of Valencia, Tarragona, Cullera, Sagunto, Barcelona, Badalona and other coastal areas. These were to help future negotiations and to pinpoint the exact sites for military bases.

To provide social stability, Spain needed economic aid. After clarifications in Washington, loans were made more accessible to Spain and by May Spain had received $52.5 million out of the total $62.5 million Export–Import Bank credit. Chase Manhattan granted Spain $42 million and the National City Bank extended loans of over $20 million. These credits for Spain were also of some importance to American industry.

On 7 June 1951, the State Department, issuing NSC 72/5, argued that in order to achieve the objectives of NSC 72/4 certain changes had to be made concerning economic and military assistance. The Department agreed that the development of Spain's military potential was no longer to be governed by political considerations. Thus US officials should no longer have to emphasize that the primary role envisaged for Spain was supporting the defence of Europe. The State

Department even agreed to provide military assistance and the necessary and appropriate economic assistance to Spain. Here the State Department had gone one step further than in NSC 72/4. Spain was not only to receive military but also economic assistance as long as this was compatible with two restrictions. First, any assistance provided to Spain was guided by the simple principle that NATO countries had priority. Second, any military or economic assistance given to Spain had to be given under such terms and conditions as to advance and not retard her participation in NATO. NSC 72/5 allowed the Defense Department to release through the Civil Aeronautics Administration, either directly to the Spaniards or through the US airlines operating in Spain, as much as possible of the air-navigational aids and other electronic equipment which the Spanish government had requested during the negotiations of the Civil Air Agreement. Compared to NSC 72/4, the State Department abandoned its opposition to bilateral agreements.

Shortly afterwards the Joint Chiefs of Staff wanted to make certain changes to NSC 72/5. General Hoyt S. Vandenberg believed that NSC 72/5 gave the impression that if Spain was not to be included in NATO and no alternative arrangements could be made then no alternative mutual defence arrangement would be concluded. On 27 June 1951, the NSC senior staff issued NSC 72/6 as a response to the State Department's proposal. The changes were dramatic. Political considerations no longer governed the development of Spain's military potential. US policy no longer emphasized the defence rather than the liberation of Europe. Spain's inclusion in NATO was no longer a long-term aim but fell under the section of immediate objectives. The paper clearly stated that if Spain's integration was delayed, alternative mutual security arrangements should be made. The paper suggested that military and air aviation aids were to be granted by the Defense Department. Although the NSC still considered NATO to have precedence over Spain, NATO no longer had priority if aid for Spain would assist the acquisition by the US of military sites. American negotiators could approach Spain for military bases, disregarding European opposition. The NSC staff had decided not to go along with the State Department's proposal that before initiating discussions, agreements had to be reached with other NATO countries. NSC 72/6 was approved by President Truman on 28 June 1951, becoming US policy.

France and Britain were informed of these changes. Washington hoped that London was ready to enter military talks with Spain. On 21 and 22 June talks were held between the US and the two European nations.

This time the military aspects came under scrutiny. Admiral Sherman and McGuire E. Perkins of the State Department outlined the US position to the British Air-Chief-Marshal Sir William Elliot. The British could not help feeling that the State Department had been pushed into an uncomfortable position by the Defense Department. The next day the two Americans met with the French General Murtin to update him.

Shortly afterwards France and Britain compared the information given to them by the State Department. It became clear that France had received less specific information about the planned US bases and airfields. This was done because US authorities knew that France was still concerned about a withdrawal of US troops behind the Pyrenees. Britain, on the other hand, had not been informed that the US saw little need to issue a tripartite statement before signing agreements with Spain. This was the most important issue for London and by keeping London in the dark, the US hoped to avoid complications with Britain. After this exchange of information, Britain and France decided to delay the talks between the US and Spain as long as possible.

On 25 June, the State Department cleared Sherman's visit to Spain. He was to depart not later than 15 July and was instructed specifically to discuss base facilities. His talks were to be followed by a small group to continue the negotiations. This group was to include high-ranking officers from the Navy and Air Force. Griffis was told that he should inform the Spaniards that the talks interrupted in March 1951 would be resumed.

After being worn down by Sherman and Marshall and after approving NSC 72/6 in early July, Truman authorized the visit by the Chief of Naval Operations to Spain. The decision whether to send Sherman or Carney was not made until the last days of June and finally came down to a personal preference by Ambassador Griffis who, after all, was to coordinate the negotiations. In fact, Griffis had already invited Sherman to Spain in April 1951 but at that time political objections had overruled the visit. Now, after NSC 72/6, nothing stood in the way of the talks.

In the meantime and as agreed with France, the British Embassy expressed a desire for the Americans to delay their planned bilateral talks with Spain in order to give the British Cabinet more time to reach and express its opinion. This was a trap by London to delay the talks indefinitely. Mr Homer Byington, Director of Western European Affairs at the State Department, assured the British Embassy that the US would wait until HM Government's view was received. However, Sherman's visit had already been approved and confirmed by the

President. In fact Sherman had been instructed not to leave for Madrid later than 15 July.

Britain was in no hurry to make its view known. Finally, on 6 July, the Americans informed the British Embassy that talks were to be resumed with Spain. The US could not wait any longer. If Britain wanted to make her policy known, she had to do so quickly. For the US this mattered little, as under NSC 72/6, Washington had decided to go ahead with bilateral talks whatever the position of her NATO allies.

The British Ambassador in Madrid urged London to make its policy known. He knew that Sherman had gone on a trip to the Far East for a week, and upon returning briefly to Washington for final instructions would depart for Madrid.

Under pressure, the British Cabinet and France finally issued a statement. In an *aide-mémoire* on 10 July 1951, the two European nations made clear that they opposed close relations with Spain. They admitted that Spain had strategic value but claimed that material and morale considerations were more important. They saw unilateral action by the US as a severe blow to NATO countries whose morale suffered because of a possible American withdrawal to Spain. The two countries saw more urgent needs elsewhere, above all in West Germany. In their note France and Britain agreed that the impossibility of keeping negotiations secret would complicate the whole matter.

This mattered little as NSC 72/6 overruled European opposition. Dean Acheson, George C. Marshall, General Bradley from the Joint Chiefs of Staff, Admiral Sherman and President Truman reconfirmed their decision to go ahead. Accordingly Acheson informed the British Ambassador on 12 July 1951 that the US had considered the *aide-mémoire* from London and Paris but decided to go ahead. The decision to go ahead with the talks had been taken long before Britain and France had voiced their concern. In order to reduce complications, Griffis was instructed to keep the visit as quiet as possible.

The Foreign Office and the Quai d'Orsay successfully increased the pressure on their governments to issue another *aide-mémoire* to the State Department stressing the seriousness of the situation. All these attempts were in vain. NSC 72/6 had settled that matter. On 19 July 1951 Truman confirmed that the policy towards Spain had changed due to advice from the Department of Defense. However, he made it clear that he had done so reluctantly – "I don't like Franco and I never will, but I won't let my personal feelings override the convictions of our military men."[4]

NOTES

1. NA, Civil Branch, NSC 72/2, 15 January 1951, Secretary of State.
2. NA, Civil Branch, NSC 72/4, 1 February 1951.
3. NA, Civil Branch, NSC 72/4, Progress Report.
4. *Public Papers of the Presidents of the US: Truman*, 19 July 1951.

8 Admiral Sherman in Spain

The US realized that Spanish generals, such as Juan Vigón, were very optimistic about bilateral talks. A year earlier they could not have expected more than some aid in the event of war between the US and the USSR. Now Spanish soldiers could go to the US for military training.

Washington knew that a bilateral agreement with Franco would stabilize his regime, removing the army as a possible source of internal opposition to him and improving Spain's economic position and military strength. For Washington, the time had come to consider Spain's military potential and find out how much aid was required.

Several studies were being made. The US Navy considered the area between Cartagena and Valencia best suited for its purposes. For the Navy this area was 600 miles closer to the USSR than French Morocco. It was easy to protect and well suited for submarine warfare. Next, the triangle El Ferrol–Lugo–Vigo, in north-west Spain, was being considered. It had a good harbour in Vigo. Yet the port at El Ferrol, Franco's birthplace, was obsolete and Lugo lacked a decent airport. The Cadiz–Huelva–Seville triangle, at the southern tip of the Peninsula, had great advantages. It was on the Atlantic coast, helping transatlantic shipment. After further studies, it was considered by the Navy and the USAF as the most attractive option.

The USAF was also looking for air bases elsewhere. A USAF officer commented that Madrid airport was 230 miles from the sea over some of the roughest country and the worst railways and roads in Europe. It was also 2300 feet above sea level and all the fuel-storage space there would not keep a squadron of B-47s in the air for a single day's operation. It was a fine field in the wrong place.

The Air Force had considered 350 airfields and showed most interest in the area Cadiz–Huelva–Seville. This area would have been the last to fall on the Continent in the event of a Soviet invasion but was still close enough to be within the bombing range of the industrial areas of the Soviet Union.

In the meantime, on 5 July 1951, Secretary Louis Johnson sent a letter to the Executive Secretary of the National Security Council. He pointed out that US policy towards Germany and Spain, NSC 71 and 72 respectively, were to be acted upon by the National Security Council as a matter of urgency.

Throughout the summer of 1951, the armed forces bombarded Congress with argument after argument in favour of Spain's integration into Western defence policy. General George C. Marshall, then Secretary of Defense, argued that Spain, Turkey and Greece would increase the strength of the Mutual Security Program. Marshall repeated his argument before a Committee Hearing of the Senate. Before Congress, Admiral Donald B. Duncan, the Deputy Chief Naval Operations, claimed that Spain was important for the defence of Europe and the Iberian Peninsula was an important factor in anti-submarine warfare. Lieutenant-General Alfred M. Gruenther, Supreme Headquarters Allied Powers Europe, argued that Spain had considerable value for air and naval bases. It was also pointed out that Spain could mobilize 2 million men each at a cost of around one-third of that of a US GI.

General Omar N. Bradley, Chairman of the Joint Chiefs of Staff, told the Foreign Committee that he would like to see Spain in NATO. The Army Chief of Staff General J. Lawton Collins admitted that Spain was important from a military point of view, but he believed that an adequate defence could be upheld without her. He realized that Spain had a large standing army but he pointed out that this army was armed and trained for low technical wars. However, the US military was concerned about Franco's willingness to give away Spanish sovereign rights and if a post-Franco government would revoke these rights.

In the House, two criticisms against closer relations with Spain were constantly brought forward: the political implications for other commitments such as NATO and the usefulness of the bases themselves. More opposition came from the State Department. George W. Perkins, Assistant Secretary of State for European Affairs, claimed that bringing Spain into the European Cooperation Administration would agitate Europe against Spain and complicate America's military aims.

In Britain, the Foreign Secretary, Herbert S. Morrison, told the House of Commons that the UK had informed the authorities in Washington that the strategic advantages which might accrue from associating Spain with Western defence would be outweighed by political damage which such an association might inflict on the Western community of Nations.

Manuel Estrada, the former Chief of Staff of Spain's Republican Army, argued that because Spain was so far from enemy centres it was not an easy target for air-strikes, but it was also hard to hit the Soviet centres from Spain and Spain's infrastructure in any case would render any strikes useless. Furthermore, Estrada said that an agreement with Spain would demoralize troops in France and Central Europe.

He concluded that Britain and North Africa were easier to defend and better suited to recapture Europe.

There were enough Congressmen who argued against these fears. Senator Harry P. Cain from Washington said that Spain and NATO were impossible to separate. He saw Spain, similar to Britain, as an enormous airfield which could also provide vital naval port facilities. Carlton Hayes, former Ambassador to Spain, recommended including Spain in the Western defence, extending foreign aid and treating the Mediterranean nation similarly to the Latin American countries. He predicted that the force of circumstances in the world at large would increasingly make for betterment of relations between Spain and the US.

Other military considerations concerned Spain's armed forces. Senator Tydings said that Spain's great national army could be used for the mutual security of Europe. In a cabinet meeting on 31 January 1951, General Eisenhower had told Truman that he could use Franco's 20 or so divisions for Europe's defence. Later the same year Colonel Shipp, Army Attaché in Spain, told a Senate Committee that a Spanish private received $5 and a colonel $100 a month. Spanish soldiers were cheap compared to their American counterparts. Colonel Tower, Air Force Attaché in Spain, praised Spanish pilots for their past achievements but pointed out that they lacked training with modern equipment. Furthermore, the Attaché speculated that a Spanish pilot would cost only one-fifth of an American pilot in Europe.

In March 1951, the Senate Committee on Foreign Relations and Armed Services concluded that Spain's potential would greatly add to Europe's defence. Thus on 4 April, the Senate asked for a revision of Europe's defence plans, which included Spain's military and natural resources.

In order to gain military concessions from Spain, more financial resources had to be made available. McCarran claimed that loans under the Export–Import Bank were insufficient and more funds were needed. This put considerable pressure on the State Department.

In February 1951 NATO members had been informed of the new US approach to Spain and both France and Britain strongly disapproved of the new turn of things. Britain rejected close links between NATO states and Spain. The Foreign Office feared for commercial interests and for the military value of Gibraltar. The French remained concerned about their strategic position in France and North Africa. Crucial for France was the possibility that the US might retreat behind the Pyrenees and across the Channel, leaving France undefended.

All these concerns were amplified by meetings in Washington between the Spanish Air Force Minister Gonzalea Gallarza, Thomas K.

Finletter, USAF, and General Omar N. Bradley, and by Admiral Forrest Sherman's visit to Spain. Admiral Sherman's analysis of Spain's strategic value and his tragic death are important to the understanding of the final arrangements between Madrid and Washington.

Forrest P. Sherman was born on 30 October 1896 in Merrimack, New Hampshire. He graduated second out of 199 of the class of 1918 at Annapolis, the famous navy college. Upon graduation he was given an evaluation which ended "Above all, Sherman knows his job; when he is given a thing to do he finds out all there is to be found about it and the job is well done."

Francis P. Matthews, who succeeded John Sullivan as Secretary of the Navy, described Sherman as shy in manner but driving himself very hard. Admiral Sherman was described by his own roommate and travelling companion Admiral Arleigh Burke as very open and talkative. He considered the Admiral to be a remarkable man with extreme drive.

Early in his career, Forrest P. Sherman developed an interest in naval aviation and became an aviator in the Navy in December 1922. Twenty years later, in May 1942, he was given the command of the CV *Wasp*, an aircraft carrier in the Pacific. On 15 September 1942 the *Wasp* was hit by three torpedoes and Sherman had to order the ship to be abandoned. Despite this setback, he became Deputy Chief of Staff to Admiral Nimitz. In 1946 Sherman outlined the threat of a Soviet advance on Europe and the Middle East. This analysis contributed to the Truman Doctrine and the programme of aid to Turkey and Greece. In December 1947, he was appointed to take charge of the US Naval Forces Mediterranean.

When Denfeld, then Chief of Naval Operations, spoke out against Truman over the cancellation of the US Navy super-carrier programme, the President forced him to resign. After Truman consulted with Nimitz, Sherman was appointed CNO on Nimitz's recommendation and initiated the CV *Forrestal* nuclear carrier programme. Himself a student of naval history and believer in containment, Sherman realized that the US had to achieve control of the sea to allow forward deployment of the fleet. This, he asserted, was to be achieved through naval aid to allied nations. He also saw that it was necessary to make Britain realize that her navy would only play a secondary role in policing the sea. Under Sherman, the US Navy broke the USAF monopoly on nuclear capability when in February 1950 the AJ-1 *Savage*, a carrier-based plane, was armed with nuclear bombs in the Atlantic.

In only two years as Chief of Naval Operations he repaired relations between the Navy and other US military services, and improved relations with other NATO navies. He also laid down a healthy ground for a shipbuilding programme. Next, Sherman wanted to solve the command problems of NATO forces in Europe. He hoped that the army command would be placed under General Eisenhower, the overall Navy under Admiral William M. Fechteler and naval operations in the Mediterranean under Admiral Robert B. Carney and a British admiral.

In Europe, Sherman saw two strategic choices for the US, either to accept the necessity of deploying forces and to fight overseas if necessary, or alternatively to withdraw, abandon Europe and liberate it later. He personally believed that the first course offered the greatest prospect for survival.

Sherman realized that NATO's southern flank would be vulnerable without friendly relations between Spain and NATO. He concluded that it was necessary to gain Spain's support. In May Sherman had an idea about how to improve Washington's bargaining position with Madrid. He wanted to start negotiations with Lisbon to obtain military bases on mainland Portugal. This would have put enormous pressure on Spain to conclude similar agreements with the US. When he asked the State Department if this was possible, George Perkins informed him that indeed it did not violate the Treaty of Friendship, nor the Non-Aggression Pact between Spain and Portugal, but that due to the negotiations concerning the Azores bases, the suggestion was not practical.

After the outbreak of the Korean War, Sherman and Admiral Carney, Commander in Chief US Naval Forces in North Europe and the Mediterranean, were strengthened in their belief that the US urgently needed bases in Spain, both for its Navy and Air Force. In order to avoid publicity, Sherman had toyed with the idea of sending Admiral Carney to Spain in civilian clothes to initiate the talks. This idea was, however, abandoned. Instead, Sherman convinced Truman to agree on a visit by himself to Spain.

Sherman was not an unknown in Spain. His son-in-law Lieutenant-Commander John Fitzpatrick was appointed Assistant Naval Attaché to Madrid in 1947, shortly after military studies in Washington had highlighted Spain's strategic value. The very same year, Dolores Sherman, wife of the Admiral, visited Spain on a trip to see her daughter and son-in-law. She was not only introduced to Spain's hospitality but also to several Spanish high-ranking officials. In February 1948, Admiral Sherman, after having been appointed commander of the Sixth Fleet, visited the Spanish Navy and several officials and took part in exercises by the Sixth Fleet. The speed with which Sherman's wife and then Sherman himself visited Spain implies that John Fitzpatrick's appointment to the post in Spain was made in order to establish contacts and to avoid Sherman's visits being blown out of proportion by Spanish propaganda.

Before Sherman left, US military requirements in Spain were clearly defined. The USAF was interested in peacetime air rights and bases to rotate air groups between Madrid, Barcelona and Seville. In the long run they hoped to gain further bases near Cádiz, Cartagena and on the Canary Islands. The Navy wanted port facilities near Valencia, Malaga and Alicante. Both branches also desired guarantees to the use of bases in case of war.

Shortly before Sherman departed, a Subcommittee of the Senate Committee on Foreign Relations visited Spain. The Senators met with Ambassador Griffis, the Marqués de Prat, Foreign Minister Martín Artajo and General Franco himself. The day this Subcommittee left Spain, Admiral Sherman left Washington in a DC-6B, together with his wife and son-in-law.

Upon Sherman's arrival, on 16 July, he and Ambassador Griffis met with General Franco and the Marqués de Prat from the Foreign Ministry. Sherman outlined the importance of the deployment of the Air Force in Spain and the vital control of the Mediterranean. He also mentioned the problem of evacuating civilians in the event of war, a problem which was to be handled outside the military negotiations. He listed some of the US requirements such as transit permits, air operating rights and naval facilities. Sherman commented that the US wanted to survey installations, exchange military information, mutually consult each other, give technical advice, use certain airfields and assist in the training of Spanish soldiers. Franco showed more interest in material aid than in rights, permits or cooperation. He was concerned about the equipment of the Spanish army and saw the need to obtain military and economic aid. The Spanish dictator pointed out that there was a possibility that a Portuguese–Spanish treaty would be signed as an alternative to arrangements with the US. This was an attempt to put Sherman under pressure. Franco even told the American Admiral that he thought France might join the USSR in an attack against Spain. The Spanish dictator was hoping to create an atmosphere of military urgency which would force the American government to act.

Despite the usual Spanish hospitality extended towards visitors, Sherman emerged from the talks with Franco pale and tired. Maybe this was the effect of the flight across the Atlantic and the insufficient rest before the meeting. It is more likely that he had simply fallen victim to Franco's long and tiring monologues which, for the Spanish dictator, constituted diplomatic skills. These presentations by the Spanish dictator were, according to Adolf Hitler, worse than a visit to the dentist. In the evening the Admiral attended a reception and went to bed late. The next day, 17 July 1951, Sherman met General Vigón together with several military attachés. They discussed the similarities between the Joint Chiefs of Staff and the Spanish High General Staff. Then the conversation turned and Vigón said something along the following lines: "It is difficult for me to understand why the French oppose the arming of Germany and Spain, which is definitely in the interest of the common defense. . . . Many of my friends in the French Armed Forces have indicated that they do not feel that way." Sherman pointed towards the historical experience of France with Germany as a result of which French people feared a rearmed Germany. The American continued:

On the other hand, it is more difficult to understand, why they oppose the arming of Spain. I feel that two factors will tend to reduce this opposition in France, as its forces, and those of other Western European nations develop a strong military posture, (1) the confidence in the prospect of successful defense will counteract panic and the desire for neutrality and (2) as French Armed Forces receive more arms, they will be more willing to see other countries receive some also.

The conversation between the two generals moved to the threat posed by the USSR. Sherman asked for an indication of the needs of the Spanish army. Vigón admitted that Spain needed artillery, and transportation for the army; guns and electronic equipment including radar and sonar for the navy; and everything that was needed by a modern air force. This was a confession that Spain lacked a modern army. Despite this Vigón claimed that Spain had good personnel in its air force. Sherman explained that with every programme that would require an additional expenditure of funds, he had to go before the Congressional Committees to justify it in great detail. It was a sign that the US would not launch itself head-first into relations with Spain. Vigón feared that discussions in Congress would stir up considerable publicity which would develop further opposition in other European countries. The Spanish general obviously favoured a more clandestine approach. Sherman replied: "I have had many discussions on matter[s] of this nature, and I want to assure you that I am quite cognizant of the need to be discreet. I also want to assure you that I am a very discreet man, and you can talk to me freely and openly about any matters you desire, and I will not violate your confidence."[1]

The conference ended with many warm and friendly adieux. For Sherman, the meeting with Vigón was more pleasant than the one with Franco. That same day Sherman attended two receptions. One of them was a relaxing garden party at La Granja Palace, the other was more formal. After the two meetings, he wrote to the Joint Chiefs of Staff to inform them of the progress made during the talks. Sherman believed that Franco had indicated an agreement in principle. He predicted that the US could get the desired operating arrangements but that Spain would ask for considerable military and economic aid. Sherman had finished his job in Spain within only a few hours. Over coffee he confessed to one of the American service attachés that he had to hang around Madrid so that the public would not get the wrong impression.[2]

On 18 July, Sherman saw Franco again, this time briefly. Then the Admiral departed for Paris. During the two-hour flight Sherman updated the American Air Attaché in Madrid about Spain, the Mediterranean, NATO and the Middle East. Once in Paris he described the conversation with the Spanish dictator to General Eisenhower. The next day, Sherman left for London where he again outlined his talks to the American diplomatic personnel.

For a variety of reasons, Ambassador Griffis went to the US for a fortnight shortly after Sherman had left. He was therefore able to inform others in the State Department personally about the talks and at the same time escape the criticism by France and Britain for initiating talks with Spain.

On 21 July, shortly after midnight, Sherman flew from London to Naples for a conference with Admiral Carney and other local officials. At around 7.30 a.m. the plane, together with Admiral Sherman, his wife and four other passengers, landed safely in Naples. The Shermans were rushed to the city-centre Excelsior Hotel. After a short time refreshing himself, Sherman received some local Italian dignitaries at 9.30 a.m. Half an hour later he gave a press conference in the hotel lobby. He was still tired from the flight to Naples. Shortly after 1.00 p.m. he lunched in the hotel and spent the rest of the afternoon in his room relaxing. At 8.00 p.m. he and his wife left the hotel and took a car to Pompeii to see an opera. Sherman was in good spirits, at ease and relaxed, but he left the opera rather tired-looking. He and his wife returned to Naples where they had dinner at an open-air restaurant on the Bay of Naples. In the car on the way back to the hotel he fell asleep. Feeling weary, the Admiral reached the hotel at around 3.00 a.m. He went straight to bed.

Early the next morning, Sherman got up. At 10.00 a.m. he told US Major Smith, in charge of his trip arrangements, that he had spent a

good night and wanted to leave at 11.00 a.m. to catch the plane half
an hour later for Madrid. Then suddenly at 10.40 a.m. Sherman was
overcome by the stress of the previous week. He felt bad and lay down
on the bed in his hotel room. Forty minutes later it was obvious that
Sherman showed symptoms of heart difficulties and exhaustion. Nevertheless, Dr Burkhardt, a medic who was at hand, told Mrs Sherman
not to worry; her husband was simply overworked and needed a little
rest before leaving for the US. But Sherman did not recover. During
October 1950, Sherman had had his annual physical examination and
his doctor had already warned him about his low blood pressure. At
12.50 a.m. an oxygen tent was brought. Admiral Carney stepped out
to the balcony and contemplated actions which had to be taken in case
of Sherman's death and the possible consequences this might have on
the negotiations. At 1.05 p.m. Admiral Sherman fell unconscious and
suffered another two heart attacks before eventually dying. He was
only 54 years old.

Major Smith accompanied the Admiral's corpse to the USS *Mount
Olympus*, where he was piped over the side at 3.30 p.m. just as the
plane carrying Mrs Sherman to Spain passed overhead. The plane stopped
in Madrid, where John Fitzpatrick boarded it.[3]

Sherman received high praise from the Secretary of Defense, George
C. Marshall, the Chief of Staff of the USAF, General Hoyt S. Vandenberg,
and the President himself. Unfortunately, Sherman's death meant that
the friendly personal relations he had formed in Madrid were lost and
future talks with Madrid were somewhat colder.

Two days after Sherman's official meeting with Franco, Acheson
had declared in a press conference that the US guaranteed the defence
of any NATO country and still saw NATO commitments as the most
vital agreements for US defence policy. "There will be no change in
this procedure. In other words the North Atlantic Treaty is fundamental to our policy in Europe, and the closest possible cooperation with
our NATO allies will remain the keystone of this policy." Acheson
continued by referring to the Sherman visit: "Any understanding which
may ultimately be reached will supplement our basic policy of building the defensive strength of the West" and "if Western Europe is
attacked it will be defended – and not liberated". His statement was
confirmation that he had acted against French and British opposition
and that he was now trying to reassure them.

Three days later, the British and French were informed of the meeting between Franco and Sherman. France pointed out that an agreement dating back to 27 November 1912 provided for demilitarization

of the Spanish zone in Morocco and French control over foreign relations of both the Spanish and the French zones. Thus any base agreements between the US and Spain had to be limited to the mainland.

The Americans reassured France that arrangements with Spain did not mean that the US had plans to retreat behind the Pyrenees, nor that it would reduce military aid to NATO.

General Omar H. Bradley, the Chairman of the Joint Chiefs of Staff, put it simply that the more countries the US could put together to build up a collective defence the better.

In the meantime the Spanish military were deeply impressed by Sherman's visit. General Muñoz Grandes confessed to a reporter that Admiral Sherman had come to Spain in 1951 to give Spain a hand when the rest of the world had isolated her, and he added that it was more a question of psychology than price.

Just before Sherman's visit to Spain, three credits worth almost $10 million had been extended at generous terms to make his visit easier. Two of these carried 3 per cent interest, and had to be repaid over 20 years, starting 5 years after being extended.

Despite the success of Sherman's visit to Spain, complications remained. Even the military establishment was divided in its opinion. The Army tended to continue to doubt Spain's value due to her badly equipped army. The Navy and the USAF had split opinions on the usefulness of ports and airfields. Admiral Norman Finletter reported to Congress that bases in Spain were not essential for US defence plans. He argued that the possible three B-29 airfields were only good for let-down stops or in the event of the fall of France, and all three required extensive logistical improvements. As for the ports, the Admiral argued that Cádiz was too close to Gibraltar to add anything new, El Ferrol was too small and, finally, the ports at Cartagena and Mahon were not needed because of existing facilities on Malta and in North Africa.

In the meantime, the success of the talks between Sherman and Franco allowed the US administration to send two study missions to Spain to gather more information about the economic and military situation. During the two teams' stay, a series of issues and complications emerged which had not been considered up until now. As a result, the friendly atmosphere of the initial meetings soon turned more hostile as both sides put their own national interest first.

NOTES

1. NA, Military Branch, Army Chief of Staff Decimal File 091, Spain, 1951–1952, 17 July 1951, Sherman to Vigón according to Military Attaché.
2. NA, Military Branch, CCS 092, US Joint Chief of Staff, Spain (4–19–46), Section 1–8, 17 July/23 July 1951.
3. Forrest P. Sherman Papers, DoD, 27 July 1951, Sequence of his death.

9 The Study Groups

In early August, as a direct result of the talks between Franco and Sherman, a Joint Military Survey Team (JMST) and an economic study group were set up by the Joint Chiefs of Staff. The JMST was made up of a team of six officers, two each from the Army, Air Force and Navy, and headed by an Air Force officer with around 30 support staff. On 22 August, the military team arrived in Spain. Air Force Major-General James W. Spry headed the Military Survey Team, with instructions to survey Spanish air and maritime facilities which might meet US requirements. The primary interest of the US was to acquire air transits and anchorage rights. Nevertheless, under no circumstances was Spain to be encouraged to demand large military aid, as this would lead to complications with other NATO countries.

Spry pointed out to the *New York Times* that any funds for Spain would be in addition to other aid programmes. He wanted to make clear that there were no plans to reduce US military assistance to NATO countries which were getting nervous at the development of the relations between Spain and the US.

In London, the Foreign Office feared that Washington was planning to grant economic as well as extensive military assistance, altering the military picture in Europe. It was speculated that Madrid's demands for more aid were a direct result of the visit of Admiral Sherman, who was accused of having handled Franco clumsily, giving him reason to believe that more could be wrung out of Washington. London had good reason to feel betrayed. The American Ambassador in London and the State Department had told Whitehall about a limited mission by Admiral Sherman to Spain, when in reality they had known that Sherman had instructions to talk about important military matters with Franco. The Foreign Office initially assumed that this had been a personal blunder by Sherman. As the Spanish authorities had great interest in keeping up the appearance of a *rapprochement* between Madrid and Washington, the Marqués de Prat told Miss Ursula Branston, Head of Research at the British Embassy in Madrid, that agreements with the US could be signed within two to three months.

In order to avoid being sidelined, the Foreign Office urged closer cooperation with the French Foreign Ministry, which naturally was as alarmed about the new developments as London was. Yet the two

European nations were unable to stop the two American study missions from initiating talks with Spanish authorities.

On 24 August, Spry saw Vigón to outline his overall mission. Following the meeting he sent Vigón two letters. The first summarized his mission to Spain, a written confirmation of the conversation held that day. The second asked for a commitment and contribution from Spain to the defence of Western Europe.

Six days later, Spry received a letter from Vigón in which the Spanish general pointed out that US bases in Spain would convert her into a belligerent nation. Therefore she needed logistical assistance to defend herself. He pointed out that the bases in peacetime would be under exclusive Spanish command and would only be of a temporary nature until the USSR threat dissipated. Overall, the tone of the letter was encouraging, but made no commitment to the overall defence of Western Europe, and only mentioned Spain's willingness to defend certain strategic islands in the Mediterranean.

Parts of the JMST had arrived in Spain on 22 August. The first week was spent in taking up contact with Spanish and American authorities in Spain. On 29 August the JMST was increased to its full strength by the arrival of officers from the European Command. Further lunch meetings and written correspondence with the Spanish authorities followed. From 4 to 7 September, the JMST conducted a survey of potential air- and naval-base sites in the area of Valencia. The following week the team surveyed the area of Barcelona and Bilbao, including the Ebro valley. From 17 to 22 September the most important regions of all, Seville, Cádiz and Malaga, were surveyed. Finally, the team looked at sites near Cartagena, Alicante and Almeria. The heads of the services would usually leave with the rest of the survey team for the studies in the different areas but would return to Madrid within a day or two. In Madrid they would communicate with the Spanish authorities while the survey team inspected the sites. During the first week in October the Navy, Air Force and Army conducted miscellaneous surveys for the development of an overall airfield complex in Spain. From 6 to 31 October the three parts of the JMST, still staying in Spain, combined their material and drafted the final report.

The Air Force Group of the JMST had shown a special interest in the Valencia–Huelva area (for strategic bombers), the Barcelona–Ebro area (for fighter bombers) and in the Central Plateau (for interceptors and long-range fighters).

The Navy Group of the JMST had worked out its requirements in Spain by early September. These were naval anchorage rights at Algeciras,

Alicante, Malaga and Cartagena, escort facilities at Barcelona, Cádiz and El Ferrol and, most importantly, offloading facilities for aircraft and an airstrip. These last facilities were likely to be situated at Cádiz, but Cartagena and Valencia were by no means ruled out. Further studies had to be made.

The Spanish High General Staff informed General Spry in September that he should also survey Spanish Morocco. Nevertheless, the Navy had shown little interest in North Africa and it was decided that no such survey should be conducted there. The decision was influenced by complications over Morocco's position regarding foreign policy arising out of the Spanish–French agreement from 1912, under which the foreign policy of Spanish Morocco was handled by France. The US was aware that the talks had not been welcomed in France and thus wanted to avoid further complications.

Brigadier-General Frank S. Besson, who had replaced General Conley of the JMST Army in early September, sent a letter to General Barrón, Spanish Central General Staff. He stressed that before Spain could receive aid, the armed forces had to draw up TO&Es ("tables of organization and equipment") to determine the exact needs of the Spanish forces. Initially the US wanted to send military material for training purposes only. In the second phase, US material was to be granted for defensive purposes. It was therefore vital to determine Spain's needs.

This came up in a conversation between Colonel Fisher, member of the JMST, and Lieutenant-Colonel Martín Alonso of the Spanish army. Fisher avoided making any commitment on military aid to Spain because he knew that the Spanish forces had done little planning on the mobilization requirements and thus were themselves in the dark about their needs. The American knew that Spain's forces needed general training, heavy equipment, production guidance and technical advice. To meet these requirements, specific demands had to be made by Spain. An American study concluded on 1 September that Spain would not even survive a short defensive war due to its weak national economy. It was estimated that in order to fully mobilize her forces, Spain needed some 18 000 sub-machine guns, roughly 90 per cent more than Spain currently possessed. Spain also required substantial amounts of anti-aircraft guns, anti-tank guns and heavy artillery, as well as deliveries of ammunition. In the meeting between Martín Alonso and Fisher, the Spaniard claimed that the army already possessed TO&Es but as only limited copies existed it would take some time to prepare the necessary reproduction. Considering that Martín Alonso did not even possess a firm figure for Spain's divisional strength, it is likely that no TO&Es existed.

The very next day, 6 September, Colonel H. Fisher met Lieutenant-Colonel Luís Garrera-Rollán. The Spaniard presented a TO&E for a single Spanish infantry division. Fisher believed that this had been drawn up overnight. The Spanish staff had worked furiously throughout the night to prepare the document, which copied the exact structure of the US TO&E presented as a sample the day before.

On 7 September 1951, the senior navy officer of the JMST had lunch with Admiral Estrada. The American outlined the port facilities and in return offered training to Spanish officers. Estrada mentioned his worries about the dated equipment used aboard the ships of Spain's navy.

The very same day General Besson received a memorandum from the Spanish Brigadier-General de Soto. The Spaniard claimed that Spain's military industry could produce most equipment if technical aid was given (apart from heavy artillery, tanks and radar). He urged that training be given to two tank companies and to two tank troops. In the short term, Spain required bazookas, anti-air batteries, heavy artillery, radar, anti-tank mines, anti-personnel mines and mine-clearing equipment. Furthermore, ammunition and equipment for airborne units were needed. While Americans offered technical aid and training, most Spanish officers were more interested in military end-products for prestige rather than for real military use.

After most of the surveys had been concluded, General Spry met General Vigón. The Spaniard assured the American that Spanish troops would fight in the Mediterranean area in the event of war. This implied that Spain would occupy and defend certain islands but there was no commitment to send Spanish troops north of the Pyrenees. In return Spain demanded military equipment.

On 2 October, Spry had another meeting with General Vigón. Spry mentioned and the Spaniard accepted another US military mission which was to go to Spain. Vigón expressed his concerns about a US offensive aviation presence near Madrid as this would become the target of Soviet bombers. He admitted, however, that in the event of war, the USSR was likely to attack Madrid with or without airfields. He concluded that there was little hope for Spain to remain neutral.

After these meetings with Vigón, General Spry held a friendly chat with Franco which lasted about 80 minutes. They started talking about the internal situation in the Soviet Union. Franco mentioned rumours about the French Ambassador's cooperation with the USSR. The Caudillo pointed out that Spain could not join NATO but he would welcome bilateral agreements with the US. He asserted that Spain would require military assistance as well as help for her ammunitions industry.

He welcomed the support from the US military which, according to him, looked towards the future while the State Department neglected long-term developments completely. Finally, Franco stressed Spain's geographical importance and the strategic value of Morocco.

In order to assist the JMST throughout its studies and inspections in Spain, several military training circulars (TCs) had been released to Madrid. These TCs not only covered such specific military information as "TC3 Organization and Employment of 280mm gun", "TC12 The Panoramic Telescope" and "TC13 The Fuze [Fuse] Mine" but also more important strategic studies such as "FM110-5 Joint Action Armed Forces" and "FM30-25 Counter Intelligence".

During autumn 1951 and while the JMST was still in Spain, a group of five US army officers visited Spain. The trip was designed to enhance bilateral goodwill. The brief report read that the Spanish army was similarly structured to the US but lacked the necessary equipment for a modern army.

The more extensive final report by the JMST was completed at noon on 31 October and passed to the Joint Chiefs of Staff by Colonel Tibetts, USAF. It was more than 350 pages long. Tibetts, with this report in hand, left Spain on 4 November for Washington, where the study was to be scrutinized.

The report argued that Spain would welcome an early exploitation of her facilities without joining NATO. It suggested obtaining facilities as a quid pro quo before granting any military or economic assistance programme for Spain. It also recommended that all future negotiations with Spain should be governed by NSC 72/6 and that a permanent US military mission was to be established. The report favoured a single US governmental agency to organize all US agreements with Spain.

The report consisted of one main conclusion and seven annexes (annex a to annex g). The reports of the Army (annex a), Navy (annex b) and Air Force (annex c), as well as Spain's request for military assistance (annex d), remains classified. The other parts are Spain's participation in the defence of Western Europe (annex e), the means of accomplishing the required developments in Spain (annex f) and the résumé of conferences and letters between the JMST and Spanish officials (annex g). The team had surveyed Spain's air and naval facilities and talked to the Spanish government about air operations, transit privileges, deployment of US aircraft and rights to overfly Spain. In the naval field they had discussed anchorage rights and the use and improvements of air, naval and other military facilities.

Spanish requests from the US were divided according to their priority into three categories. The first group covered equipment needed for immediate training, with a cost of about $10 million. The second group covered weapons of all types, ranging from 105 mm artillery to fire-control equipment to arm six divisions. In the final group, Spain asked for the complete equipment for its forty divisions.

The report declared that Spain's position was not pro-NATO, rather she was inclined towards a bilateral agreement with the US or at least a continuous liaison with Washington. There existed some complications concerning Spain's commitment to sending troops outside Spain in the event of war. Vigón, willing to send troops north of the Pyrenees, claimed that Franco had agreed to defend Mediterranean islands, while Minister of Air Major-General Gallarza argued that Franco would not permit Spanish troops to fight on French soil, nor was he happy about committing troops in the Mediterranean.

The report by the JMST concluded that the Spanish government was willing to grant military rights. The time had come to approach Madrid for airfields, ports, petroleum storage and ammunition depots. In order to get these, US military assistance was to be granted to Spain. The report advised the Department of the Army to supply a limited amount of training equipment to improve relations. The study also outlined the requirements of the three services. These included the construction of facilities and securing rights of way for pipelines, roads and bridges. The financial costs were to be met in a variety of currencies.

It was argued that the responsibilities should be divided between the three armed forces while a single US agency was to conduct the negotiations. Finally the report read that any aid to Spain should be based on a quid pro quo.[1]

Annex c of the report, concerning the US Air Force, was partly repeated in a study titled "Planning for the base development of Spain". In this study it was made clear that the USAF wanted to station six medium bomber wings; one each at San Pablo, Moron de la Frontera, Los Palacios, Manijas and Los Llanos; three fighter wings at Getafe, San Jurjo and Muntadas; and one strategic reconnaissance wing at Torrejón. It was recommended that the administration offices for these bases be located near Madrid. Copero, near Seville, would hold an air depot. While previous studies had emphasized the need for fighter planes, the final version favoured bomber planes. The report confirmed that all airfields in Spain lacked adequate parking areas, taxiways, fuel storage, and distribution facilities. Nevertheless, most had adequate housing, hangars and administration buildings.[2]

The survey team estimated total construction costs to exceed $463 million. In comparison, the bases in Morocco had been constructed in 1951 at a cost of $200 million and required an annual expenditure of roughly $45 million. During the construction phase 4500 people had been employed. It was expected that personnel at the bases in Spain would number over 43 000.

The report mentioned problems concerning transportation, distribution facilities, lack of construction material, labour and quality of locally produced items required for the construction of the bases. It is clear that these considerations ultimately decided the sites of the bases. The Deputy Assistant Secretary of State Bonbright confirmed this in a letter on 21 November 1951. He suggested that due to financial reasons the US was to avoid a major reconstruction of Spain's railway, road and communication system by concentrating bases in two areas, Cádiz and Barcelona. He argued that bases close to ports were easy to supply and thus cheaper than existing alternatives. It was deemed better to construct new military facilities near the coast than to improve existing airfields inland.

Seville, the main USAF base area, would require during a military conflict over 5000 tons of general supplies, 440 000 barrels of fuel, 11 500 barrels of motor fuel and 1300 barrels of diesel. These had to be delivered along winding roads from Cádiz, Cordoba and Huelva. The situation at Madrid and Valencia was just as desperate. The logistic problem was considerable.

Even peacetime requirements of the USAF could only be met through a newly constructed pipeline, extensive air transportation and additional transport vehicles. It was known that in the event of war the lines of communication would be saturated. In order to solve this a system of pipelines and a petrol distribution network had to be built. A 280-mile-long pipeline was to connect Seville and Madrid and another was to connect Cádiz with Seville. The cost for this petrol storage and distribution system was estimated at $27.75 million.

Despite this, concerns over transportation by road and rail remained, and more transport by air was required. The logistic problems were paramount in the selection of the base sites.

The report specifically claimed that there would be no problem in finding enough Spanish labour for construction work at the site of the bases as long as these were close to cities. Labour was in abundance in almost all areas where construction was to take place. Spanish construction was considered of good craftsmanship but labour-intensive. There was, however, a lack of technological experience, and materials such as steel, paint, timber, and electrical and plumbing materials were scarce.[3] Despite this, construction costs were only 10–30 per cent of costs in the US. To lay one square yard of runway in Spain cost $2.20; in the US it was $12. One gallon of fuel storage required an expenditure of $0.076; in the US $0.10. One cubic yard of earth was moved in Spain for $0.24 and for $0.75 in the US.

One of the problems which the report considered was the inefficiency of Spain's petrol industry, operating under the monopoly of the "Compañía Arrendatoria Monopolio Petróleos Sociedad Anónima" (CAMPSA). The only other institution to store petrol in Spain was the Spanish Navy. CAMPSA controlled a total of 18 tankers with an average capacity of 7180 tons. Fifteen ports had facilities for these tankers: the largest was Barcelona, with a storage capacity of 641 800 barrels. In total Spain could store between 3 and 9 million barrels. Furthermore, CAMPSA had 70 tank cars with an average capacity of 5000 gallons, but the majority of these had been on the road for 20 years or more. All CAMPSA's trucks, storage capacity and distribution network were needed to meet Spain's requirements. An increase of demand created by petrol consumption at the bases made it necessary to increase the overall number of vehicles and storage capacity in Spain.

Another consideration was Spain's lack of an aircraft industry. The largest company, Construcciones Aeronáutica SA, only had factories in Madrid, Seville and Cádiz. It was capable of producing around 300 outdated transport and medium bomber planes. Aeronáutica Industrial SA, based in Cuatro Vientos, produced some 180 small trainer planes and the company Hispano-Suiza, based in Seville, could produce up to 200 Me109. The lack of critical materials, manufacturing licences, engines and modern tools meant that the planes still had designs predating 1945. As a result Spain was unable to produce spare parts for modern fighter and bomber planes which therefore had to be imported from elsewhere.

Shortly after receiving the report, the Joint Chiefs of Staff gave their impression. General S. Conley, from the US Army, informed the Army Chief of Staff that he believed that Spain would fight in Europe if her armed forces received the necessary military equipment. It became clear during the discussions that the Joint Chiefs of Staff favoured most of the administrative recommendations made in the report which included the creation of a Joint Military Liaison Group (JMLG) Spain, later called the Joint US Military Group (JUSMG). It was recommended that the JMLG was to be composed of 13 officers and 8 support staff. The new group was to provide data to the Joint Chiefs of Staff, just as the JMST had done. Furthermore, it was to establish Spain's military needs and to evaluate the usefulness of US training, economic and military aid. The JMLT was not to be placed under the Joint American Military Assistance Group, based in London, which played a similar role in Western Europe as JUSMG was to play in Spain. It would have been only natural to combine the administration of the two to cut red tape. The reason why the Joint Chiefs of Staff decided against this was because Spain had expressed little desire to join NATO, and the Western European powers likewise had expressed little interest in Spain joining NATO. To avoid political controversy with Europe, the JUSMG was to be fully independent, reporting to the American Embassy in Spain and to Washington directly. As had been recommended in the report, the Joint Chiefs of Staff agreed that further negotiations were to be governed by NSC 72/6. Restrictions applying to the JMST were lifted and a negotiation team under a USAF officer was to be set up. The Ambassador to Spain was to be in charge of the coordination of the JUSMG. However, the Joint Chiefs of Staff disagreed with other points of the report. It was argued that sending training equipment to Spain was premature. The Joint Chiefs of Staff were unwilling to see the negotiations as a quid pro quo and believed that the talks had to be based on general reciprocity and trust, rather than on hard bargaining.

The Joint Chiefs of Staff also wanted to know how costs for improvements of inland bases compared to those of newly constructed coastal facilities. The JMST report, by favouring coastal bases, gave a clear priority to the geographical position over the convenience of existing bases, but had not established cost differences.

Apart from the geographical value of the Iberian Peninsula, the Joint Chiefs of Staff claimed that Spain could also help to fill the vital need to increase Europe's military manpower. At the same time they argued that Spain's contribution of military power to the NATO cause would be sufficient to advance the defence of Western Europe east of the Rhine, thus ensuring Germany's participation in that defence.

On 1 October, Lequerica, Charles P. Clark, Colonel Andrew Samuels (Pentagon) and Frank C. Nash from the State Department held a conversation in which the Spaniard claimed that he too would prefer to see a war fought on the Rhine or Elbe, or even further East, if possible, and with Spanish troops included rather than one fought in Spain.

During August five Spanish Army officers were flown to the US to attend military courses and another eight were expected in October. On 26 September the *Sunday Times* claimed that the first cadres from the Spanish Army and Air Force were expected in Germany before the autumn to receive training in the operation and maintenance of US military equipment.

On 27 September, the State Department confirmed to a British MP that 30 Spanish officers were going to receive training in Germany. The Department claimed that this was not special treatment for Spaniards but was part of an old programme which was open to many nationalities.

Despite this assurance, the incident caused an outcry in the British Foreign Office. In order to limit the diplomatic damages, General Omar N. Bradley informed the Secretary of Defense that no plans existed for the training of Spanish military personnel in the American Zone of Germany. The project was cancelled and the British Foreign Office was informed.

The UK was willing to accept the new US policy towards Spain as long as no military end-products were sent to Spain. France had similar concerns. The two countries hoped that they would be able to use NATO as a lever against Washington. But after a study of the position of other member states it became clear that only Norway and Denmark supported Whitehall and the Quai d'Orsay.

Diplomatic pressure by London and Paris forced Acheson in Washington to assure the British and French Embassies that they would receive more information about US intentions in Spain and that the ensuing talks between the two countries would receive low publicity.

This did not convince the Foreign Office and it was suggested that the UK should take part in the negotiations. Sir John Balfour in Madrid opposed this as he feared demands by Madrid to participate in the administration and political life of Gibraltar.

British fears were confirmed after a conversation between Erice, Director-General of Foreign Policy, and a British official in Spain. The Spaniard claimed that he was confident about the progress in Anglo-Spanish relations over Gibraltar and over an agreement between the two nations. Erice hoped that Spain could link the two issues. For the British Foreign Office there could be no deal between Spain and the UK because there was no vital military advantage.

The Chiefs of Staff feared that the American–Spanish agreements would lead to renewed demands by Madrid on Gibraltar and extensive military assistance. The Joint Planning Staff argued that any military agreement between Washington and Madrid should be limited to the use of ports, airfields, overflight rights, exchange of military information and the granting of military equipment. In the long term the military planners were not against Spain joining NATO as long as no question of the rendition of Gibraltar to Spain was discussed.

The other American study group to go to Spain was the Temporary Economic Survey Group under Dr Sidney C. Sufrin. Before going to Spain, he visited Paris, where he was informed that France had no interest in the American economic programme for Spain. The French government itself faced economic difficulties due to US cuts in aid programmes. It was feared in Paris that if Spain was to receive economic aid, even fewer dollars would be available for France.

Sufrin was an academic at Syracuse University. By 1951, he had published two books, *Labor Policy and the Business Cycle* (1943) and *Union Wages and Labor's Earnings* (1950). In 1952 he published a 62-page study titled "The Economy of Spain". During his mission he was to analyse the projects financed under the $62.5 million loan, look for future possible investments and, finally, to study Spain's economic requirements. He was not suited for this assignment as he lacked leadership qualities as well as diplomatic skills. Shortly after arriving, he had a conflict with some American diplomats after he had contacted the Embassy concerning certain questions about the Congressional debates on the Mutual Security Act. The Embassy sent a cable to Washington, which Sufrin thought appeared to portray him as the only one who had failed to grasp the technicalities of the debate and which, furthermore, had mistakes in the technical language. Sufrin was outraged. Ambassador Griffis had to settle the dispute between the two sides.

Next Sufrin made a blunder out of a meeting with the Duke of Alba. The Spanish Ambassador had returned from London and Sufrin invited him to a buffet. The American expected the Duke to arrive with four or five members of the Foreign Ministry but was horrified when he turned up with more than 25. Naturally food and drink had not been prepared for so many and consequently ran out. The Duke of Alba greeted Sufrin with a handshake and a slap on the back. When Sufrin wanted to return the friendly slap his hand got caught in his pocket and, as he forced it out, he lost control and hit the Duke, who in the meantime had turned away, on his backside. During another meeting with Spanish authorities one of the economists working with Sufrin lectured the Spaniards on the Marshall Plan, despite having received specific instructions not to do so.

The State Department was rightly worried about Sufrin's ability when the Spanish authorities appointed nine subcommittees to assist him during his research. He was unable to escape from their influence. This was despite the fact that he had been instructed that the study should be prepared on a confidential basis, in view of its relationship to and effect on negotiations for military facilities.

Sufrin also failed to free himself and his team from the influence of the INI, whose delegates stuck to the American team like leeches. This failure meant that he could not gather the necessary material he wanted and was unable to produce a new and interesting analysis of Spain's economic situation and prospects. In the end he relied heavily on an earlier study by the State Department. Furthermore, his inability to keep information away from the Spanish authorities meant that once the negotiations started, Madrid knew more about the American interests than Washington had desired.

The final report, passed to the European Cooperation Administration on 20 December, consisted of 13 chapters analysing, among other issues, national accounts, foreign trade, industrial sectors and infrastructure.

Dr Sidney Sufrin's conclusion was that the Spanish economy was "being held together by bailing wire and hope".

In a lecture to the Law Faculty of Madrid University in December he expressed concerns that foreign currency investments in Spain would overdevelop industry compared to agriculture. Spain lacked general industrial machinery, a modern electric power grid and a healthy infrastructure. Before these were improved, substantial industrial investments would increase the strain on Spain's economy and would create an even more unbalanced economy. A capital rush, if not properly channelled, would lead to inflation. Sufrin pointed out that Spain had to reorientate her trade and increase mineral exports to the US.

In his report, Sufrin asked for Spain to receive $150 million a year for raw materials, transport and power supplies. As a result it was estimated that Spain's GNP would increase by 3–4 per cent during the first year alone and aid for irrigation and fertilizers would increase agricultural output by 20 per cent alone. Other funds were required for an estimated 40 000 tractors. Only 0.5 per cent of farms used tractors, while 90 per cent of the grain was still sown by hand. Out of 13 500 tractors registered in Spain most were 30 years and older.

Sufrin asserted that industrial production in Spain could be increased by 10–15 per cent with US technical aid, advice and help for the electricity industry. While Spain produced enough electricity, she lacked the national power grid to transport it from areas of supply to areas of demand.

Another problem concerned Spain's infrastructure. There were insufficient railways, roads and airport facilities to overcome the mountainous transport routes through her interior. RENFE, the Spanish railways, was described by Sufrin as terrible. Before the Civil War,

Spain had 3000 steam locomotives; by 1950 there were only about 3400. As old trains were not being replaced, many of them were almost 100 years old. Unsurprisingly, almost 15 per cent were in constant repair and in 1950 alone more than 471 derailments occurred. A high ratio of 26.5 cars per train meant that the average speed was only just above 10 km/h (about 6 mph). Yet on average a locomotive travelled 104 km per day, and thus was in service for, on average, ten hours per day.

Spain's banking system was also in need of reform. Financial agreements were made by handshakes rather than official contracts. Banks required no legal minimum reserves and there was no debt ceiling for the government. Informal governmental pressure required banks to hold 40 per cent of their securities in government bonds, thus providing the regime with cheap loans by creating artificial demand for governmental paper. The banks naturally passed the extra costs to their customers, private clients as well as corporations.

One of the more favourable points was that Spain slowly developed into Europe's sunny tourist centre. In 1950 a total of 38 000 tourists came to Spain; one year later 750 000 and, in 1952, a total of 1.5 million were expected. These tourists brought foreign currency with them and helped develop commercial areas along the coast.

Sufrin strongly argued against the damaging interference of the government in the economy. The iron-ore industry, for example, was adversely affected by government intervention. The fixing of multiple exchange rates in December 1948 discouraged exports of iron ore by paying exporters less in pesetas for dollar proceeds than they could receive from exporting other products (e.g. a dollar's worth of iron ore did not have the same value in pesetas as a dollar's worth of olive oil). Spain had only a limited domestic consumption for iron ore and with the introduction of multiple exchange rates, which discouraged iron-ore exports, production fell to such an extent that economies of scale were lost and prices increased. As a result other industries were now faced with higher raw material costs. A liberalization of the exchange rate would have increased exports, recovered economies of scale and increased production, as well as productivity, of related industries. At the same time this would have created more foreign currencies for imports as well as removed iron-ore scarcity in Spain.[4]

Sufrin pinpointed the problem of over-regulation by the INI which believed that a move from an agricultural to an industrial state could not be achieved by private enterprise but by the government alone. During the previous years, Spain's economic and trade policy had been determined to a large extent by Juan Antonio Suanzes, head of the INI. Sufrin expected an increase of foreign investments once the maze of regulations had been removed. However, even Suanzes's resignation in 1951 as Minister of Trade and Industry, and a split of the ministerial post between Manuel Arburúa and Joaquin Planell did not improve the situation.

Liberalization of production, of ownership and of trade would have encouraged foreign investments. However, as long as these were limited to 25–40 per cent and as long as cases like the Barcelona Traction bankruptcy were possible, foreigners stayed away.

Barcelona Traction, partly a Canadian company, was declared bankrupt despite returning to profitability in 1948. This had been due to the distorting exchange rates which gave a false picture of foreign capital gains and foreign capital investments. The fact that the case was not referred to arbitration but that its assets were seized and transferred directly to the industrial group of Juan March, further indicated the unfair treatment foreign capital was receiving in Spain.

For the time being, Spain's economic situation remained dire. Low rainfall over three years (1948–50) meant that the reservoirs were at less than 10 per cent of their full capacity. Water shortages meant poor crops and lack of electricity. In Catalonia, factories had to close due to electricity shortages. In order to avoid social disorder, the Falangist syndicates forced employers to pay wages throughout the closure, thus causing financial losses and, in certain cases, bankruptcies. Unemployment rose from 1947 to 1950 by 43 per cent. As a result, the state had to increase its social expenditure which in turn lead to inflation. In 1949, inflation stood at 6.5 per cent; in 1950 it rose to 18 per cent and in 1951 it had increased to 30 per cent.

Some improvements came in 1951. In February, the first $12.5 million under the McCarran credit was granted. Rain in the autumn filled the reservoirs to two-thirds of their capacity and solved the electricity and irrigation problems. The potato production doubled, dried fruit and olive harvests tripled. Tomatoes, cotton and tobacco increased by between 12 per cent and 40 per cent.

Due to the conflict in Korea, raw material prices advanced. One ton of tungsten was sold at $2300 in 1950; one year later it was purchased at $4740. Mercury rose from $55 per flask to $200. As a result Spain had its first trade surplus in the post-war period. However, due to monetary growth of 12.6 per cent and resulting inflation, and an increase of expenditure abroad for military equipment, Spain's balance of trade deteriorated the following year. The economic prospects improved and a $50 million long-term debt to the International Telephone and Telegraph Corporation (ITT) for the 1945 nationalization of Telefónica could be paid back eight and a half years before schedule in 1952.

In August/September the Export–Import Bank granted $18 million for an electric power station, steel and fertilizer plants and for RENFE. Furthermore a good harvest combined with better trade and diplomatic relations with Portugal, Latin America and the Arab nations helped the economy and real national income increased by 17.6 per cent.

While commercial relations improved, political concerns remained. Francis Williamson, Deputy Director of the Office for Western European Affairs, told the House of Representatives on 18 October 1951 that there remained two complications; the opposition by European states and the fact that there was no alternative to Franco. He argued that NATO countries opposed the American *rapprochement* to Spain because the Spanish Army could not fight efficiently without substantial military aid which, if supplied by the US, would reduce America's commitment to NATO.

The Assistant Director of the Mutual Security Agency, John H. Ohly, told other State Department employees that the negotiations for bases in Spain were closely linked to the $100 million aid which had already been appropriated for Spain. On 21 November, he requested the State Department to send him information about the availability of these funds and the administrative procedures.

The very same day the Deputy Assistant Secretary of State for European Affairs, Bonbright, informed Ohly that NSC 72/6 essentially provided guidance for the $100 million aid. Under NSC 72/6 the money was to develop the military potential of Spain for Europe's defence, assist Spain in improving relations with NATO countries and obtain early participation of Spain in NATO or help conclude mutual security arrangements between the two countries. It was clear that NATO countries were still given priority under NATO, the Mutual Defense Assistance Program and the European Recovery Program. He also confirmed that all military aid to Spain had to take political considerations into account. Bonbright informed Ohly that US officials should stress that Spain's role was to defend, not liberate Europe and that one should avoid reaching a quid pro quo. While this policy was being discussed with France and Britain, the US approached Spain for long-range bomber and naval operation facilities.

Finally, Bonbright made it clear that the current negotiations in Spain would determine what facilities the US would seek, what aid would be given and what tactics were to be employed. He considered economic aid as one of the most important means available to ensure that Spanish forces would be included in the common defence.

While discussions in the State Department continued, the Joint Chiefs of Staff came under time pressure to include Spain in the Mutual Security Act of 1951. Before negotiations or economic aid could be granted, the Joint Chiefs of Staff had to decide on the volume and composition of military aid. Freeman Matthews, Deputy Under-Secretary, raised this point in December at a meeting between the State Department and Joint Chiefs of Staff representatives. The Joint Chiefs of Staff representative pointed out that the report by the JMST had only been finalized in November and was still being considered. Bonbright called the attention to the January deadline when a new Mutual Security Agency plan had to be sent to Congress.

The Mutual Security Act allowed funds to be appropriated for Spain, as this would promote the foreign policy of the US to assist friendly countries in strengthening the overall defences of the West. The President had a total of $5028 million available during FY 1952 for European countries which were parties to NATO and for any country in Europe which the President determined to be of direct importance to the defence of the North Atlantic area.

In order to administer the fund, the Mutual Security Agency had been set up. It replaced the Economic Cooperation Administration and was designed to sustain and increase the military effort.

As requested by the International Security Affairs Committee, the Mutual Security Act included a $100 million allocation for Spain. Nevertheless there was no obligation to use this fund. There had been a clause in the Mutual Security Act which called for an approval by NATO members when credits were to be extended to non-NATO countries. This meant that Britain and France could have blocked any funds for Spain. However, the clause was struck out in autumn 1951, allowing Congress to appropriate the first $100 million for Spain.

It was necessary to get Truman to approve these funds for Spain and Griffis did everything he could to encourage the President to do so. The Ambassador's advanced age (65) and biased support for Franco during his short stay in Madrid made him retire in early 1952, though he continued to support Spain wholeheartedly during his last weeks in office. When President Truman stated that he was not very fond of Spain, Griffis went as far as to explain away the comments made by his head of state, claiming that the President was only referring to the unfortunate delay of the talks between Spain and the US.

To improve his international image, Franco re-formed his government on 18 July 1951. The cabinet shuffle favoured the Monarchists. The Industry and Trade Minister Juan Antonio Suanzes, who was greatly disliked by the American authorities, was replaced by Joaquin Planell and Arburúa. At the same time Franco released 250 imprisoned demonstrators. A series of political blunders by the Americans also helped Franco to improve his image. Paul A. Porter, the Director of the Mutual Security Agency, publicly announced the beginning of negotiations which Madrid claimed were to seek "a pact of mutual aid based on equality of rights".

A Special Subcommittee of the House Committee on Foreign Affairs toured Spain and wrote a report claiming that Congress believed that Spain belonged in the Western community of nations, and that the US had to unite the efforts of all peace-seeking nations.

In the meantime, the military and economic surveys by Sufrin and Spry were being used by the agencies concerned in making detailed preparations for negotiations with the Spanish government. Also, the Joint Logistics Plans Committee put together an extensive initial study on American expenditure in Spain which heavily focused on the needs of the US Navy and Air Force.

Apart from its own economic and military considerations, the US had to think about Spain's role in a military confrontation. Concern also remained over Franco's willingness to give up sovereignty after having hailed Spain's national past for over a decade. It was therefore only natural that the negotiations during the following two years focused on this issue and complicated matters for the American negotiations team.

NOTES

1. NA, Military Branch, CCS 092, Spain (4–19–46), Report by the JMST.
2. NA, Civil Branch, 59D108, Air Base Expenditure Abroad.
3. NA, Military Branch, G3091, USAF "Planning for the Base Development of Spain."
4. Sufrin and Petrased, *Economy of Spain,* pp.12-58.

10 Analysis in Washington

Sufrin's report recommended that aid for Spain should be spread over five years and split 57 per cent for economic aid and 43 per cent military. The report estimated that this would increase Spain's industrial product by 6–8 per cent and agricultural production by 12–20 per cent. He suggested that during the first year $20 million should go towards military-related industries such as a power grid in Seville, steam-generating stations, and road repairs; $15 million should be spent on the railways; and $95 million should be granted to other industries. He concluded that aid was required to put the Spanish economy on a firm enough basis so that it could support a growing US and Spanish military machine with all the incidental positive adjustments to the civilian economy.

Sufrin also suggested a limitation on the Spanish government's inflationary policies by restricting the money supply, the building of unnecessary structures and the production of luxury goods. In addition he wanted a package of essential goods to be sent to Spain soon after military agreements had been signed. The American academic hoped that this would ease inflationary pressures.

Sufrin's report was similar to a study by the Western European Affairs branch of the Department of State conducted in March 1951. Sufrin did have a look at this report before he departed for Spain. Given the difficulty with which he had to gather information in Spain, the State Department's study was of great help for Sufrin once he had to draft a summary of his visit to Spain.

On 7 April 1952, the House of Representatives was presented with another report, prepared by a Congressional subcommittee and outlining Spain's dire economic situation. It stressed the difficulties caused by the many different exchange rates and claimed that Spain's purchasing power was still only about 50 per cent of its pre-Civil War level. Inflationary financing of public spending had resulted in a spiralling of prices and in a shortage of food and consumer goods. The development of a free economic market had been prevented by the control of the government over vertical syndicates in almost all sectors of the economy.

In October 1951, Spain's total national debt stood at 63 billion pesetas or roughly one-third of GNP. On top of that came foreign credits of around $145.5 million, from Italy roughly $5 million, 3.6 billion pesetas from Argentina and $76 million from other nations.

Annual spending of the government was financed to 84 per cent through receipts and 16 per cent through borrowing. The government deficit had increased from 320 million pesetas in 1948, to 893 million in 1949, to 1364 million in 1950, to 1655 million in 1951 and was almost 2 billion in 1952.

The Subcommittee, which drafted the report, recommended tax reforms for Spain, suggesting higher luxury tax, closure of the many loopholes, and reform of the regressive tax system so that it had to rely less on property tax and more on income tax.

Shortly after the Subcommittee had presented its report, the House of Representatives was told by the State Department that Franco was willing to commit troops to fight north of the Spanish border and would welcome the use of Spanish ports and airfields by US soldiers. Allegedly previous complaints by the Spanish military had only been concerned with US troops stationed permanently in Spain. It was argued in Congress that despite opposition by France and Britain, the US should no longer waste time and make use of the advantages Spain had to offer. Thus the report concluded that in order to oppose the Communist threat Spain and the US should join forces in the form of a mutual security pact as soon as possible.

On the other side of the Atlantic relations between Spain and the European NATO members showed little signs of improvement. Apart from Dr Paulo Cunha, the Portuguese Foreign Minister, no European representative at the Ninth North Atlantic Council argued in favour of Spain's inclusion in NATO. Britain remained concerned about Gibraltar. In November 1951 Franco had made some comments to the *Sunday Times* which were as absurd as they were offensive. He suggested that Spain should lease out Gibraltar to Britain in return for Spain's sovereignty over the colony. The religious problem in Spain continued to unsettle Britain. In March 15 young men stormed a religious service in Seville and injured the priest and two ladies while burning bibles and prayer books. Protestants were still banned from importing religious non-Catholic material and were denied the right to contract civil marriages in foreign-owned churches.

Apart from the religious issue, Westminster was also worried about the diversion of military aid away from NATO countries to Spain, but did not oppose granting military advice, training equipment and obsolete war equipment as long as this did not decrease the amount of military material available for NATO countries and for Germany's re-militarization.

France had similar concerns. Both nations feared that the American Defense Department had increased its interest in Spain and had become willing to grant Spain military end-products as well as financial aid in return for a base agreement. London and Paris feared that this would result in a decrease of military help for NATO countries and a possible withdrawal of troops stationed in Central Europe. Washington was aware of its Allies' concern and, when the time came, secretly instructed the head of the JUSMG to ensure that in all discussions there was no indication of a possible course of action to withdraw US forces from Germany and France to Spain in the event of war. These international issues were further complicated when the Mutual Security Agency stressed that before economic aid could be granted, liberal trade unions and free enterprise had to be established in Spain.

Given the diplomatic complications, the head of the negotiations team for Spain was to be a person with exceptional diplomatic skills, business experience and prior European Cooperation Administration background. On top of these professional skills, they had to be almost unknown to the public in order to avoid unnecessary publicity.

After Sufrin's report, the State Department worried that it might lose control over its policy towards Spain for several reasons. If limited economic aid for Spain was the result of a concession for the achievement of specific military objectives then the State Department could see itself sidelined. Clearly it was considered important, even by the State Department, to link military and economic aid. However, if it was decided that bilateral agreements between Spain and the US could be entered into, the State Department ran the risk of being swept aside by military considerations during the negotiation process.

Military cooperation between the two countries increased. From 4 to 9 January 1952, 16 Spanish naval officers embarked on two American ships, the *Tarawa* and the carrier *F. D. Roosevelt*, to observe the Sixth Fleet exercise in the Mediterranean. Shortly afterwards, 31 ships of the US Fleet, including a carrier, visited several ports in Spain. This was the largest naval visit to Spain since the end of the Spanish Civil War.

On 14 January 1952, Secretary Acheson told Congress that what Admiral Sherman had taken up with Franco were anchorage, landing and overflight rights. It was clear that some of the airfields in Spain required extensive work before they could be used by large USAF bombers, but this was of minor concern. More problematic, though clearly solvable, was Spain's desire to obtain military end-products. Acheson explained that in return for granting base rights, Spain wanted equipment which was hard to obtain. He told Congress that the administration would go ahead with the talks. The Secretary agreed that Spain would add to the depth of the defence of the Atlantic area but made it clear that this was not the central issue at stake.

Two days later the Joint Chiefs of Staff instructed Secretary of Defense Robert A. Lovett to establish a Joint US Military Group Spain (JUSMG). The JUSMG was to start military negotiations and decide how to use the $100 million appropriated for Spain. The Joint Chiefs of Staff wanted to split the available $100 million for Spain as 15 per cent for the US Army, 13 per cent for the Navy and 72 per cent for the Air Force. During the first year of the construction programme, the USAF hoped to station three medium Bomber Wings and one Reconnaissance Wing in Spain. Construction of air-force bases at Torrejón, San Pablo, Moron, El Copero and Matagorda would be initiated. At the same time, new air depots and POL (Petrol, Oil, Lubricants) storage facilities near Matagorda and Seville would be constructed. During the same period the Navy hoped to build the off-loading dock and fly-away strip near Matagorda as well as add to the existing storage facilities. The Army hoped to improve roads and railways near the area of Matagorda and Seville.

The Joint Chiefs of Staff outlined long-term US military requirements in Spain. These were based on a note by the Secretaries of the Services, dated 7 January 1952. The requirements included air bases for peacetime rotation and a wartime ten-wing detachment. In order to do this a series of airfields had to be improved. Furthermore a HQ near Madrid was to be built. The total costs of these USAF projects came to $285 million. The US Navy wanted an aircraft support dock near Cádiz for $11.8 million and a logistics base near Rota. The cost of the latter was expected to be $45.8 million. The Navy also wanted anchorage rights, port repair facilities, and subterranean storage facilities. Additionally, the US hoped to gain access to an amphibious training area, improve rolling stock and build POL terminals and a pipeline system. On top of that the US Army required additional facilities to secure and protect all US operations. Generally speaking, the US wanted to develop Spain's military potential at a total cost of around $400 million. To assure flexibility, the Joint Chiefs of Staff wanted to include a statement that the US also had the right to demand additional facilities as might be considered necessary in the future. In the short term, the Joint Chiefs of Staff recommended entering negotiations with Spain on the military aspect and lifting previous restrictions, as under the limited approach agreed by Truman, Acheson, Marshall and Sherman. In order to conduct negotiations at the military level and to coordinate

them with the Mutual Security Agency, the Joint Chiefs of Staff wanted
to dispatch the JUSMG under an Air Force officer reporting to the US
Ambassador in Spain.

The State Department agreed that combined economic and military
negotiations should start as soon as possible. It wanted to seize the
initiative over the negotiations by agreeing prior to the departure of
the negotiations team on the topics which were to be covered. It therefore stressed that military plans had to be defined before they could be
endorsed.

The State Department also wanted to avoid any complications with
NATO countries arising out of the negotiations with Spain. Acheson
argued that it was best to leave the Spanish matter outside NATO.

Economic aid was to be the carrot for military negotiations. As for
the exact use of the $100 million aid, it had not yet been determined,
but the Mutual Security Agency and the State Department were convinced that the loan would benefit the Spanish economy. It was feared
that Spain might come to see the $100 million already appropriated as
a minimum rather than a maximum of aid. The State Department argued that the US should not hesitate in disappointing the Spaniards
over their false assumption.

Theoretically, the $100 million appropriated for the Mutual Security
Agency could not be used directly for the construction of military facilities in Spain as this would have been against the purpose of the
Mutual Security Agency. Nevertheless, the chairman of the Mutual
Assistance Advisory Committee mentioned that counterpart funds, created
through the purchase of dollar commodities for the Spanish economy,
could be used for military constructions. The Spanish government would
deposit pesetas in an account, as a counterpart for American economic
and technical assistance. The American government would be able to
draw money on this account to pay for peseta expenditures in Spain
and could thus use them for the planned military constructions. Funds
generated through Spain's purchase of goods in the US could be indirectly used for military purposes. The Mutual Assistance Advisory
Committee approved the idea and on 2 February it gave a rough estimate on how to break down the $100 million: $40 million for com-
modity purchases which would generate counterpart funds; $25 million
for the purchase of military training equipment; $15 million for mate-
rials for the railways; $20 million for the ammunitions industry.

By now, January 1952, it was clear that the planned $57 million-
worth of military end-products were not available for quick delivery
due to the great demand created world-wide by the Korean conflict. It

was clear that Spain would receive military aid. Yet as for military end-products, hardware deliveries to NATO were given priority and Spain would only receive modern military equipment once it had made a commitment to support NATO.

The State Department wanted to reconsider aid plans for military end-products and minimum training equipment. The Department feared that if the current plans for the negotiations were not reconsidered, Spain's hopes would be raised and Madrid would ask for more military items and thus complicate negotiations further. The State Department asserted that if Spain received large amounts of military aid, complications with NATO would come about and delivery of this equipment would have to be delayed until Spain was committed to the defence of the West.

Fearing European opposition, Secretary of State Acheson informed Secretary of Defense Lovett that his Department was not in agreement with the Department of Defense on entering negotiations with Spain under the plan outlined by the Joint Chiefs of Staff. Acheson asked for a decrease of minimum base requirements and US personnel stationed in Spain. He asserted that if this was not possible, two problems would arise. The gradual increase of the implementation of a programme of the considered size would dislocate Spain socially and economically. High inflation and conflict between the Spanish people and US personnel would create difficulties. Acheson argued that the second problem was the lack of military information passed on to the American Ambassador in Spain concerning the required military facilities. It had been agreed that the Ambassador would be involved during the later stages of the negotiations and therefore had to be kept informed throughout the talks. However, the Department of Defense, concerned about national security of the military project, wanted to keep US military demands secret from the State Department and the American Embassy in Madrid. By scaling down the project, Acheson hoped that the Pentagon would make more information available.

Acheson agreed with Lovett that the negotiations should get under way once Lincoln MacVeagh, future Ambassador to Spain, had presented his credentials to Franco, presumably around the middle of March. Until then, he considered it of utmost importance that the two Departments reached an agreement.

Included in his letter, Acheson sent Lovett a counter-proposal on US military requirements in Spain. This agreed with most of the Joint Chiefs of Staff demands apart from the size and composition of military deployment in Spain, nor was it agreeable with the demand or concessions by Spain for the US Army to secure future US operations. Acheson did not favour the possibility of asking Spain in the future for additional facilities not outlined in the military report. Most importantly though, the Secretary felt that it was not appropriate to develop Spain's military potential to the maximum.

The State Department knew that Spain had carefully studied bilateral agreements and US aid programmes to other European countries. Madrid was fully aware of the kind of assistance which was going to its neighbours. As a result, the Counselor of the American Embassy in Spain believed that military talks were not going to be easy unless the US was willing to spend more than just $100 million. The US Chargé, John W. Jones, hoped that if this money was not going to be enough to provide facilities in Spain, the US would use the $5 billion base construction funds of the Department of Defense. Jones also recommended that technical assistance should only be granted in fields which were covered by economic assistance. That meant that advice on the textile industry in Catalonia and Mutual Security Agency funds for cotton, as well as insecticides and advice on how to combat the olive fruit fly, should be combined. Jones claimed that the delay of talks was due to the failure by the military to adhere to NSC 72/8. According to him, NSC 72/8 had opened the question of US military policy towards Spain and caused a split between the economic and military talks. This was exploited by Franco and delayed the negotiations by a year.

In the meantime two new reports by the Joint Logistics Committee to the Joint Chiefs of Staff recommended a different breakdown of the $100 million. This would have created a total of $83 million, instead of only $75 million, of counterpart funds. The rest of the money would go towards military end-products and strategic material. The suggested changes meant that an extra $8 million were available in counterpart funds, which could be spent on the construction of military facilities. The $83 million in counterpart funds was to be spent as $78 million for base constructions and $5 for the Mutual Security allocations. The base construction costs, adding up to $390 million over three years (annual costs of $130 million), were to be covered during the first year by the counterpart funds ($78 million) and by the Department of Defense ($52 million).

Hoyt S. Vandenberg, the USAF member of the Joint Chiefs of Staff, informed the Secretary of Defense that he favoured the new distribution of military end-products as suggested by the Joint Committee. Nevertheless, Vandenberg also suggested that if Spain disagreed with the arrangements concerning counterpart funds, the Department of Defense would have to pay more than the $52 million for the base construction. The same day, 15 February 1952, the Department of Defense under the Mutual Defense Assistance Program started planning how to split up the $55 million worth of military end-products.

On 26 February 1952, the Interdepartmental (Defense–State) Working Group sent a report to the Chairman of the Mutual Assistance Advisory Committee. It supported the Joint Chiefs of Staff's earlier suggestion by stressing that the $100 million should be used in such a way as to create enough counterpart funds to meet the construction costs. In FY 1953 alone about $78 million had to be covered in this way. If Spain refused to accept a proposal which channelled $88 million into construction and $12 million into military training then the Mutual Assistance Advisory Committee would not use the funds for the construction of bases, but would have to finance them completely through the Department of Defense. It was expected that Spain would complain about the counterpart arrangement, as no other country received aid for the construction of military facilities under such an agreement. Other nations used the money created by counterpart funds for their economy, while base construction was paid for exclusively by the US. The report speculated that Spain might agree to the military proposal but not to the administrative arrangements.

The report claimed that the fundamental problem was the financial inability of the Department of Defense to pay for the base construction plan during the first year. The US was trying to make use of the $100 million appropriated for Spain twice, once by creating counterpart funds and then by paying for the construction of their own bases. If Spain had found out that this had not been done elsewhere, it would have complicated the negotiations considerably.

In Washington three scenarios were envisaged. The Spanish government would be unwilling to grant all bases, which would reduce the total costs to merely $152 million, a sum small enough to be financed without counterpart funds. Second, the US could simply slow down the construction during the first year to an investment of $52 million, which the Department might be able to finance. Finally, the Department could provide funds, which were not specifically earmarked for Spain, to pay for the costs during the first year, thus leaving the overall base construction costs at $230 million for coming years.

The Mutual Assistance Advisory Committee would have to balance these aims while taking into consideration that any action taken should not have inflationary effects on the Spanish economy. The Committee was to give priority to US military requirements and avoid peseta expenditure on the railways, labour, and facilities. Nor were pesetas to be spent on military end-products or for training.

On 4 March 1952, the USAF spelled out what the Mutual Defense Agreement Program's objectives should be in Spain. It was to provide a broad base and well-trained nucleus for future expansion of the Spanish Air Force. This meant that the programme had to train Spanish pilots and provide modern training equipment. It also had to increase the air–sea rescue capabilities of the Spanish Air Force. In order to achieve this, the USAF estimated that a total of $27.6 million, spread over three years, was required. The money was to be spent as $15 million for aircraft; $6 million for electronics and communication and $4 million for general equipment. The rest of the $27.6 million, i.e. $2.6 million, would go towards administrative charges. The total aid would be delivered to Spain between 1953 and 1955, with the bulk arriving in 1954.

On the same day the Mutual Assistance Advisory Committee reconsidered the report by the Interdepartmental Working Group on Spain from February and decided to continue discussions.

On 20 March 1952, the Interdepartmental Working Group issued its new statement of policy. This document was to serve as instruction to the Mutual Security Agency negotiation team during the first few months. This policy paper, known as DMS D-7 (FRUS, 1952–54, VI, p. 1824), argued that the aid programme was based on the assumption that there was only $100 million available for FY 1953 and that no new funds would be made available. Furthermore it saw the US's primary objective to obtain base rights in Spain. Moreover, it considered that the $100 million had to cover the base construction costs as well as economic, technical, and military aid. The report estimated base costs at $390 million spread over three years. The costs could be covered 40 per cent in US dollars and 60 per cent in pesetas, resulting in annual costs of $52 million and the equivalent of $78 million in pesetas. There was still hope that during the first year the Department of Defense would cover the entire $52 million. The alternative, using the Mutual Security Program funds, was undesirable as it appeared to breach the terms of the Mutual Security Appropriation Act.

However, the report also read that it would be appropriate for counterpart funds, generated through the purchase of dollar commodities, to be used for the construction of military facilities in Spain. This too had been part of the Mutual Assistance Advisory Committee's decision on 2 February. The $100 million was broken down along similar lines as before.

It was expected that the assistance for Spanish private industry and the ammunitions industry would create a total of $22 million in counterpart funds, as would the $50 million spent on consumer goods to offset inflationary effects. Thus the assistance would place no additional burden on the Spanish economy. After further studies, it was decided that the money flowing into the railways and the technical assistance would not create counterpart funds because it became obvious that most of the rolling stock had to be purchased in the US and paid for in dollars. The exchange rate for the counterpart funds was not to be determined under the Spanish multiple exchange-rates system but fixed beforehand.

The US Embassy in Madrid was convinced that Spain would not accept the method of counterpart funds because it had not been applied to other countries. If Spain objected, the negotiation team was instructed to point out to the Spanish authorities that Spain was not a member of NATO and thus bilateral agreements would be based on a quid pro quo. Should Spain continue to oppose, then the negotiation team was allowed to reduce the funds Spain had to deposit from $78 million to $50 million. If this concession was necessary, constructions would have had to be slowed down, lowering expenditure and spreading costs over a longer period.

In the meantime in Spain, Artajo and Marqués de Prat had a conversation with the US Chargé in Spain and others from the American Embassy. The Spanish Foreign Minister outlined Spain's struggle against Communism as well as Spain's vital strategic location in the Mediterranean. He claimed that Spanish soldiers were brave but lacked modern equipment. In order to strengthen Spain militarily, Spain needed a healthy industry as well as arms and ammunition. The Spanish Minister claimed that his country had no immediate interest in joining NATO. The American Embassy Representative Perkins pointed out that 1952 was an election year in the US, which would cause delays in the negotiations. Despite problems between Britain and Spain, which could further complicate matters, Perkins told Artajo that MacVeagh's team might have instructions to initiate negotiations.

As the date of Lincoln MacVeagh's departure drew closer, discussions in Washington heated up. Due to the possibility that Spain might reject the idea of counterpart funds, Lovett tried to take all necessary steps to ensure the $52 million from the Department of Defense funds for the construction of the bases in Spain.

The Secretary argued that as the Department of the Air Force was the main benefactor, it should carry the burden of the costs. The Air Force was expected to pay $44 million out of the $52 million for the first year. Nevertheless, when the Department of the Air Force was informed about financing Spain's bases through its defence funds, it told the Secretary of Defense that neither the allocated $44 million to the Department of the Air Force nor the subsequent annual $110 million had been included in any funds appropriated for the Air Force, nor did it contemplate reprogramming its funds for FY 1953. Straightforwardly, the Department was not willing to bear the costs required to finance the base construction now or in the future without further appropriation or reallocation of funds.

The Air Force had received $82 million for base construction in Europe during FY 1953 and was currently requesting a further $120 million for military bases in Portugal and Northern Ireland. The Department of the Air Force argued that if the Department of Defense had to finance the costs of construction in Spain, then the European base construction fund would have to be split between Spain, Portugal and Northern Ireland. The Air Force suddenly thought that Spain was of no greater interest as a location for air bases than other areas of corresponding distance to possible targets, and made it clear that it only wanted to invest in Spain after full political agreements assured access to the military bases in times of difficulty.

The base project was in serious difficulties if the USAF refused to bear its costs. The Joint Chiefs of Staff had recommended economic and military assistance to Spain on the assumption that the Department of Defense would partly finance the base constructions. William C. Foster, member of the Joint Chiefs of Staff, now put pressure on the Chief of Air Staff to get his Department to approve the necessary costs. He wrote to the Secretary that if the Department of the Air Force desired the development of the bases in Spain, it should make the necessary budgetary provisions.

The Secretary of Defense took note, and his office informed the Air Force that in order to initiate construction without undue delay the reply by the Secretary of the Air Force was requested.

Similar problems arose with the Navy. On 11 April 1952, the US Navy reviewed the Public Works Authorization and the Appropriation Acts. The Chief of Naval Operations concluded that the Navy would be unable to recommend a reprogramming of costs to cover either the initial $8 million or the subsequent annual $20 million. Suddenly the Department of Defense itself was hard-pressed to finance the construction. The Army too became involved. None of the three armed services wanted to come up with the funds.

Given that the Defense Department was denied the cooperation of its Air Force and Navy Departments, it became clear that the availability of funds for the construction depended solely on the progress of the negotiations. If Spain refused to go along with the idea of counterpart funds, the Defense Department would be unable to finance the construction.

This led the Joint Chiefs of Staff to consider possible alternatives if Spain rejected the idea of using counterpart funds. In such a case, the $100 million aid for Spain would have been split differently.

As these financial considerations in the Pentagon were being discussed, other important developments had taken place. On 12 March 1952, Acheson announced in a press statement the beginning of negotiations between Spain and the US. Britain was pleased that he did not mention possible military aid for Spain. In fact the State Department had assured the Foreign Office only days before that if any military equipment was provided it would not be such as to affect existing NATO priorities.

In his press release Acheson claimed that negotiations had been delayed until the analysis of the two reports had been concluded. Shortly afterwards the talks could go ahead under the newly created JUSMG. Major-General Garvin Crump would represent the Army, Captain H. G. Sanchez the Navy and Colonel Jack Roberts the Air Force. Major-General A. W. Kissner, USAF, was to head the overall American military team. Kissner was an old friend of William Dunham who was in charge of Western European Affairs at the State Department. Kissner had only recently gained important practical experience skills when assisting the Azores negotiations with Portugal. He was a quietly spoken and very cooperative man who got on well with the American Ambassador in Spain.

This was important as the JUSMG was to work under the Ambassador in Madrid and report through him to Washington. Later, it was expected that the Ambassador would personally assist the negotiations. It was notable that by 19 March, the JUSMG still did not have any final instructions from the State Department on the breakdown of the $100 million, despite their planned departure six days later. Finally, the next day, DMS D-7 was issued, which was to serve as rough instructions for the negotiation team while interdepartmental discussions in Washington continued.

The Department of Defense claimed that one major point of disagreement left with the State Department concerned the limitations on the scope of negotiations. The State Department still wanted to operate under the limitations agreed upon by the President, the Secretaries for Defense and State and Admiral Sherman prior to the Admiral's visit

to Spain. If the US wanted to avoid unnecessary delays, they had to
sort out the differences between the two Departments soon.

Nevertheless, it was clear from the start that negotiations would take
a while due to Spain's peculiar position. Already before any delays
became apparent, the press speculated about problems such as Franco's strong negotiation position.

Franco was not a bad tactician. In order to strengthen his position,
he pre-empted any criticism by Truman on the religious intolerance in
Spain. In a letter to President Truman he wrote:

> I hope that the negotiations which are about to start shall attain a happy
> ending and will draw our two peoples nearer each other. . . . I do
> not believe there is any essential matter between our two nations
> which can estrange us since friendship and understanding between
> countries have always been above peculiarities of each people. These
> differences of a religious nature which enemies of our understand-
> ing seek to exaggerate respond to a natural difference in feelings
> and traditions of a country fully united in its Catholicism and where
> dissident confessions do not amount to one per thousand of its popu-
> lation, and of those other countries which, due to their diverse and
> numerically important confessions, are compelled to live under a
> system of mutual concessions and balances. . . . Our system does
> not interfere with the private practice of other cults, which are guar-
> anteed in our nation by its basic laws. (FRUS, 1952–54, VI, p.1799)

Franco also asked for $750 million industrial credit. Delegations of
the Export–Import Bank estimated that $400 million would be more
than enough and recommended this sum to the Senate. This sum threw
the Department of Defense back to the beginning of the *rapprochement* period. Bases in Spain seemed too costly. It became known through
General James W. Spry that parts of the USAF had become indifferent
towards obtaining bases in Spain. One of the main reasons for this
was because the Department of the Air Force had to bear most of the
base construction costs.

In February 1952, Lincoln MacVeagh officially replaced Griffis as
Ambassador to Spain. For Britain as well as many Spaniards, Griffis
had not been a popular ambassador due to his strong support for Franco's cause. During his last months in Spain, Griffis received so many
threats against his life that the Spanish authorities had to provide him
with a permanent security escort. The British Ambassador was pleased
when he saw the back of him and wrote about the new American

Ambassador: "Unlike his predecessor ... McVeagh [*sic*] ... appears to assess matters in a realistic light and to be confining himself to securing the limited objectives which the United States Government have come to set themselves [in Spain]" (PRO, FO 371.10214). The new Ambassador arrived in Madrid on 23 March and presented his credentials four days later. As he was being driven in the ambassadorial convoy to meet Franco for the first time, his limousine was being followed by a lorry picking up garbage. Even if unintentional, the British Embassy joked that this was a metaphor for MacVeagh having to pick up the mess left behind by his predecessor. Spaniards chaffed that this Lincoln undoubtedly was unrelated to the Lincoln who had freed the slaves. As for Griffis, the rumour spread that he had not resigned out of personal or health reasons but due to his handling of Franco.

When MacVeagh arrived in Madrid, Artajo went to visit the Middle East, to express his gratitude to the Arab nations for their support in the UN. This encouraged scaremongers to speculate that Artajo wanted to form a third world power, a combination of Arab and Latin American countries and Spain. The Spanish diplomatic corps did not discourage these wild rumours as they gave the appearance of strong Arab support. This increased Spain's importance in the coming talks. The Americans were not impressed. Indeed the American Ambassador to Turkey stated that good relations between Spain and the Arab states were desirable.

Shortly afterwards in Madrid, during the annual military parades, the army once again ceremoniously revealed its obsolete war material. Each year this ceremony was getting more and more embarrassing for Spain. That very same day, at 7.30 p.m., Artajo and MacVeagh held a conversation in French at the Foreign Ministry. Artajo believed that MacVeagh was ready to start negotiations and had brought with him the proposed plans. In the conversation he made clear that Spain would never be willing to lease or sell bases to the US and all military facilities would be used jointly. As had been feared by Washington, the Spanish Minister saw the $100 million as a drop in the ocean and said in French that "The soil of the Spanish economy is so dry that it would take torrents of financial assistance to wet it." He encouraged the Ambassador to send the two special US military and economic groups to Spain as early as possible.

Shortly afterwards, on 4 April, the military group JUSMG under General Kissner arrived. Nine days later, the economic group, MSAEG, under George Train from the Mutual Security Agency, landed in Spain for talks. The negotiations were under way.

11 Kissner and Train in Madrid

The arrival of the JUSMG and the MSAEG was followed by several meetings between General Kissner and Lieutenant-General Vigón. On 7 April, the first conference between the two took place. In another meeting on the following day, General Kissner presented Vigón with an outline of the proposed contents of a base agreement. This and other questions were subsequently discussed. In one of the early sessions, the Spaniards asked for grants to train pilots before any agreements were signed. The Americans refused. They had not come to Madrid to make easy concessions. Over the next 18 months the two sides would be engaged in hard bargaining.

On 16 April, during the third meeting between the two, Vigón expressed that he was satisfied with the military aspects presented so far and accepted the fact that the appropriation of money was a Congressional not a military matter. He also urged that the improved installations be under a joint agreement. Kissner still did not mention any particular installations. However, he confirmed that end-product equipment was being considered for all three military branches of the Spanish forces. At that moment, Washington planned to extend an aid programme to Spain for three years. Vigón feared that three years might be too long if an emergency arose. He was also concerned about Spanish public opinion if bombers were stationed in Spain. Kissner assured him that US requirements did not include peacetime stationing of full capacity. He estimated that by rotating planes, an approximate detachment of 500 soldiers per base was required. Vigón seemed happy with this but insisted on Spanish control over these bases. The Spanish general, due to the forthcoming meeting of the National Defence Council, the top military policy making body, asked for a delay of the negotiations by one week.

After their meeting, Kissner wrote a letter to the Spanish negotiation team, in which he stated that the US was still uncertain about Spain's role in the Western defence. Furthermore, Kissner claimed that military aid was to be discussed by the economic teams but he could not guarantee that funds would be allocated for military training equipment. He explained that if base agreements were reached, Congress would naturally want to see the appropriate defence of these bases. Unfortunately for the American negotiations team, Kissner's letter, trying to create a friendly atmosphere, followed the wording of discussions by the Joint Chiefs of Staff more closely than it did his official instructions from the State Department. In his letter, despite having been instructed not to do so, he gave away the list of 11 items, agreed upon by the Joint Chiefs of Staff and the Departments of State and Defense, and outlining US requirements.

After seeing these demands, the Spanish negotiation teams were assured of strong, long-term US interests in Spain. Thus they had no problem accepting the idea of counterpart funds to finance the base construction. This was an important step forward for the agreements as it solved one of Washington's main concerns. Funds were available for the first-year construction plans. However this was only solved by creating another problem; Spain was now certain that they could increase their demands without Washington pulling out.

On 26 April, Vigón had a fourth meeting with Kissner. This time they talked about Kissner's letter. Vigón exposed Spain's position towards this document. He assured Kissner that Spanish forces could be mobilized in a short period and even before the full mobilization of NATO divisions. This was important because, according to the Spaniard, the American demands meant that Spain could no longer remain passive in a European conflict. This situation, he continued, would naturally result in air strikes and might induce a possible large-scale operation by the enemy against Spain. This line of thought developed into one fundamental tenet of the Spanish position throughout the talks. Granting bases to the US would make Spain a belligerent nation and thus increase her vulnerability. The Spanish government therefore considered it essential that the US accept the principle that there had to be a considerable amount of military equipment available for Spain's national defence. Such equipment and the granting of bases were regarded as an indivisible whole.

Eventually, Spain would contribute to Western defence, but due to the urgency of the military requirements, Vigón argued that his country should get war material from the existing NATO stocks. He claimed that the delay of the creation of NATO divisions made the material unusable for the time being. Analysing Kissner's specific requests, he seemed willing to grant the USAF and Navy airbase installations as long as they remained under Spanish control. Both nations would use them simultaneously. However, he wanted more details on the American demand to develop, equip, man and use facilities as required by any projected US Army operation and furthermore, the Spanish general demanded that the Americans should be more precise about their demands for additional facilities because of developments in negotiations with other countries. He strongly objected to the demand for an amphibious training area because there did not seem to be a suitable spot. He claimed that Spain's coast was either too rugged or too densely populated. He also demanded that US aircraft in Spain should rotate from base to base and only a minimum of US personnel should be stationed at the bases. As for the duration of the treaties or agreements, he proposed to have them run for five years with a possible prolongation at the end of this period.

Once Vigón's reply was received in Washington, the State Department realized that Kissner had made a blunder in his negotiations. Instead of presenting the arguments of Acheson's letter to Lovett, dated 11 February 1952, he had exposed the point of view of the Joint Chiefs of Staff. The State Department concluded that the Spanish negotiation was nicely off the rails. Kissner also admitted that the US wanted to develop Spain's military potential to the maximum degree possible within existing limitations. The State Department feared that "the trap that we sought to avoid – asking the Spaniards for rights in the Army area, which will invoke requests for army equipment" had been sprung. The State Department knew that it could not meet NATO equipment needs, and it would have been murder to engage in a major end-product programme for Spain. It was questionable if they could put the negotiations back on track and avoid a similar blunder in the future.

In the meantime, the Secretary of State responded to the developments in the negotiations by contacting the Spanish Embassy. On 2 May, Acheson complained that Madrid failed to see the difference between the European Cooperation Administration and the Mutual Security Act 1951. The difference was crucial as it determined the way in which money was being allocated. He disliked Spain's multiple exchange-rate systems, which would have had an inflationary impact during the construction phase and make an increase of trade impossible.

These multiple exchange rates were inhibiting free trade with Spain. Britain also favoured putting pressure on Madrid to abolish these. The International Monetary Fund (IMF) or the International Bank for Reconstruction and Development (IBRD) were considered appropriate institutions to do so. The Bank of England suggested that if the US only extended aid to Spain under the condition that Spain joined the IMF, the Fund could in turn force Spain to review its exchange rates. The British Treasury supported this but it was doubtful if Washington agreed.

Initially, the State Department was in favour of abolishing multiple exchange rates through the IMF. However for Washington, the essential problem of the talks concerned military, not economic issues. Train had confirmed this to the UK Commercial Counsellor in Madrid, admitting that Washington subordinated economic aid to US military requirements. On top of that the timing was inopportune. After Kissner's initial blunder, Washington was interested in stalling the talks. In fact, with his note to the Spanish Embassy on 2 May, the Secretary of State wanted to complicate the talks and throw the Spanish side off balance in order to correct Kissner's mistake.

Acheson was more successful in achieving this in a note to the US Ambassador in Spain four days later. In it, he claimed that Spain was trying to offer a quid pro quo for the bases but that the Spanish negotiation team was asking for too much aid. Countering Spain's argument of being converted to a belligerent nation, the American hypothesis emerged that Spain would inevitably be involved in hostilities, even in the absence of US bases. He concluded that from a military point of view, Spain's best defence was north and east of the Pyrenees and thus she should welcome the chance to contribute to this defence line. At the same time, if a quid pro quo was reached, Spain should not forget the value of the economic and technical aid she was going to receive. Acheson believed that the discussions were concerned with the amount of aid and the control of the facilities. It was only natural for the Secretary to claim that as Spain had less military value than NATO, military supplies should go to NATO countries first, and before any new training material could be allocated, the $100 million had to be used. Finally, Acheson tried to prevent further discussion of Kissner's mistake. He ordered that the two demands concerning requirements of the army for projected operations and for additional facilities were scrapped altogether from the negotiations. Acheson claimed that they were no longer needed. More importantly, Acheson gave instructions for no further discussion of the US proposal to develop Spain's military potential to a maximum. Spain was of course unwilling to forget these important demands and concessions by the US team.

With the two discussion fronts clearly drawn, the talks became more concrete. On 9 May 1952, Kissner handed General Vigón a draft of the proposed base agreement. Without delay, Madrid started its analysis.

One week later, John Wesley Jones, Counselor of the US Embassy, had an informal conversation after dinner at the French Embassy in Madrid with Manuel Arburúa, the Spanish Minister of Commerce. Arburúa told the American that Spain needed urgent equipment for "no more" than 20 divisions. The Spanish Minister believed that France and Italy did not have the will to fight because of the large Communist groups within their countries. He stated that Spain was unwilling to defend areas like Cádiz while leaving Barcelona unprotected, thus implying that a commitment to the defence of all of Spain was needed. Arburúa supported the military point of view wholeheartedly while not even bothering to mention the economic talks. One can conclude that the Spanish negotiators were more interested in the military than in the economic aspects.

The economic talks had started on 17 April when the head of MSAEG, Mr Train, held a first meeting with Jaime Argüelles, Under-Secretary of Commerce. The Train–Argüelles talks were usually held at the Ministry of Commerce in "Don Jaime's" green-walled office. In this first meeting, Train claimed that the US government intended to request the reappropriation in FY 1953 of the $100 million allocated by Congress the year before. His Spanish counterpart made it apparent that they had hoped for additional funds. In fact, Spain wanted the immediate payment of the $100 million without any conditions.

Shortly after their first informal discussion, Train sent an *aide-mémoire* to the Spanish Economic Aid Negotiating Group on 19 April 1952. He described the legal authority under which US assistance was provided and outlined the view of the US government concerning the proposed use of that assistance in Spain. He made clear that aid to Spain was limited to the Mutual Security Act, which granted Spain a maximum of $100 million, split into 88 per cent economic aid and 12 per cent military aid. In order to receive the $12 million for military aid a separate "Mutual Defense Assistance Agreement" had to be signed. This agreement was separate from any agreements concerning the use of bases and the agreement covering economic and technical assistance. From April 1952 onwards, it became clear that three separate contracts had to be signed. Train hoped that the aid would be issued to the most profitable short-term investments and would counter possible inflation. As for technical assistance, the US negotiation team asserted that aid could only cover the dollar costs. Any costs in pesetas had to be borne by Spain. Train also believed that a $15 million loan to the railways was required, as well as some aid for the Spanish ammunitions industry. He told the Spanish team that all economic assistance, which was made on grants, required counterpart funds at an exchange rate to be agreed upon in advance. It was expected that the counterpart funds would finance all military construction costs for 1952/53.

In response, the Spanish team formally requested that the $100 million should be extended completely during FY 1952 and that the US administration should request Congress for an additional appropriation for the following year. Argüelles argued that this should be done as recognition in principle of the change in mutual relationships resulting from the opening of the negotiations. It is clear that Madrid considered the proposed amount as an initial aid package, soon to be followed by more substantial funds.

The US economic negotiation team advised their counterparts that this was not possible. They argued that the availability of further funds provided during FY 1953 and additional funds for FY 1954 could only be determined after a specific economic programme had been worked out and agreed.

On 3 May, six days before Kissner handed in the military proposal, Train provided the Spanish representatives with a written draft for the economic assistance agreement. These two drafts were discussed extensively over the next few weeks. In a statement on 16 May 1952, Franco said that he was hoping for a Spanish–American agreement in the general area of mutual security and corresponding military and economic assistance without any infringement of mutual sovereignty. He was asking for a friendly relationship with Washington, as well as for substantial aid, without granting anything in return. Franco was trying to make the best of his position and Kissner's initial blunder had encouraged further demands by Spain. For Franco it was important to maintain the appearance of full sovereign control so that his position remained unchallenged.

After these initial two months of negotiations, the US informed Britain of the progress of the economic and military talks and about the position the US was to take in the future. This was done during a meeting of Foreign Ministers in Paris on 26 May, attended by Acheson and Anthony Eden.

Major problems remained for the American negotiation teams. On the economic side Madrid asked for more money. On the military side the most pressing problem concerned the duration of the bases. Kissner demanded twenty years while General Vigón only offered five, with a possible extension of another five years.

Soon after the Foreign Ministers meeting in Paris, further complications arose in the military negotiations. All had gone relatively well until a meeting between Kissner and Vigón on 1 June 1952. During this meeting the Spanish general raised the question of US continuity of military assistance after the successful conclusion of the agreements.

Kissner could not guarantee this as ultimately the decision had to be made in accordance with the corresponding Committees in Congress or by the President. As it was clear that Truman would not continue in power beyond January 1953, Kissner was unable to reassure Vigón. The Spaniard kept pressing for an answer which Kissner refused to give. Naturally the Spanish team concluded that once the agreements were signed without such an assurance Washington would not grant more than the $125 million. During the next meetings and in order to get assurance for long-term military aid, the Spanish team decided to go back on concessions made earlier, such as peacetime use of the bases. It was unfortunate that the legal position simply did not allow Kissner to make these concessions.

The Ambassador to Spain informed the Spanish team of Acheson's argument in the letter dated 3 June. The US agreed to Vigón's statement that US bases meant an automatic belligerency for Spain in the event of war. Washington also realized that it was politically impossible to include Spain in NATO or to sign a tripartite pact with Portugal and Spain. MacVeagh believed that the complications which arose had to be ironed out by force. However, he suggested that pressure should be kept to a minimum so that the talks concerning military bases remained friendly. He realized that Spain considered the $100 million insufficient but would take anything they got. A lot of time had been consumed but the Ambassador considered it better than to press and risk losing what had been gained so far. MacVeagh also confirmed that the US team had to reconsider proposals several times and communicate with Washington, which had caused delays.

In their seventh meeting on 5 June, General Vigón handed Kissner a note, in which he pointed out that Spain had already revealed the weaknesses and deficiencies of the Spanish Army to Sherman and Spry and further studies were unnecessary. The Spanish general repeated the argument that US bases in Spain would be attacked by the Soviet Air Force. He asserted that the numerical advantage of the USSR meant that the US air crews stationed in the Elbe/Rhine area would not stop aerial attacks on Spain by Soviet planes from the Balkans and across the Mediterranean. From the Spanish military point of view, Spain needed to be able to defend herself. To do so, she needed a radar network during the first year after the completion of the agreements. Vigón also argued that as the USAF would be required elsewhere Spain needed her own national air force. He asserted that this was indispensable and that collaboration for production of jet engines and spare parts as well as training material was crucial. The US had already agreed to send more training aid for AA-artillery. Vigón argued that this only made sense if Spain also received more material for real defence purposes. The Spanish general continued to argue that arming Spain's divisions to the standard of other nations would not place a burden on NATO stocks because most war material could be produced in Spain, given adequate financial and technical aid. The $12 million for military end-products was expected to cover only the training period, and more material was to follow later. The Spanish team assumed that the $100 million of aid only covered the first year and were interested in working out a full assistance plan for the coming three years. Vigón even proposed that the Mutual Aid Agreement should be five to nine years long, with a possible extension. He also wanted to reduce the number of US soldiers stationed in Spain, and argued that it was natural for other European countries to see permanent US soldiers stationed on their territory as they had been exposed to years of struggle and occupation, while Spain had remained under a national regime. In Spain, the note claimed, US soldiers would be welcomed only by the Communist propaganda machinery. The airbases, he claimed, did not need a permanent presence of wings and their operation could be verified by frequent visits of less than a wing of planes.

The Spanish negotiation team had so far only expressed in vague and general terms their military needs. In view of the importance of Spanish interest in such aid, and after General Vigón had pushed for long-term US commitment, General Kissner suggested in their eighth official encounter, on 9 June, that it would be helpful to have more specific information regarding Spain's material requirements. Agencies in Washington had encouraged this and had informally informed Kissner that they were considering an increase in the amount of military aid for Spain by $25 million.

After Congress had approved the extra $25 million, the State Department wanted the President to issue a statement relating to these funds. It was felt that such a statement would help the negotiations by providing a link between the economic and the military talks. Otherwise the Spanish authorities would assume that they did not have to give military concessions to obtain the $125 million assistance. This would undoubtedly weaken the position of the Ambassador and the negotiation teams.

Secretary Acheson told the American Embassy in Spain that it was now possible to give more military aid from the newly appropriated funds. He therefore suggested that Vigón should submit a detailed plan for Spain's military requirements. It was possible that Spain was going to receive $25 to $30 million for military aid. The Secretary of State claimed that anything greater was out of the question. Nevertheless, Acheson made it clear that those figures should not be mentioned to Vigón.

In late June, Vigón submitted his estimate for Spain's military requirements, trying to take advantage of Kissner's earlier blunder. Vigón claimed that the Spanish armed forces required substantial military hardware, with a total cost during the first year alone of almost $650 million. In the long term the Spaniard was talking about total assistance of $2 billion.

The amount was far above anything Washington had contemplated. It was time to consider how to decrease this astronomical figure. Kissner had indicated after talks with Vigón that Spain was not only after military end-products but also wanted to gain full international recognition. Kissner argued that if the US expressed the intent to develop a programme of military assistance for Spain, which would run over a period of years, then this would materially assist in the advancement of an early conclusion of a satisfactory base rights agreement with Spain. It had also become important to explain that Spain had important differences compared to NATO member states and thus had to be treated differently.

The survey team had previously looked into potential sites for US facilities. The Torrejón airbase, 15 miles east of Madrid, had a runway of 8500 by 197 feet, four hangars and a gas storage capacity of 52 000 gallons. Torrejón was chosen above Barajas to avoid confusion with heavy civil air operations and to eliminate duplication of aircraft and maintenance facilities in the Madrid area. It was considered a good site because it was near Madrid and thus was linked up with the rest of Spain for communication and transportation because Spain's road network reached out from Madrid towards the coastal centres. At the same time, the survey team wanted the military headquarters to be situated in Madrid to provide easier communication with the US Embassy.

Another site considered for a base was San Pablo, five miles east of Seville, which was considered an excellent site because it was connected with good rails and roads. At the same time it could be logistically supported through the ports of Cádiz and Seville. Moron de la Frontera, 34 miles south-east of Seville, had the advantage of being easily extendable because land was available. It only had three hangars and a gas storage capacity of 30 000 gallons but was accessible by rail and road. El Copero, five miles south of Seville, was also considered a good site because it lay on the shipping channel to Seville, making unloading at the base itself possible. Furthermore, El Copero was not subjected to flooding like nearby Tablada. These were the chosen sites for airbases near Seville.

Matagorda, across the harbour of Cádiz, was chosen because it had access to the protected deep-water harbour on the Atlantic coast. Furthermore, it was accessible to the mainland by good roads and railways and the purchase of land did not cause civilian hardship. The existing Spanish naval facilities were also useful. The dock would be expanded to 600 by 60 feet and 40 feet deep. The Navy required a 8000 by 200 feet airstrip and storage facilities for 54 000 barrels of gas. Rota was the closest deep-water harbour to the naval air station and thus chosen as a very suitable site.

Most of the bases were chosen for their rail, road and sea connections. In the long term, this was a wise economic choice because expensive construction costs for Spain's infrastructure and long-term projects were avoided.

However, it was long-term commitment by the US that Vigón was seeking. The Joint Chiefs of Staff would not decide on Spain's suggestion with the Department of Defense alone and urged the Secretary of Defense to pass on Vigón's demand to the Secretary of State. The Joint Chiefs of Staff recommended that a note should be sent to Vigón along the following lines: "The Government of the United States considers that military relations between the United States and Spain should be on a continuing friendly basis in support of the policy of strengthening the defense of the West." The Joint Chiefs of Staff realized that this policy would be limited by annual Congressional appropriations, existing priorities, Korea, the status of supply and the overall international situation.

Out of the three armed services, the US Navy was most likely to welcome a long-term commitment to Spain. On 1 July 1952, the Chief of Naval Operations outlined the aims of the US Navy to his Commander in Chief in the East Atlantic and Mediterranean. The Navy wanted facilities in Spain and suggested that, even before an outbreak of war, storage facilities at El Ferrol, Tarifa, Cádiz, Cartagena, Soller and Port Mahon should be obtained. He also wanted anchorage rights almost everywhere in Spain. Furthermore, the Navy required an amphibious training area, possibly on the Balearic Islands. At the same time, the Naval Chief wanted to improve Spain's logistics.

In case of war with the Soviet Union, the Navy would require more facilities and bases at Barcelona, Almeria and on Lanzarote. In addition, the Plans Division wanted a ship-repair area and airbases near Cádiz, Majorca and Cartagena or Albacete.

As a result of the Spanish Cabinet Meeting on 4 July 1952, the US and Spanish representatives had another meeting in Madrid. Argüelles told Train that Vigón and Arburúa had held lengthy discussions all week long. Vigón believed that the $12 million plus the entire new $25 million aid were still inadequate for national defence purposes. Both the Spanish negotiation teams, as well as the cabinet, agreed to the idea of having four different agreements: an economic aid agreement, a Mutual Defense Assistance Program agreement, an airbase construction agreement and an agreement covering the utilization of the bases (the last two would be combined into one). Argüelles continued in an open manner to point out that there existed no public opinion on the subject, and the position of the Spanish government depended mainly on the armed forces, who would be unsatisfied with bases unless they received enough modern war material. Argüelles mentioned that some people in the government did not want to see any agreements at all. In return, Train pointed towards NATO's priority and the scarcity of equipment. The talks had almost come to a standstill because Spain was fearing that the $125 million was all the US was willing to give and under the circumstances was not going to grant facilities. It would have been possible to start constructions of the bases if a Mutual Defense Assistance Program or an economic aid agreement, assuring financial aid for some years, had been signed. Nevertheless, even if this had been the case, the use of the bases was still unresolved. The US believed that it was possible to get the bases on their terms for annual military aid of $50 million over three years. Spain was not willing to settle for that amount.

At a meeting between Train and Argüelles, on 5 July 1952, the American position had changed slightly. The total aid had been increased from $100 to $125 million. For military end-products this meant a possible increase from $12 to a total of $37 million. The rest, $88 million, would still be economic aid. Train proposed to sign three agreements; for economic cooperation, mutual defence and bases.

For Spain the $125 million was still not enough, as it did not even cover her economic demands. Likewise, the $37 million for military aid was inadequate. As an alternative Spain sought an assurance of continued military aid for several years. A comprehensive outline of Spain's position was sent to the US team on 9 July 1952. This was the first time that the Spanish government had coordinated its position regarding military and economic discussions. Parts of this memorandum had been drafted by Franco himself.

Franco believed that difficulties encountered in the negotiations arose from the disproportion which existed between the amount offered and the obligations for Spain resulting from an eventual agreement. Franco also claimed that if aid already granted had to be subordinated to the existence of an agreement under the Mutual Security Act then such aid should have been negotiated beforehand. The Caudillo believed that the funds were already his because they had been appropriated specifically for Spain. It also offended him that aid granted to other nations was higher than the amount offered to Spain. He demanded that an assurance of continued aid for a period of several years was given. The Spanish general also argued that if the military threat to Spain increased due to the new base agreements, then his General Staff and the public would not be interested in the negotiations. He wanted sufficient military aid to equip all 22 Spanish Army divisions, the Air Force and the Navy and the coastal defences.

If this aid was forthcoming, he guaranteed that Spain would be willing to conclude an agreement for the construction and organization of Spanish bases whose eventual utilization by American forces in the event of emergency would be the subject of a later agreement. The use of Spanish bases in time of peace by a foreign power, inasmuch as it was not indispensable, conflicted with his and Spain's national feelings and dignity and was considered harmful to the understanding between the two countries.

Franco believed that the inability to advance in detailed negotiations was because the base agreement had not been signed and the fact that the proposed assistance was in any case insufficient.

The Spanish dictator argued that the talks should continue even if a fundamental agreement was not reached, i.e. the US should grant the full $125 million to advance the negotiations. Furthermore, he suggested that Spain should study the texts for the economic cooperation agreement and the Mutual Security Agreement presented by the US delegation to effect their modification where necessary. He hoped that the execution of the draft base agreement could be postponed until adequate aid had been provided. He confirmed that Spain was willing to use the counterpart funds for the construction costs of the military facilities. In the meantime, he suggested that a "fundamental agreement" or "little agreement" should be signed to show goodwill between the two countries.

In the light of these arguments made by the Spanish dictator in his communiqué, MacVeagh's earlier suggestion to increase the newly appropriated aid for Spain from $25 to $30 million lost its importance. The positions of the two negotiation teams were so different that in the absence of further instructions from Washington, the US negotiation team was unable to continue. Spain clearly demanded financial and military concessions which were outside the instructions of the negotiation team. The talks were dangerously close to breaking off.

However, after a meeting with Argüelles, MacVeagh could assure Washington that Spain had shown no intention to terminate the conversations with the Americans. The problem was that the American experts in Madrid could not act beyond their instructions. Thus, MacVeagh believed that it might be time to hold official governmental talks with the Spanish Foreign Minister Artajo.

In a private meeting, on 17 July, Artajo argued that the negotiators seemed to confuse two issues: on one side Spain as a factor in the defence of the West; on the other Spain granting bases to the US. For the Spanish Minister, granting bases would convert Spain's position from "neutrality" to "pre-belligerence", and this could not be undertaken without assured defensive commitments by the US similar to those made to NATO countries. A Mutual Security Agreement could be worked out, according to Artajo, which would add Spain's resources to the Western defence. In the short term, his country not only required an increase of military aid but also desired the conclusion of a "little agreement" which would give Spain some advanced assurance of US support in case of war. MacVeagh inquired if Spain expected to remain neutral in case of war. Artajo answered that it was very likely that Spain would be attacked by parachute regiments in the event of war but bases in Spain would be more threatening and might lead to aerial bombardment of Spain's cities.

After the conversation, MacVeagh concluded that Spain was not asking for too much. He claimed that Madrid was not anxious to receive foreign military detachments on Spanish soil and that bases posed an external threat in wartime and an internal threat in peacetime to the survival of Franco's regime. The Ambassador believed that US failure to treat Spain on the same basis as other NATO countries would be seen as a continuation of the diplomatic boycott of the late 1940s. Thus an overt reversal of policy was required. Spain had to be considered as a partner in the common defence effort rather than as an unacceptable dealer possessing vital facilities for sale. In order to conclude the negotiations, it was vital to find a formula which met American requirements and provided Spain with her essential needs. MacVeagh concluded that the US should grant Spain the defence guarantees she was asking for and in the meantime a "little agreement" should be signed to reassure the Spanish negotiation team in relation to America's long-term commitment.

As MacVeagh was forming his opinion, a draft reply to the Spanish memorandum was being prepared in Washington which came under

consideration by the relevant agencies and subsequently by the negotiators in Madrid. It was decided not to broaden the policy on which
the negotiations had been based. The idea of a "little agreement" was
rejected to avoid committing a future President. It was considered advantageous to reply to the Spanish memorandum by giving notice of
the plans for continuous aid programmes over a long period and placing Spain on the same or similar level as other nations. Hopefully this
would reassure Spain of US long-term commitment. This was a very
delicate matter as it clashed with the usual procedures adopted in relation to other countries. It was thus unclear how much assurance could
be given without conflicting with US laws and policies.

Much earlier in the year Franco had written to Truman concerning
Spain's religious freedom. Now, two months later, Truman sent his
reply. Though this letter was similar to one drafted by Truman and
Acheson on 14 May 1952, a week after Franco's letter had been received, it had been kept in Washington for two months. The letter was
only sent when the American Embassy in Spain requested it. It read:

> In this country the tradition of civil liberties, particularly freedom
> of speech, of assembly, of the press and of worship, is deeply in-
> grained, not by compulsion of circumstances but by the choice and
> conviction of the American people . . . I share your hope that they
> [the negotiations] will come to a successful conclusion.[1]

On 30 July, in their eleventh meeting, Vigón handed Kissner lists of
Spain's requirements for her Navy and Air Force. These lists supple-
mented the Army list previously submitted. The total cost of the required
aid was $1 360 952 000. In return, Spain was willing to give the
US Navy and USAF the base facilities demanded. MacVeagh suggested
to Washington that the US should reverse its policy and instead of
buying the base facilities, the US should treat Spain as an equal partner in defence, arguing that nothing less than injured national dignity
was involved. MacVeagh was certain that if the US did this then the
negotiations could be successfully concluded.

In response to Spain's outrageous military demands, Acting Secretary of State Bruce summarized Madrid's position in that Spain, in
return for aid, was willing to conclude an agreement for the construction of bases whose eventual use by American forces in the event of
an emergency would have to be the subject of a later agreement. However
the Spanish government wanted to deny to the US the use of these
bases in peacetime and made wartime use subject to a later agreement.

Madrid further proposed an immediate extension of the $125 million of aid, already appropriated by Congress, without giving any commitment in return. The Secretary stressed that under these circumstances an increase of $125 million would not be enough to bridge the gap between the two countries. A new approach was therefore required.

Bruce argued that Spain's defence should start further east than her borders and that military bases in Spain would eventually add to this defence. He claimed that the bases would not increase Spain's involvement in a war because of Spain's strategic importance in the Mediterranean. The Acting Secretary also asserted that weapons and economic aid would go to the front-line countries first, Korea and Indochina in particular, and this was not a discrimination against Spain but simply a policy based on necessity. However this would result in Spain's pride being dented, which had to be rectified. The Ambassador was encouraged to avoid mentioning Italy, France or Britain as having priority over Spain so that Madrid would not feel further sidelined.

Bruce continued to argue that due to the current world situation there could not be extensive grants of military aid to Spain. Washington had also made up its mind that funds could not be granted without guarantees in return, because such action would constitute a violation of the Mutual Security Act.

These reconsiderations resulted in a reversal of the US approach to Spain. The paper DMS D-7, which had formed the body of the instructions to the negotiations team, was, *de facto*, dead. Secretary of State Acheson had ruled on 31 July that DMS D-7 was obsolete after the $25 million increase of aid to Spain. He had then instructed the State Department not to decrease dramatically the $50 million allocated to offset inflation in Spain. DMS D-7, a hastily drawn-up document which had set the requirements and the scope of the negotiations until August, was now of no relevance.

After receiving a summary of Bruce's position, MacVeagh told Washington that something had gone wrong in the negotiations with Spain. He argued that Spain did not need vast military aid but simply adequate aid to organize a national defence and that if this aid was phased over five years then it could be acceptable to both Spain and the US. The Ambassador also believed that Spain did not really require, nor expect a military alliance with the US. Madrid simply sought a statement for the purpose of public opinion. As in other fascist regimes, appearances were vital. Linked to this was the fact that Spain did not reject US usage of the bases but simply pointed towards a possible internal conflict which might be caused by US soldiers being stationed in Spain. Furthermore, MacVeagh argued that Spain's proposal was not to receive the $125 million without commitment but was to sign a modified economic aid agreement and a Mutual Defense Act Agreement, which would lead to certain obligations for the two countries. The Ambassador asked the Secretary of State whether the US wanted to change its policy in the light of this new interpretation or if Washington wanted to stick to the policy expressed in the letter from Bruce.

On 22 August, Bruce decided that a new reply should be drafted to replace his original letter. Almost a month had passed since the Spanish proposal had been received and Washington had still not decided on new instructions for their teams in Spain. A rift seemed to have opened between the State Department in Washington and its Ambassador in Madrid.

Train supported McVeagh's new interpretation in a memorandum to the Deputy Director of the Mutual Security Administration, Kenney, who had been in Madrid on 14 August 1952. Train wrote that Spain was entitled to demand to be treated like other nations. The head of the economic negotiations team asserted that the $125 million was of little importance and that bases in Spain were not an asset for the Mediterranean country because Spain would not have, in the foreseeable future, any heavy bombers to fully make use of these facilities. Train knew that Franco had realized that Spain could not be part of NATO but, nevertheless, the Spanish dictator wanted at least to be associated with the NATO security concept. And so far, the American approach had been unacceptable to Spain.

A new US policy had to be found and it was important to fully understand Spain's demands and objectives. In the meantime the Air Section of the JUSMG in Spain came to the first arrangement with the Spanish Air Force. The military end-product aid earmarked for the Spanish Air Force was to be used for the purchase of four jet engines, to equip three flying and two technical training schools and to commence limited base construction. This was a small sum in proportion to the total expected by Spain.

The JUSMG sent a report on Spain's position and a proposal of policy to Washington. It told the State Department that Spain required $349 for the Army, $302 for the Navy and $710 million for the Air Force, a total of $1361 million. The JUSMG had studied these requests and in the report recommended to the Joint Chiefs of Staff that a counter-proposal should be submitted. General Kissner recommended granting $214 million to the Army, $100 million to the Navy and $127 million to the Air Force, a total of $441 million. He suggested that this aid, which was to increase the capability of the Spanish armed forces to defend Spain was to be phased over four years. It was, however, less than one-third of the aid the Spanish had demanded as "indispensable". But Kissner claimed that Spain's "indispensable" sum was not their lowest bid. He was convinced that Spain would be willing to sign even if she were offered less than the "indispensable" amount. Kissner suggested that the US should assign certain tasks in the Western defence to Spain, such as for two Spanish military corps to operate outside the Peninsula. General Vigón had indicated that the divisions in the Pyrenees could be used north of Spain and now Washington was to take up this offer. Ultimately, the Joint Chiefs of Staff had to decide how badly they needed military bases and how high a price they were willing to pay for them.

This report by the JUSMG on the list of Spanish military aid requirements reflected a new concept of strengthening Spain's armed forces. Rather than placing emphasis on the concept of military aid for the development and protection of the desired base facilities and training, the JUSMG wanted to strengthen all Spanish armed forces for military use outside Spain. A careful study and review of this report needed to be made. It was clear that a reversal of policy would have to be discussed with Britain and France before it could be implemented and it was likely that these two European nations would not be in agreement. In relation to Britain, the Foreign Office feared for British trade with Spain, and the British Chiefs of Staff had concerns about Gibraltar. The Chiefs were opposed to the creation of a single Iberian Atlantic Command as this would further America's influence. They also opposed the proposals made earlier by the American Admirals Sherman, Fechteler and McCormick, to create a joint command, as this would have had similar results. The British Chiefs were still hoping to create an independent British command with headquarters in Gibraltar for operations in the Mediterranean.

Washington realized that the international climate in Europe still did not favour Spain's integration but, nevertheless, the negotiation teams were instructed to proceed with the talks without awaiting the review of and final decision on the JUSMG report.

The Regional Affairs Section of the State Department argued in favour of the JUSMG report: to seek Spain's military commitment outside its own territories. NATO policy had always been to operate defences as far north and east as possible. If Spanish troops remained behind the Pyrenees, Spain's role in this defence would be negligible, and the money spent would be going to troops which would therefore not be acting as a deterrent. Naturally, this would create a problem with NATO partners and with Germany's defence plans. If the policy of the State Department towards Spain had been implemented before 1952, it would have made sense because a fallback towards Spain would have been necessary in the event of a Soviet attack. However, after 1953 this made little sense, because NATO had already established a reasonable number of units which guaranteed a defence of Europe. Military retreat to Spain or the UK was no longer necessary. Thus if money was to be given to Spain, the country would need to have a specific role in Western defence. Otherwise, US defence plans would not benefit.

The Ambassador in Madrid urged Washington to recommence talks at the highest level. MacVeagh informed the Office of Western European Affairs that Argüelles was tending towards higher-level discussions in his conversation on 5 July 1952. It seemed to the Ambassador that the fundamental conflicts involved in the negotiations were irresolvable by the informal talks between the teams in Spain. He suggested, therefore, that the parties should take a step towards governmental negotiations, in order to establish the exact relationship between Spain and the US and to positively influence the negotiations. It would also provide an answer to the question of whether military end-products were to be included in an aid package for Spain. MacVeagh pointed out that Spain would be more flexible in governmental talks than they had been in the current talks.

Given the advice of its Ambassador, the State Department had to determine its future commitments to Spain. In early August 1952, Nash (Pentagon) advised Lovett (State Department) that assurance should be given to Spain that she would receive long-term credits, but in return the US would require control over the use of bases in peacetime and Spain should not expect more than $125 million during FY 1953. This advice was supported by the view of the Spanish General Alonso Vega, who was touring the Caribbean and the US in August. On 28 August, in a lunch meeting with General Omar Bradley, member of the Joint Chiefs of Staff, Alonso Vega told the American that Spain did not really require the amount of assistance she had been demanding but simply wanted a reassurance of Washington's long-term commitment and moral obligation towards Spain. The Spanish general seemed to indicate that Franco needed this assurance in order to persuade Spanish public opinion that the agreements were a diplomatic coup. If this was so, the proposal put forward by Nash, to grant long-term credits in return for the bases, was very sensible.

In order to clarify US policy, representatives from Washington and the negotiators in Spain, Perkins, Draper, Anderson, MacVeagh, Kissner, Garvin and Train, had a meeting in Paris on 29 September. They drafted a response to Argüelles's July letter. It had taken from 9 July, when MacVeagh's report was received, until 7 October to do so.

Several governmental agencies and departments had spent a full three months in consultation. As MacVeagh had suggested, it was decided that the negotiations should move one step up. It was also decided that from then on, US policy would include support of Spanish defence efforts for agreed purposes by the provision of assistance to Spain over a period of several years, subject to limitations imposed by Congressional appropriations, existing priorities and commitments, the exigencies of the Korean situation, the status of supply and the international situation.

It was clear that military aid would go first to countries participating in the common defence of Western Europe. During the meeting in Paris, the two sides, the State Department and the negotiation team, came to an agreement and were able to decide on their response to Artajo's letter. Back in Madrid, the Ambassador sent this response directly to Artajo, who received it on 8 October. The US reply did not mention specific military supply to Spain, the only limits being available funds and supplies. All the other limitations had been omitted in this note for Madrid. It was clear that Spain had already been a part of the US security policy plan, which was to aid all those countries which could defend themselves if attacked. Clearly, the Ambassador hoped that Artajo would agree that Spain should not be given the same aid as front-line countries for strategic and not political reasons. This constituted the informal part of the letter to Artajo. Included was an official memorandum to the Spanish Minister for Foreign Affairs, Martín Artajo.

This formal reply was divided into nine points. It stated that America's policy towards Spain should support the Spanish defence efforts for agreed purposes by the provision of assistance to Spain over a period of several years. Spain was to be treated as other countries under the same restrictions because of her strategic location. This implied that if resources were required elsewhere more urgently, then Spain would have to wait her turn. Western defence was deemed to be Spain's defence, and under this concept Spain could make a valuable contribution to her own defence as well as that of Western Europe by granting the US the use of military facilities. The letter argued that in case of invasion of Western Europe, Spain would also be attacked due to her geographical position and strong anti-Communist stance. This argument was simply to increase Spain's belief that the US was taking her seriously.

The note continued, pointing out that the possibility of a sudden attack made peacetime preparations necessary. Then, in point eight, came the ultimate bait. If the agreements were signed, the Executive Branch was prepared to include suitable provisions for assistance to Spain in its presentation to the Congress. To smoothen the hard road ahead, the note finally asked for an official statement of friendship between the two countries. Now it was Washington's turn to wait for a reply from the Spanish negotiations team.

On 24 October 1952, Kissner and Vigón had another meeting. They discussed the letter from the American Ambassador to the Spanish Foreign Minister. Vigón seemed to be pleased with the reply. After being briefed by Kissner, MacVeagh wrote a report on the conversation which he sent off to Washington. The Ambassador claimed that if Spain received US assistance over a period of years on an equal basis with other nations then Spain would not be unreasonable about base rights and military aid. MacVeagh speculated that the best way to achieve the agreements was by seeing them as on an equal basis and not just as buying rights. He considered that not increasing the funds earmarked for Spain during FY 1954 would be ruinous to the progress of the talks.

It seemed that time and political acceptance would reflect the seriousness of America's commitment towards Spain. This perception would have been disastrous if Spain had really been after money rather than recognition of status because it would have offered Spain the possibility of receiving more aid than required. As this was not supposedly the case, MacVeagh pointed out that aid should be sufficient to show that the US was serious. MacVeagh argued that aid in the military sector should be based on Kissner's recommendation of not less than $80 million in new funds over several years. He also suggested that economic aid should be based on Train's estimation of not less than $57 million in new funds. Both should be in addition to the already earmarked $125 million.

The US negotiators also commented on the military aid programme during FY 1954 for Spain. Originally, it had been designed to build up the Spanish military potential for territorial defence. However, under the revised programme the primary purpose was to provide assistance to develop and protect the bases and to develop military conditions in Spain for future associations under the programme of US–Spanish negotiations with NATO.

In less than one month, on 31 October, Madrid officially replied to the American note. Spain was pleased with the cordial tone of the letter and underlined again that there was no distinction between Spain and other countries and that she agreed to establish a friendship which included assistance over several years. The Spanish armed forces were willing to contribute to Western defence through the defence of the Peninsula which could only be guaranteed through US aid. Therefore, Spain should receive complementary military means sufficient to assure the defence of the Peninsula territory. Artajo argued that the Communist threat, the oscillation by various countries, Soviet affiliation and other factors made the strengthening of Spain the most essential factor for restraining and lessening the dangers thereof. The Spanish government also claimed that because of Spain's strategic position and her anti-Communist posture, she might constitute an objective of Soviet aggressive action. However, in the event of war, the pressure on Spanish territory of joint bases and military personnel of the US would necessarily aggravate and accelerate the aggression.

Madrid considered air defence vital for all Western European countries, but above all for ports, industry and populations in strong anti-Communist areas. Therefore the argument continued that Spain should receive aid for its air force and air defence. This was all a rebuff to the American argument that Spain's anti-Communism was enough for a *causa belli* with the USSR. The Foreign Minister stressed the urgency of the situation, which called for immediate military aid. It was suggested that only later should the two countries work out texts for the military base agreements. On the other hand, Artajo believed that the economic aid and Mutual Defense Agreements should be signed in the near future. Spain also hoped for an increase of annual aid from $25 million to at least the $100 million of the previous year, as well as a quick investment of the previous $125 million credit. It was unclear from Artajo's comments whether US use of Spanish military facilities in peacetime as well as in wartime would be allowed. Nevertheless, oral assurance concerning the use of bases in Spain was given on 3 November, except for details regarding construction and personnel utilization.

On 4 November 1952, MacVeagh passed on Spain's reply of 31 October to Washington. In the light of this reply, MacVeagh expected that, as a result of Spain's need to complete the two agreements concerning economic and military aspects, it would not take long before the US would procure the third, the base agreement. Only two weeks earlier, Vigón had told Kissner that he was confident that the disagreement over the usage of bases in peacetime could be resolved soon. On

3 November, Vigón had gone even further and claimed that the US had usage in principle of bases in peacetime as well as during a war. Spain was giving in to the American demands in relation to the military bases. Vigón, Argüelles and Arburúa all expressed their willingness to sign all three agreements but preferred to delay the base agreement for political reasons. Clearly Spain benefited from hailing the success of these two agreements as another diplomatic coup by Franco. Weeks later, when the base agreement would have be signed, public interest would be discouraged. As for the Americans in Spain, Kissner and Train agreed that all three agreements should be signed at the same time because they feared that their negotiation team would have no bargaining power once it had committed itself in the agreements on economic and military aid. MacVeagh agreed with this in principle but also urged flexibility and encouraged considerations of the impact on NATO countries. He believed that signing the agreement separately would not enhance the image of the US with NATO countries. By signing them together, Washington could at least claim that it was done for security reasons. Nevertheless, the mood was optimistic. Train suggested January 1953 as a possible date for conclusion of the agreements once the go-ahead for the base agreement had been received by both sides.

On 7 November, the British and French representatives in Washington were informed of the status of the negotiations. After a statement by Franco in November, the British Foreign Office had been speculating that the American–Spanish agreements would be signed by the end of the month. The State Department openly dismissed these speculations.

While Spain was formulating its position on the base agreement, the US Department of Defense was reconsidering the JUSMG report of 20 August on military aid to Spain. On 8 December, the Department of Defense informed the Department of State that the Joint Chiefs of Staff had reviewed and approved the report recommending $440 million in military assistance for the defence of the Iberian Peninsula as a long-term military programme. As money for Spain was limited for the time being to $125 million, the Joint Chiefs of Staff and the JUSMG (Spain) recommended that the new $25 million aid package should be used exclusively for military end-products. This was partly because Captain H. G. Sanchez, heading the Navy section of the JUSMG, had already guaranteed $57 million worth of military end-products to Spain.

In return the State Department pointed out that certain basic concepts of the JUSMG report had already been altered in October and November and there was no longer the need to adhere to the report in its entirety. Instead it agreed to the October recommendations, according to which a military programme of $85 million in FY 1954 should pay for equipment to the Spanish forces to assist the protection of the US bases and the training of the Spanish armed forces. This was now being considered by the Department of Defense. These were concessions by Washington which improved Franco's bargaining position during what appeared to be the final phase.

In the economic sector, the US still wanted to import Spanish raw materials and to remove the foreign investment limitation of 25 per cent, as well as the restriction on profit transfer. Furthermore, the US wanted a guarantee for a stable foreign exchange, new oil drilling rights along the Ebro valley and larger quotas for imports to Spain to secure markets against foreign competitors such as Britain, Italy, France and West Germany.

Minor issues remained unresolved. In November, Lieutenant-Colonel González-Camino, a former service attaché, told the JUSMG that friction between US military personnel stationed in the bases and Spanish troops could develop due to differences in pay between the two.

Vigón and Kissner had a series of unsuccessful meetings on 5, 6 and 10 November. The problems persisted and the two sides seemed to have come to a deadlock. Then, on 20 November, Kissner, talking directly to Artajo, was able to break this deadlock and pave the way forward. Problems concerning jurisdiction and duration of the lease over the base facilities were discussed and solved.

In Washington, Propper de Callejón once again, though with less enthusiasm than Vigón, expressed the desire of the Spanish authorities to sign the military and economic aid agreement before the base agreement. Propper picked up on a small blunder by Lincoln MacVeagh. The Ambassador had been instructed always to stress that the agreements would be signed together, yet in a letter, written on 7/8 October, he wrote that the agreements were to be concluded in one official ceremony or closely consecutive signature. Propper took this statement as a suggestion that the agreements could be signed separately. Naturally this suited Madrid, as it could stress the diplomatic success of the aid agreements while ignoring publicity for the price Spain had to pay in the base agreement. Washington, however, still wanted to sign all agreements at the same time.

Artajo initially complained about the proposed agreements, including the suggested period of the lease for the facilities. However, the American team remained unmoved and soon the Spanish side abandoned the complaint. On 2 December 1952, Artajo gave Lincoln

MacVeagh a clear indication that the talks should be wound up and the agreements signed.

Vigón indicated that his team would accept a lease of ten years with one extension of five years. There were no objections to US wartime use or to limitations on personnel.

The State Department was confident that the agreements would soon be signed. Bonbright wanted to inform the Secretary of State in waiting, John F. Dulles, about the expected success of the negotiations. Washington saw Spain's letter, dated 31 October, as an agreement in principle. Vigón seemed assured and was happy to conclude the talks. Only Franco's confirmation was awaited and the State Department speculated that it might express minor complaints about the current deal: first, the number of US military stationed in Spain during peacetime and secondly, the scope of use of the bases by US troops. Ambassador MacVeagh also feared that relations might become tense as a result of the decrease of allocated funds for Spain during FY 1954. Other concerns centred on issues such as the jurisdiction over US personnel stationed in Spain and tax relief for the Military Aid Agreement. However these were minor considerations and would not take long to solve.

Then, almost out of the blue and taking full advantage of the positive international developments for Spain and US concessions, came a shattering note from the Spanish negotiations team. This had been initiated and encouraged by Franco. On 23 December, Spain submitted a counter-draft of the base agreement proposing to Kissner a link between base construction and military end-products for Spain's forces "on a parallel basis", so that as soon as the moment of utilization of the desired facilities was reached, the minimum necessities required for the defence of Spanish territory would have been covered. These included air defence, the security of her maritime communications, and the completion of the armament of her land, sea, and air armies. The Spanish armed forces were to be equipped with modern material which would allow them to independently defend the whole of Spain's territory, waters and airspace. In late October and November the Spanish negotiation teams had given the impression that they would be satisfied with some military aid unlinked to any base programmes or specific defence requirements. During these months, the JUSMG had been sure that $440 million in aid was enough to satisfy Spain. Now the Spaniards were returning to their earlier demands for more substantial and specific aid. In addition the demand for a parallel development of bases and aid posed a serious legal problem.

The American administration was legally unable to guarantee in an executive agreement with Spain any long-term financial commitments for which Congress had not allocated funds. To do so would violate Congressional taxation and spending rights. Furthermore, Spain wanted the use of bases during war to be joint and based on prior consultation. The counter-draft omitted concrete provisions for peacetime use of the military facilities. Here again Spain was returning to previous demands. The oral assurance from early November concerning the use of military facilities had been revoked. The note made it clear that during times of conflict consultation for the use of these facilities was required and peacetime use was left altogether vague. The Spanish Foreign Minister told MacVeagh that the two requirements of "parallel development" and "prior consultation" were "essential" to Spain. These were unacceptable demands to the US and shattered any hopes of signing the agreements in 1952 or even in early 1953.[2]

NOTES

1. FRUS, 1952–54, VI, p. 1865.
2. Condit, *Test of War,* p. 356.

12 Waiting and Hoping

During early 1953, many foreign diplomats, including staff at the British Embassy in Washington, believed that the three agreements between the US and Spain were about to be signed and only minor details had to be worked out. It was assumed that Lequerica's opportunism and oversimplifications had been abandoned by the Spanish negotiation team in favour of honesty and frankness. This ignored the Spanish negotiation efforts during December.

Spain's counter-draft of the base agreement, dated 23 December 1952, had necessitated a reconsideration by the American negotiators. Kissner presented a revised draft which was designed to accept as much as possible of the Spanish version while not departing in any essential respect from the US position. This revision was analysed by Franco and the Defence Minister. In a letter, dated 14 January, General Vigón advised General Kissner that the American revision was considered inadequate. He argued that the American draft still was a concrete military pact for one side, and a benevolent political declaration of vague military content for the other. Vigón suggested that the Spanish redraft should be submitted to the US government.

Subsequently, the Spanish draft was sent to Washington where it was given careful consideration. The appropriate agencies of the State and Defense Departments felt that the changes were substantially different from the previous Spanish position in the negotiations. This indicated that there might be a considerable degree of bargaining in their counter-proposal, done to sound out the new administration in the hope of getting a better deal. Therefore it was decided that the matter should not be placed before the National Security Council for review but rather, further discussions should be held to determine how firmly the Spaniards intended to hold to their new position.

This decision, to wait and see, was supported by the fact that some Senators feared that entering agreements with Spain without the approval of public opinion would cause political difficulties. These Congressmen continued to argue that to test public opinion, the US should not enter agreements with Spain but a treaty instead, the difference being that treaties have to be approved by Congress, while agreements do not.

In his last appearance before the Senate Foreign Relations Committee as Secretary of State, Dean Acheson made a series of interesting statements. He outlined that it had taken the West until now to enlist enough troops to make it impossible for the existing Communist forces in Europe to overrun Europe. Europe would still be under threat in the event of an all-out mobilization by the USSR. Nevertheless, a surprise attack could be stopped. This was important because, as Acheson pointed out, it would require some considerable degree of mobilization to augment the forces in East Germany to make a successful attack, and that was something observable and something to which the US could react.

NATO was now ready to meet the Soviet threat with existing conventional forces in Europe. Acheson also pointed out that the negotiations with Spain were well advanced and would soon be concluded, but he also confirmed that John Foster Dulles would carry out the last steps under the new administration.

The new military situation which Acheson outlined was not without consequences to European member states of NATO. France was reassured that an improvement of relations between the US and Spain would no longer threaten her own national security. Promptly, she started to suppress clandestine broadcasting stations run by Spanish exiles and prohibited political meetings by Spanish refugees. The government even considered compensating the Spanish victims of the 1945 train incident in France.

Simultaneously, Britain relaxed her trade relations with Spain. During 1952, the UK had lost her market share in Spain to France and the US. Naturally, London was interested in preventing further losses and trade of military items was directly relaxed, leading to a contract between the Spanish Navy and Vickers-Armstrong of over £1.5 million for submarine equipment and fire-control gear. The UK also increased Spain's currency receipts from the sterling area, which in turn increased imports from Britain. The decreasing sterling receipts by Spain had already led to the cancellation of a deal for 50 Spitfire planes. According to the Bank of England, in 1952 Spain had received goods worth £59 million but had only paid £54 million. The rest was financed by drafts and drawings on Spain's account balances. This meant that Spain had already drawn the entire £2 million of her exchange facilities, normally used to facilitate trade and payments. If Britain wanted to export manufactured goods to Spain, London had to increase Spain's sterling receipts. Thus Britain was becoming increasingly interested in relaxing OEEC trade restrictions with Spain.

The Board of Trade claimed that Spain had an interest in playing down her exports to Britain. The undeclared sterling earnings of these exports were not used to pay off imports, but were invested in Britain, held in Spanish accounts, spent on consumer goods in the UK and on UK goods and services imported into Spain. After further discussions with the Ministry of Food and the British Ambassador in Spain, the Foreign Office decided not to take strong actions against Spain. While sterling transfer facilities remained unchanged, draft facilities were increased to £4 million, and indirect pressure was put on Madrid through economic talks between Argüelles and Mr Cotton from the British Embassy.

Franco could be satisfied with these developments. Additionally, the election of a Republican candidate to the White House seemed to favour Spain's position concerning the military negotiations in Madrid. Lequerica was still convinced in March 1953 that the new administration in Washington was more lenient towards Spain. Madrid was so confident about Western support that it tried to rally Latin American, Arab nations and the US for Spain's candidature to the UN.

With the election of President Eisenhower, the Truman containment policy came to an end and Washington planned to roll back the Communist threat. John F. Dulles, who had been favourably inclined towards fascist regimes before the Second World War, was appointed Secretary of State. After the Civil War, Spain had made an effort to recover silver, which had been shipped abroad by the Spanish Republic. John F. Dulles had represented the National Bank of Spain, which tried to recover the silver for Franco. As a result Dulles was accused by Democrats of having acted on Franco's behalf.

Concerning the UN December resolution, Dulles had always opposed it in principle but once it was passed, he realized that it was a symbol of opposition to all right-wing totalitarian regimes and revocation would be difficult. He was aware of Spain's strategic value for the West and would support the military in its endeavour to obtain bases in Spain.

While generally getting on well with the Department of Defense, Dulles had problems with people inside the State Department. Sometimes he upset the civil servants in the Department due to his jealousy and ambition. In return, he thought the Department was a disaster due to its excessive paperwork, and he bypassed the State Department in favour of the Joint Chiefs of Staff or the Pentagon more than once.

The change of Secretary of State was important but not as important as the change of President. Truman was from the very beginning anti-Spanish and had expressed his dislike for the Franco regime on many occasions.

Eisenhower was different. His army career in Europe, and above all the days of the Allied landings in North Africa during the Second World War (Operation Torch), had shown him the necessity to deal with Spain. He had feared during Operation Torch that the military campaign might bring Vichy France and Spain into the war on the Axis side. The experience proved to him how vital Spain's geographic position was. No wonder that he harboured the belief that security in Europe was only possible if a United States of Europe, including NATO countries, West Germany, Sweden, Spain, Yugoslavia and Greece could be formed.

Nevertheless, Eisenhower recognized that it was also in the interest of Spain to help defend Western Europe and her commitment to assist NATO's defence effort was assumed by the President. For Eisenhower, there seemed little reason why Spain should not accept the deal offered and he was unwilling to compromise on Spain's new demands. It became obvious that the new administration in Washington would not shift from its previous position, even though the State Department changed the Ambassador in Spain, appointing James Clement Dunn as MacVeagh's successor. The Spanish administration was concerned about the newly appointed ambassador's religious background and the impact on the negotiations. Despite this concern, the Spanish propaganda machinery claimed that the US was sick of the poor showing of France and had thus decided to move their best diplomat, James Dunn, from Paris to Madrid. In reality, the appointment had more to do with Dunn's past experience than with any disappointment in France.

James C. Dunn was born in Newark in 1890 and studied architecture and, later, law. During the First World War he had served in the Navy. After getting married, he became Special Assistant to Secretary of State Hull in 1935. After the war he was sent to Italy as an ambassador and subsequently to France. In 1919 he had an assignment in Madrid which later made him a good candidate to assume the role of Ambassador to Spain. All hoped that the transition would be smooth and John W. Jones, American Chargé-d'affaires, stayed on after MacVeagh had left to introduce James Dunn to the necessary protocol.

Spain's hopes of a lenient approach by the new US administration were shattered and the negotiations were criticized by the nationalists, who claimed that foreign troops in Spain were an offence against Spanish sovereignty and would put an end to Spain's neutrality. The Spanish Air Minister González Gallarza vehemently asserted that "We do not want American soldiers here. We are not a liberated nation. We won't tolerate it." Admiral Salvador Moreno, Minister of the Marine, was more positive about the prospects and enthusiastically proclaimed that the time had come to sign the agreements.

The Catholic Church opposed a treaty with a Protestant nation and Cardinal Segura saw the Catholic faith in the US at the same level as "heretical dollars". Franco would calm religious opposition by entering a treaty with the Vatican shortly before signing the agreements with the US.

Concerns over religious freedom in Spain remained. Since 1948 12 British-owned chapels had been seized, closed or assaulted; 2000 British bibles had been seized and Spanish authorities caused problems over clothing for charities imported by Protestants. A Baptist pastor was fined the equivalent of £16 for public proselytizing. As it turned out, he stood accused of having given details of the times of worship to a non-Protestant in a public market. However, in a State Department study, "Spain: Current Problems", dated 11 February 1953, it was stated that the Protestant problem was not so important as to merit being placed alongside the negotiations.

As the Cold War was getting hotter, Washington paid less attention to these issues and focused on military aspects. In 1952, American aid to Europe under the Marshall Plan ended and further aid was governed by the Mutual Security Program. This meant that the Mutual Security Administration rather than European governments were in control of aid for Europe. As a result military aspects became more important for foreign policy decisions.

It was suggested that the USSR had to be fully encircled with US bases to deliver a vital blow from the air at any time. For this purpose, Spain in particular had many advantages. There was little air traffic and few flight restrictions. The weather, with few and short periods of rain in the south, was suitable for flight training. There already existed airports which could be extended through cheap Spanish labour. Furthermore, to become more cost efficient, the responsibilities of maintaining a standing army in Europe had to be delegated to other countries. Spain, with an army of 400 000 soldiers, would allow the US to cut overall defence expenditure in Europe.

However, Spain's infrastructure was weak and its economy needed large investments to bring it up to Western standards. The American journalist Walter Lippman described Spain as so weak, so poor and so primitive that to make it into a base would take years, and a programme of capital investment on a grand scale.

Spain's transportation system had improved little during Franco's early period in power. In 1953, Spain had 60 000 cars, 50 000 trucks and 7000 buses, about 250 people per car. In the period 1949–53 only 69 miles of new railways were laid. Nevertheless, there had been some good economic developments. Spain's exports increased steadily between 2 per cent and 16 per cent annually from 1946 to 1953.

Commerce between the US and Spain, making up about 15 per cent of Spain's exports and imports, was composed mainly of raw cotton and manufactured goods. American exports to Spain of automobiles doubled during the first three years of the 1950s. Over this period Spain's trade balance was increasingly helped by tourist receipts. In 1950, 75 000 tourists went to Spain, in 1951, 105 000, in 1952, 1.5 million and in 1952, 2 million. The same trend can be observed with tourists from the US. In 1950, 30 000 Americans came to Spain, in 1951, 45 000, and in 1952 almost 100 000 Americans spent roughly $20 million during their stay. By 1953 a total of 140 000 American tourists arrived.

These aspects gave the Franco regime no reason to change the multiple exchange rates which hindered free trade. On the Tangier black market, $1 was worth about 43.2 pesetas. Yet according to the official basic exchange rate the dollar was only worth 10.95 pesetas. For exchange-rate purposes, imports and exports fell into five groups and their product exchange rates stood between 16.4 pesetas and 38.9 pesetas. The product classification depended on the desire of the government to encourage its trade flow. By allowing lower exchange rates for imports than for exports, the government was helping Spain's industry. Another industry that was aided by trade policies was tourism. The tourist rate was the highest official exchange rate at 38.9 pesetas per dollar. By undervaluing the peseta compared to the dollar for tourists, Franco made holidays comparably cheap. The Spanish population carried the burden of Franco's restrictive trade policies. The liberalization of these economic policies was one target of the US negotiators in Spain.

Another US target was to make use of Spain's strategic geographical position. On 8 January 1953, the Chief of Naval Operations informed the Secretary of State of the Joint Chiefs of Staff's decision that US objectives in Spain went beyond base rights and included increasing Spain's capability of defending the Iberian Peninsula. Spain had made it clear that she was only willing to grant bases if she was treated on an equal basis with other European nations. Hence, the Joint Chiefs of Staff argued that until Spain's role in the Western defence was crystallized, all military assistance granted should have the objective of developing her capability to defend the Iberian Peninsula.

While the State Department had decided to wait and see, the military became increasingly anxious. The USAF was fully in agreement with the Director of the Office of Military Assistance memorandum from 24 December 1952 on the MAAC D-3/5a, which urged an early conclusion of the negotiations. However, this had been written before Franco's counter-proposal had destroyed hopes for a swift conclusion of the talks. The USAF used this outdated document to propose through Major-General Haywood S. Hansell that three agreements be signed on 1 February 1953. This attempt was unsuccessful for various reasons. Franco's demands during December were one factor; another was logistical problems. Serious shortages of military material changed the aim of the aid programmes. Originally aid to Spain was designed for the defence of Spain's territory. The revised programme was simply to assist the development and defence of the bases.

The other problem concerned the use of the bases. On 16 March 1953, the American Chargé in Spain, John W. Jones, informed Artajo that the US government wanted to include in the Military Agreements a secret technical annex which would allow the US to use the bases in Spain without prior consultation with Spain in the event of Communist military attack on Europe. This was an excellent proposal. It had become clear to the State Department that Spain was concerned about the perception in Spain of the agreements. The demand for prior consultation of the use of bases originated from the same desire of the Spanish authorities to retain the perception of neutrality and sovereignty over foreign policy. By placing this right into a secret annex, Madrid would be able to hide it from the public.

On the next day, 17 March, the US reply to Spain's December counter-draft was presented. It included the US draft of the Military Facilities Agreement, a covering note and a personal letter to the Foreign Minister. The draft was a repetition of the American position, avoiding any commitment regarding future aid. It provided clear provisions for peacetime and wartime use by the US of Spanish military facilities. Furthermore, it completely separated the construction of these facilities from the development of the military aid programme. This was in direct conflict with Spain's draft. The covering note claimed that the President's 1954 budget message to Congress, presented on 9 January, contained an estimate for foreign aid which took into account potential requirements for aid to Spain. These would be extended to Spain if mutually satisfactory agreements were concluded in time. In the personal letter to Artajo, it was made clear that the provisions regarding aid to Spain were still based on the assumptions mentioned in the 7 October memorandum, i.e. that the agreements would be completed in time to permit suitable provision for such assistance in FY 1954. This included time required to permit extending previously appropriated funds. The letter threatened that if time ran out and it was impossible to obligate some of these funds, they would be carried over into the next FY, with the result that new funds which had to be justified in Congress would be reduced. Consequently the longer it took to complete the three agreements, the more difficult it became to justify previous provisions. The Federal Budget and the detailed justification for the estimates it contained were under active study and would be presented shortly to the President for approval. Thus, as indicated in the October memorandum, the time factor was essential. As a result the question of which of the two countries was responsible for the time delay arose. The letter not only blamed Spain for the delay but also rejected Spain's demands made in December. It was offensive and showed that Washington had abandoned the "wait and see" policy and was pressing for an answer. Spain's response was awaited anxiously in Washington.

Naturally the Spanish Embassy in Washington was well informed about this. Eduardo Propper was reluctant to react while Lequerica was willing to give in to the harsh treatment by the Americans. However, the final decision was to be taken in Madrid.

Martín Artajo reacted in a letter, dated 26 March 1953. The contents of the American personal letter was to Artajo of such gravity that it had considerable weight upon the execution of the proposed agreements. The Spanish Minister stated that Spain could not in any way be made responsible for the delays in the negotiations. He argued that the delays were caused by the decision by the former American administration to condition the granting of assistance upon the conclusion of a military agreement; that is, the refusal to sign the base agreement separately from the other two; and the slowness in reacting to the counterdraft by the Truman administration because of "the necessity of coordinating the points of view of the many interested governmental agencies", that is, to America's "wait and see" policy; and finally the change of the American administration; that is, to Truman's refusal to tie down his successor. Artajo tried to intimidate the US negotiators, writing that it would be a very serious matter if these complications reduced or delayed the granting of funds necessary for the defence of Spain, since this would weaken the effectiveness of the agreements themselves. He claimed that

> this is precisely the concern which inspired the text of one of the most essential paragraphs of the Spanish counterproposal of December

23, 1952 . . . which foresaw the necessary and desirable parallelism between the development and use of the bases and the strengthening and perfecting of the defensive means of the Armed Forces.[1]

He also suggested referring from now on to the military facilities agreement as the Defense Agreement, thus taking out bad publicity over the use of facilities by making it sound more like a mutual agreement between two equally important nations. Negotiations had clearly become unfriendly. One side or the other had to back down to avoid further heated exchanges. The Americans had misjudged Spain's reaction. Their hopes of pressuring Spain to make certain concessions were shattered. A more subtle approach was needed.

The situation was so serious that the British Embassy in Washington wrote of the possibility that the talks would end without an agreement because Spain seemed to have lost interest.

On 26 March, the State Department suggested to the American Embassy to reply that the letter by the Chargé, dated 17 March, which resulted in the Spanish outcry, had been drafted with the most friendly motive – to share with the Spanish government information regarding more difficult problems confronting the US negotiation team. In no way was it meant to assess responsibility for any delays of the talks. Washington was retreating. However, at the same time the US could not accept the statement that Washington was responsible for delaying the negotiations. Therefore the State Department argued that the talks had required considerable time and effort on both sides as a direct result of the many important issues and considerations which had to be taken into account. The State Department argued that the responsibility for the delay was no one's in particular. It was assessed that further talks on whom to blame for the delays would only waste time and thus should be avoided by both nations until the conclusion of the negotiations. Furthermore, the US Embassy in Madrid was advised to send a note saying that the relationship between military aid and base agreements had been made clear in the 19 April 1952 *aide-mémoire* and the October 1952 note, i.e. little or no new appropriations would go to Spain until the negotiations were concluded. Washington was not willing to give this up. Nevertheless James Dunn decided against sending such a note after a new proposal by Spain had been received in April.

On 23 March 1953, the Department of Defense agreed with the analysis of the Department of State concerning the military aid programme for FY 1954 to Spain. It was made clear that the purpose of this particular aid was to provide equipment to the Spanish forces to assist in the protection of US bases and for training purposes. Nevertheless the Department of Defense also made clear that it considered the $85 million proposed for FY 1954 as only the first instalment. Thus the report by the JUSMG from 20 August was considered compatible with the later report from October 1952. If anything, Martín Artajo's outcry had helped to draw the US Departments closer together in this matter.

During March 1953 General Hoyt Vandenberg visited Spain, and in January and April parts of the Sixth Fleet stopped at several Spanish harbours as a friendly gesture. During January of the same year, 25 Spanish Navy and Air Force officers, including three Rear-Admirals, embarked on the US destroyers *Brownson* and *Turner* and later on the carriers *Midway* and *Leyte*. These visits were an expanded version of a similar stay of Spanish officers aboard American ships the year before. The Navy could hope that relations between the two services would spill over to the negotiations.

The US military establishment still acknowledged the political complications which a treaty with Spain would cause. On 1 April 1953, General Gruenther, Chief of Staff of SHAPE (Supreme Headquarters Allied Powers Europe), told the Senate Foreign Relations Committee that SHAPE was staying out of negotiations with Spain because of the connotation of withdrawing to the Pyrenees. Gruenther still feared an all-out attack on Europe, and if such an invasion took place troops might still have to be withdrawn from Central Europe. He stated that if the US gave any connotation that there was going to be a withdrawal, NATO would no longer be interested in the liberation period. This had serious repercussions for Spain. The General made it clear that the reason why he stayed out of it was because Spain was not a part of NATO.

Problems during the negotiations between Spain and the US were partly alleviated by the arrival on 3 April in Madrid of Ambassador James Dunn, appointed in January 1953. MacVeagh's position had became increasingly untenable, as his goodwill towards Spain had led to more demands which the State Department was unable to grant. Finally the row resulting from John W. Jones's letter to Artajo left MacVeagh's staff in Madrid on bad terms with the local authorities. After almost 20 years in the State Service Lincoln MacVeagh decided to retire. James Dunn would make a new start, paying his first visit to the Foreign Minister on 6 April. On this occasion Martín Artajo stated that despite the speculation by the foreign press that the agreements were to be signed soon, he assured the Ambassador that he knew that this was not the case. Dunn assured the Spanish Minister that the US had no intention of blaming either side for the delays. Artajo pointed out that the real difficulty lay in formulating a proper balance between granting Spanish bases on the one hand and provisions for economic and military aid on the other. He vehemently defended Spain against a perceived accusation by the US that Madrid had been responsible for the delays of the talks. If Washington had hoped that James Dunn's appointment would give Spain an honourable chance to back down, they must have been disappointed. Artajo was not giving in.

Three days later, Dunn presented his credentials to Franco, whose opening remarks expressed admiration for General Eisenhower. The Caudillo referred to the current negotiations and said that in his original conversation with Admiral Sherman he had expressed Spain's desire to enter into an arrangement which would assign Spain a proper role not only in the defence of its national territory but also in Europe. Nevertheless, this was conditional on improvements made to her economic and military situation. During the 50-minute conversation, the Caudillo claimed that Spain's industry could produce 1000 planes annually at costs far below those of other European nations. He expressed regret over the delays of the talks, which according to him were due to US misunderstandings concerning Spain's capabilities to contribute to the defence effort, and to the increased risks Spain would incur with the establishment of US air bases. Dunn replied that his government too regretted the delays but that with the advent of a new administration it had been necessary to re-examine its foreign policy. According to the Ambassador this had been done and Washington had arrived at the conclusion to continue talks based on the 17 March communication – the one which had offended Artajo. Franco was appalled and said that this position was worse than any one previously taken. Dunn pointed out that Washington was anxious to be helpful but that there were obvious limitations imposed upon his government resulting from developments in other parts of the world. Furthermore, the Ambassador pointed out that the US government was reducing expenditure in order to balance the budget, an objective which had strong Congressional support.

Two days later and exactly one month after Jones's letter to Artajo, General Vigón handed Kissner the Spanish counter-draft of the military facilities agreement. In this document the Spanish negotiators clearly backed down on some of their military demands made earlier. The harsh American policy finally had some positive results. Immediately, Ambassador Dunn recommended withholding the note drafted on 26 March, which rejected responsibility for the delays and confirmed the

April and October 1952 communications, until there had been an opportunity to study the latest Spanish counter-proposal. This proposal was already under discussion between Vigón and Kissner. The Ambassador suggested to the State Department that either he himself, Kissner or Train should go to Washington to discuss the latest proposal by the Spanish team with high officials in the capital.

In the meantime Vigón and Kissner held further talks, during which the American was able to negotiate some changes incorporated in a Spanish redraft on 24 April. Nevertheless, even this new document still contained two fundamental concepts of the Spanish position which had been previously rejected by the US negotiation team. These concerned the parallel development between bases and the aid programmes on one side, and on the other the adequacy of the military aid programme designed to equip the Spanish forces for her national defence.

Dunn acknowledged these two concerns but pointed out that the concept of parallel development in the new Spanish note was only referred to implicitly and fortunately left the United States' position sufficiently protected so as to avoid legal and political complications. Furthermore he said that if the US intended to carry out its commitments to Spain as expressed in the "statement of intent" on 7 October 1952, i.e. "support of Spanish defense efforts . . . by the provision of assistance to Spain over a period of several years", then reasonable military and economic aid had to be provided to Spain during this and the following years. Otherwise the negotiations could not be concluded. Under these circumstances, he called for approval of the Spanish redraft of the Defense Agreement.

In the meantime in Washington the Department of State came to the conclusion that to accept the military aid programme of such a nature and magnitude as recommended by the JUSMG report from 20 August 1952 would require a major policy change. The negotiators had been informed about this in September 1952. The State Department advised that the long-range planning for US military aid to Spain should be considered in connection with the imminent review of all aspects of the negotiations which would take place as soon as the new Spanish proposal and the negotiators' comments were received in Washington.

The Spanish counter-proposal contained certain demands which could have been dealt with by the US negotiators in Madrid. Nevertheless, it also contained additional points which further discussions in Spain could not solve. The JUSMG was in no position to agree to the basic Spanish tenet regarding aid and US obligations. The negotiations had reached a point at which a decision by Washington, involving a fresh look at plans concerning the use of military facilities, as well as the parallel development of bases and aid, was required. Accordingly on 30 April Ambassador Dunn, General Kissner and Mr Train were instructed to return to Washington to participate in a thorough review of the negotiations and in the preparation of a paper which was to be presented to the NSC. The consultations in Washington had started earlier but after 4 May they were to include the three most important negotiators, the Ambassador and the two heads of the negotiation teams.

One day earlier, John F. Dulles had told the Senate Foreign Relations Committee that the delay of the negotiations with Spain was due to complications concerning economic aid, equipment for Spain's forces and the military bases. The Secretary of State stressed that Spain's expectations as to what they would receive had been very high. He claimed that the Spanish negotiation team was asking for $700 million extended over a period of three or four years. Dulles believed that this was way out of line. He stressed that the air facilities could be duplicated in North Africa but that the Navy facilities could not. The latter were considered of utmost importance and irreplaceable for the US. Thus, Dulles favoured new appropriations for Spain during the coming FY as well as carrying over the $125 million from FY 1953 to FY 1954. He argued that this would be necessary for a successful conclusion of the negotiations.

Ambassador Dunn had informed Franco during early May that Congress would agree to carry the $125 million through to 1954 and extend additional credits. This was in line with other nations who had given Spain credit facilities. The UK had granted £11 million, Belgium BF 700 million, France FF 15 billion and Germany the equivalent of $17 million.

On 5 May President Eisenhower presented his foreign aid programme for FY 1954 to Congress. As predicted, he asked for the carrying over of the previously appropriated $125 million as well as adding an additional $10 million in new funds for defence and $90 million for military aid. These additional funds were to help the negotiations come to a swift conclusion.

Two days later, Dunn explained to the House of Representatives that the initial delay of the talks had been due to Spain's reluctance to give up her neutrality which had kept her out of both world wars. According to the Ambassador, Spain had wasted six months deciding on this issue. He also claimed that Spain had hoped for a Republican victory in the US Presidential elections, expecting a better deal from the Eisenhower administration. This had further delayed the talks. Dunn explained that the US wanted to use military bases in Spain in return for aid. Spain, on the other hand, was afraid of becoming vulnerable in case of war and thus wanted enough military and economic assistance to guarantee her independent position during a conflict. Ambassador Dunn stated that one of the elements of Franco's strength was the fact that he had kept Spain out of world war. He asserted that Franco would need some substantial gain to which he could point if publicly he had to give up Spain's control over foreign policy.

However, Dunn was enough of a realist to see that Spain could not remain neutral during a new world conflict. He claimed that Franco did not ask for nor desired the defence of the bases to be secured by US troops, but instead by his own national force.

At the time, the USSR and its allied troops in Europe were composed of a total of 134 Soviet army divisions, 75 satellite army divisions, more than 15 000 planes (mainly Mig 15s, stationed at over 300 airfields) and over 125 submarines operating along the coasts. NATO had estimated that it would require 140 army divisions, 12 300 planes and over 3000 vessels to check this threat in the long term. So far NATO had been building up its forces from 14 army divisions in 1950 to a total of 91 divisions in 1952. Despite this massive build-up, NATO still lacked sufficient troops. However, it was very likely that these forces could slow down an attack long enough to prepare for nuclear retaliation. Under these conditions, Spain was no longer needed to cover NATO's rear but would play an offensive role. Bases in Spain could be used to launch a nuclear attack. The earlier these bases became operational, the more benefit they could bring.

C. Tyler Wood, Deputy to the Director for Mutual Security, told a House Committee in May that the negotiations had advanced encouragingly during the previous weeks. Train and Dunn had already been recalled to Washington for last consultations and to set the next stage of tactics which was under intensive study at the cabinet level. After pressure from the Air Force Department, General Kissner joined them in Washington.

The State Department and Nash, from the Department of Defense, were not happy about Kissner returning to Washington. Since December 1952, the State Department's policy had been to wait and see if Spain abandoned some of her demands. Kissner's return to Washington, while Dunn, Train and MacVeagh were already holding talks, made it obvious to Madrid that a major review of the entire US position was taking place. Under these circumstances, Spain was reluctant to accept a reply reconfirming the previous US policy. The American negotiators would lose their edge as well as waste time.

During the meetings held in Washington, a memorandum was prepared for consideration by the National Security Council. The negotiators and the State Department believed that the Spanish government would conclude and carry out a base agreement satisfactory to the US if the Executive Branch approved a programme of continuous military and economic aid to Spain over a period of several years. It was thus estimated that in addition to the $125 million carried over from the last FY and the $101 million requested by the President, a further $80 million annually would have to be appropriated for three successive years beginning in FY 1955. This would mean total aid of $466 million. The memorandum reiterated the importance to the national security of the use of air and naval facilities in Spain.

On 11 May 1953, the Planning Board of the National Security Council outlined eight major points of Spain's significance to US national security, which ranged from increased military flexibility in peace and wartime to providing continuity of the global base structure. Two days later, Ambassador Dunn, Kissner and Train presented their memorandum to the National Security Council. The National Security Council instructed (NSC Action 786) the Secretary of Defense to further study this proposal. He was granted the right to make financial adjustments to the Air Force base programme as a result of the negotiations. If he was convinced by the arguments presented in the memorandum, he was to advise the Secretary of State to proceed with the negotiations once the necessary discussions with the Congressional committees had taken place. Furthermore Charles Wilson, the Secretary of Defense, was to report his actions to the next National Security Council meeting. The terms of the agreements as proposed by the US negotiators were, generally speaking, acceptable to the Council.

Barely a week later, Secretary of Defense Charles Wilson reported that after further study, he considered that the use of air and naval facilities in Spain was of urgent importance to national security. It was clear that Spanish airbases had been part of USAF strategic plans for some time. As a result other Continental and overseas bases had already been eliminated or their construction had been deferred. To go back on the base plans in Spain would have seriously conflicted with USAF plans. The Secretary argued that there was no alternative for these bases and according to his instructions, he advised the Secretary of State to continue the negotiations after consultation with Congress. Finally he requested the National Security Council to note that he was asking the Secretary of State to move towards "early" conclusion of satisfactory agreements with Spain.

The next day, 20 May, the National Security Council, meeting in the President's Office, noted Wilson's report and decided, in Action 795, that the use of air and naval facilities in Spain was vital. This action, together with the NSC action taken a week earlier, authorized the State Department to proceed with the negotiations.

The very same month, James F. Dunn explained to the House Foreign Affairs Committee that US aims in Spain were quite simple, and if Spain wanted military and economic aid she had to accept a reversal of her non-alignment policy. Dunn felt that bilateral agreements between Spain and the US would be the opening phase of getting Spain back into international cooperation.

On 4 June 1953 representatives of the Departments of State and Defense and of the Mutual Security Agency talked with the European Subcommittee of the House Foreign Relations Committee. The Executive Branch was willing to commit itself for an aid period beyond FY 1954. However, it could not force Congress to do the same. The risk of Congress not making a financial commitment beyond 1954 and thus undermining the whole relationship, meant that the Executive Branch wanted to avoid Congressional debate on the issue altogether. Senator Knowland was one of the Senators on the Foreign Affairs Committee who initially supported the idea of establishing bases through Congressional approval, but eventually changed his mind and argued against Congressional involvement. Congress would have to approve the funds annually rather than in one lump sum, thus giving it more flexibility in the future. Senator Alexander Wiley supported the idea of allowing Congress annual appropriation of these funds. Senator George concurred that Spain was vital to the defence of North Africa and the Middle East but did not favour limitations on Congressional appropriations. In contrast, Senator Fulbright strongly opposed any alliance with Spain and proposed a motion to reduce the aid to $50 million. Only Senator Green supported him in this motion. Outnumbered, his motion was defeated by a vote of five to two.

Later that month, Mr Wood, Deputy Director of the Mutual Security Agency, pointed out that it was important to quickly get the $125 million for FY 1954 to Spain, as this would be a lever for the negotiation team. This was needed as Spain wanted to see an early and continuous commitment by the US towards the defence of the Peninsula. On the other hand, the US risked giving up a strong bargaining position by granting aid before the agreements were signed.

On 9 June the representatives of the Departments talked to the corresponding Committees of the Senate. Senator Bridges, Chairman of

the Senate Appropriations Committee, was also briefed on the negotiations. Frank C. Nash, the Assistant Secretary of Defense, made the
most revealing statements. He briefly mentioned visits to Spanish ports
by the US Navy, before stressing that Spain had no internal Communist threat like France or Italy. This, and the fact that construction
costs in Spain were low, made her an attractive alternative to other
European partners. The low construction costs were due to a number
of reasons, including the price of land and labour and the fact that no
import tax for construction or maintenance supplies was levied. Nash
conceded that the Defense Agreement in its present form might pose
some problems to the Franco regime internally, and could further delay
talks while Spain was attempting to gain a stronger commitment from
the US.

The Assistant Secretary made it clear that bases in Spain were desirable
because bases in Morocco, which might have been used for similar
military purposes, had limitations arising from the political instability
in the region. He confirmed that Rota, Cádiz and four other bases were
already in the advanced stage of planning and the services estimated
that economic assistance would generate savings for the base costs of
roughly $55 million over four years. Thus the total costs would be
around $760 million over four years.

Nash also pointed out that he believed that Spain was not too interested
in the actual financial amount but simply wanted to assure America's
willingness to enter an honest relationship. This implied a commitment of US troops and aircraft to secure bases and anti-mine and anti-
submarine assistance to keep Spanish ports open. According to Nash,
the US Army wanted geographical bases in Spain as well as to get her
on the right side. The Navy needed Rota as well as British Gibraltar
because, according to the Assistant Secretary, "we want to have our
hand in there, too".

More revealingly, Nash pointed out that "if we have that in hand
[the three agreements] by virtue of the execution of an agreement with
Spain, in my judgment, my personal judgment, it will have a strong
effect indeed in pushing the progress of the consummation of the EDC
[European Defence Council]". Apart from the strategic considerations,
Spain fulfilled the function of a possible threat to French opposition to
US plans for the defence of Central Europe. Following the outbreak of
the Korean War, America had begun pressing for a European integrated force under a centralized command which was to include German
troops. This would have eased pressure on the US defence budget.
France, feeling the impact of the Korean War less and fearing Germany's

re-militarization more than the US, countered with its own strategic plan, the Pleven Plan. It called for small national contingents integrated in a unified European army with a common budget and supranational control. Initially Washington feared that this was no more than an attempt to delay German re-militarization, and thus the State Department continued its pressure on France. Spain, by giving the US an alternative to the Pleven Plan and a possibility to withdraw from France, fulfilled a useful function. Nash asserted that "he [Adenauer] pointed out that [if] the United States was going ahead with these negotiations with Spain . . . [then] the United States might be forced to contemplate a reappraisal of its strategy in Europe". The Assistant Secretary made clear that he believed Spain apportioned an important factor to US strategy in Europe. "I think it [Spain] is an important ace in the hole in this important poker game that we are playing now, and I think if we had that ace in the hole we would have a better negotiating position [*vis-à-vis* France]."[2]

NOTES

1. FRUS, 1952–54, VI, p. 1923.
2. Executive Sessions of the Senate Foreign Relations Committee, 9 June 1953.

13 The Final Stage

On 12 June 1953 the consultations with Congress were concluded and the American negotiation teams were told that they would receive final instructions shortly. In the meantime they were authorized to inform the Spanish government that the Executive Branch had requested Congress to appropriate another $101 million. Given the complications in March this must have come as a great relief to Spain.

While these developments took place, one final concern by the US Army was voiced. The Army Chief of Staff realized that due to the political climate in Europe, Spain could only be integrated into NATO after overcoming considerable opposition by France and Britain. US military officers in Europe argued that any military command structures outside NATO were undesirable and thus Spain should be included in NATO.

Brigadier-General Bergquist from the US Army argued that no steps should be taken by the US which would endanger, or even delay, attainment of full Spanish participation in NATO. The general claimed that the proposed organization discussed in Madrid did not dovetail with existing military organizations in Western Europe, in particular not with the Mutual Security Agency organization. He concluded that entering the agreements was not in the interest of the US.

As agreed after Congressional consultations, on 20 June 1953, instructions were sent to the American Embassy in Spain to proceed with the negotiations after minor changes in the wording of the base agreement. The more important ones were the insertion in Article 1 of necessary legal safeguards regarding the furnishing of military equipment and the deletion of a phrase which might have implied Spanish priority for military end-products aid over NATO. The American Embassy was also told that Spain should be informed that the total aid envisaged by the US did not exceed $466 million and was subject to future Congressional appropriation.

Despite authorizing the Ambassador to proceed with the negotiations, he was told that the signing of the agreements depended on obtaining further legislative authority. Washington was considering whether to conclude the agreements in the form of an executive agreement without prior Congressional authorization or in the form of a treaty. One view was that the agreement, because of its importance and duration, had to be submitted to Congress as a treaty. Another was that the abandonment of the executive agreement process, as a general pattern, would seriously jeopardize most of the current base rights with other countries and critically affect the American defence position. In either case, further Congressional consultation had to take place.

The American Embassy in Madrid wanted to defer advising the Spaniards about the possible necessity of obtaining Congressional authorization because of the adverse effect this might have on the negotiations at such a late stage. The last time Spain had been informed about a similar problem, in a personal letter to Artajo on 17 March, the progress of the talks was seriously endangered by the Spanish Minister's defiant reply. Washington agreed to this suggestion by the Embassy and Spain was kept in the dark.

In the meantime, the economic teams of the two countries discussed future credits of between $200 and $400 million. This credit was not only meant for military installations but also for economic aid and to improve Spain's infrastructure. In return the Spanish government was willing to drop the strict 25 per cent limitations on foreign capital. Instead foreign investors were allowed to control between 45 and 50 per cent of Spanish companies.

Train and Argüelles met again on 2 July. The next day they were joined by General Kissner. The Spanish team presented a proposal on how to split the already appropriated funds. The newly appropriated $101 million was to be divided into $91 million military aid and $10 million economic aid; the $125 million carried over from the last fiscal year was to be split similarly into $37 million military and $88 million economic aid.

Overall, Argüelles felt that more economic aid was required. In this context, he made it clear that he did not yet understand the actual procedure of the base construction but he wanted the Spanish government to fully participate in the project. More importantly, though, he pointed out that he had not fully assimilated all of the facts which General Kissner had pointed out during the discussions. Specifically he was referring to the legal restraints under which the American Executive was conducting the negotiations in regard to the future appropriation of funds. As agreed in Washington, the American negotiators were not to disclose these financial limitations and therefore some of the explanations given had been intentionally vague.

The problem was simultaneously being addressed in Washington. On 9 July 1953, John F. Dulles had a conversation with Congressional leaders concerning the question of legislative authorization for the Spanish and other base agreements. Again the question posed was whether the US should adopt the form of executive agreements or treaties concerning the use of foreign military facilities. The latter required Congressional approval by two-thirds, the former did not.

Senator Knowland, who had become the mentor in Congress for the appropriation of the funds, approved that the President could enter agreements without additional legislation. The issue was brought up again in a meeting with eight other Senators and four Representatives later in July. There were no dissenting points of view. Evidently the view of those present was that past procedures with respect to base agreements could be appropriately continued. However, some Senators pointed out that future financial commitments were subject to Congressional appropriations and neither they nor Congress could guarantee these. Furthermore, Senator Saltonstadt said that the actual construction of bases was also going to be subject to approval by the Armed Services Committee. Overall, the conversation made it clear to Dulles and the President that they did not require Congressional support to sign the agreements. The Secretary of State informed the Senators that the negotiations would proceed accordingly and that the appropriate committees of Congress were going to be advised and kept informed about the negotiations.

On 15 July the President officially approved the course agreed with Congressional leaders. Eisenhower, his legal advisers, the Attorney General and the State Department all acknowledged that future legislative appropriations were required. For the Executive the question remained whether to inform Spain about this legal complication or not. The State Department favoured disclosure. However, the Department of Defense dissented. Particularly, the Department of the Air Force favoured to keep this secret, enabling the negotiators to secure the agreements without further complication. This, however, might have led to severe strain on relations with Spain if some time in the future Congress refused to appropriate the necessary funds. With this in mind, the other services departments were inclined to disclose the restraint on the Executive. It was only after Frank Nash overruled the Air Force that Spanish negotiators were informed of this legal issue.

The fact that no further legislative approval of the base agreements was required did not mean that Congress fully supported the agreements. Senator McCarran (Democrat/Nevada) continued his crusade for Spain, claiming that the US needed Spain and Spain needed the US. For him the Spanish government's violent opposition to Communism would assure them of their support in the crucial hour. McCarran argued that Spain really had been a neutral nation during the world war, even supporting the Allies during the North African invasion. He maintained that only the Soviet propaganda had labelled her pro-Axis and, therefore, suggested that there should be an immediate agreement with Spain as all Communism's enemies were allies of the US.

Representative Dewey Short (Republican/Missouri) supported McCarran. He mentioned 4000 Allied pilots who sought refuge in Spain during the war and were released to fight another day. He believed that Spain added valuable manpower to the West, and that aid to Greece and Turkey was intended to safeguard the eastern doors to the Mediterranean and that common sense demanded similar attention to the Western door.

Senator Owen Brewster (Republican/Maine) argued along the same lines, stressing Spain's past as the one government which had been successful thus far in dealing with Communism. He therefore advocated economic aid to Spain as the best way to stop Communism.

Senator Hickenlooper expressed his belief that Spain was the only sure thing the US had in Europe in the event of war with the Soviet Union. However, Spain had received little by June 1953 and yet, according to Hickenlooper, had been guaranteed a lot. He upheld that for every dollar spent in Spain, the US would get more ultimate long-range protection than in any other place in Europe, not only because of the Spanish government, but also because of Spain's geographical location and the determination of the Spanish government to resist to the last ditch any Communist activity.

Others, such as Representative Leon H. Gavin (Republican/Pennsylvania), simply saw the US policy as a necessity. Rather then supporting it, they tried to justify it. Senator Mike Mansfield (Democrat/Montana) maintained that Spain was a purely military issue, not a political one, and as Generals Eisenhower, Bradley and Ridgway, all military experts, stressed Spain's importance, the issue was settled for him. He would support their decision.

Not all were convinced. Many Senators continued to strongly oppose a deal with Spain. Representative Emanuel Celler (Democrat/NY) argued that the US could not subscribe to the *non sequitur* that an enemy of an enemy is a friend, and that therefore Uncle Sam had to love Franco because both hated Russia. Celler then made the point that by no stretch of the imagination would Franco support the Russian cause and no pact was needed to shape Spain's policy in that direction. The word "welcome" would be on the Spanish mat to American aviators.

However, the Spanish invitation to the US was not sufficient, substantial investments were needed to make full use of her resources. Spanish airfields were too small, so small that not all US planes were able to land there. Before aviators could use facilities, Spain had to have appropriate airfields, a modern communication system and a decent transportation network to supply a modern army and air force.

Representative Celler was not the only one in Congress who was unconvinced by the negotiations. Senator Herbert H. Lehman (Democrat/NY) argued against the agreements from a simple ideological standpoint. He drew attention to the fact that an alliance with Spain gave the USSR propaganda material. Lehman was supported by Representative Chet Holifield (Democrat/ California), who stated that until Spain changed her robes of dictatorship for garments of freedom, the US could not sign any agreements and thus feed the flames of Soviet propaganda by courting a fascist regime.

Representative Jacob Javits (Republican/NY) upheld that an agreement with Spain would give the impression that the US would withdraw behind the Pyrenees in the event of Soviet attack, which ran counter to NATO members' interests. He pointed out that Spain's economy stood for everything the US tried to avoid; regulated trade, centralized planning and an unfree market.

Representative John Kee (Democrat/West Virginia) supported this by giving the example of economic regulations concerning oil. Foreign oil imports were allowed to provide for only up to a maximum of 40 per cent of the total domestic consumption. The remaining 60 per cent had to be provided by Spain's oil companies.

Nevertheless, attempts to stop the negotiations were unsuccessful. Senator Fulbright's second attempt, supported by Senator Tobey, to cut aid to Spain from $125 million to $50 million was defeated because some, such as Senator Mansfield, greatly valued Spain's strategic importance.

It became apparent to the negotiators at this critical phase that the effect of Congressional action concerning the proposed $226 million on the foreign aid appropriation for Spain was a crucial factor. Ambassador Dunn cabled to Washington that if Spain did not get the $226 million or very near that amount, the State Department should consider the probability of a complete breakdown of the negotiations.

Senator McCarren and Senator Ferguson took opposite sides on this issue. In August Senator Ferguson indicated that the $125 million would be carried over by Congress but that it was likely that the $101 million in new funds, recommended by the Executive Branch for Spain, might have to bear a proportional share of the overall Congressional cut in foreign aid funds. McCarren vehemently opposed this on the grounds that the funds were, strictly speaking, part of the foreign aid programme. His view prevailed and subsequently the Departments of Defense and State were informed that the $10 million economic and $91 million military aid originally proposed would be retained without reduction.

Other supporters of close Spanish–American relations were former ambassador Charlton Hayes, who pointed to strong cultural links between Spain and American nations, and Dr Sidney Sufrin, who explained the economic benefits for both nations of an agreement. British opposition to the agreements had been silenced. France and Italy faced internal problems and accepted the new American initiative in Spain.

By June 1953 Spain had resumed close military contact with Western Europe. Military missions to Spain arrived from Britain under Air Commander John Fressanges, from France under General Goisland, and from Italy, Germany and Belgium. The Spanish headquarters of Allied Emergency Forces was established in Madrid. French observers were at manoeuvres in Navarra. France and Spain had even entered talks concerning allocation of French troops in sectors of Spain's defence. In the event of an attack on Europe, Spain would allow French African troops to use Spanish ports, French aircraft to use Spanish airports and French troops to pass through Spain. Paris even accepted that French troops seeking refuge in Spain would operate under Franco's and not NATO's command.

Many more countries had signed Treaties of Friendship with Spain. These included a block of four Latin American countries, Nationalist China, Liberia and Iraq. In a gesture of benevolence, the Japanese Crown Prince visited Spain during late June.

In Britain, ever since the Spanish Military Attaché had expressed interest in British military equipment, the Ministry of Defence and the Ministry of Supply wanted to relax trade restrictions further. The revision of these had been going on since late 1952. One day after the agreements between Spain and the US were signed, the Joint War Plans Committee met and decided that the agreements forced the UK to revise its trade policy and abandon coordination with France. During November, the Cabinet decided to relax export restriction to Spain.

Final discussions were held in Washington. Since the Armed Service Committee, which still had to approve the base construction, had not been previously consulted, arrangements were made to do so. Mr Smart, Clerk of the House Armed Services Committee, was briefed on 20 July 1953 by representatives of the Departments of Defense and

State. Following this the Committee itself was briefed a week later.

One day earlier, the Spanish counter-draft of the Defence Agreement was received by Kissner's team in Madrid. It contained nine minor changes which the US negotiators in Spain approved and others which were not acceptable and had to be addressed in Washington.

Spain wanted, by implication only, to make the authorization of the use of military facilities in Spain dependent on the fulfilment of the US aid programme, a watered-down version of "parallel development". Furthermore, Spain wanted to authorize the use of Spanish facilities by US forces for the effective air defence of Spain. This latter indirectly implied a US guarantee of Spanish security. Neither of these two changes were acceptable to either the US negotiation teams or Washington. Spain also wanted to eliminate a clause inserted by the US which made future aid dependent on Congressional appropriations. Washington also decided to keep this clause so that the US position would be legally acceptable.

Another change implied that Spain ranked equal to other NATO nations. The US negotiators had agreed to this at one time, but had eliminated it from the US draft on 20 June because it could be argued that, in this context, it implied that NATO was not given priority in military end-products over Spain. The Spaniards wanted the clause to be reinserted. They were worried that its omission might imply some sort of political discrimination. Washington only reluctantly agreed to reinsert this phrase in the interest of early success of the negotiations.

On 29 July 1953 a telegram was sent from Washington to Madrid which contained the reaction of the administration to Spain's counter-draft and was to be submitted to the Spanish Cabinet before their meeting on 11 August. It agreed to all Spanish demands apart from the implied parallel development bases–aid programme and the indirect obligation by the US to use bases in defence of Spain. General Kissner, who received it, realized that it was not properly marked with the official "USNEG" and thus was not an official instruction for him. ("USNEG" stood for US negotiations representing official documents relating to the talks.) As this paper would have complicated the negotiations, the Ambassador was happy not to act upon it. The Chargé John W. Jones believed that this was due to a clerical error and that the document was indeed a "USNEG" paper. The matter was further delayed as Ambassador Dunn decided to have an operation, spending four days in hospital. Kissner decided not to follow the instructions until Jones had confirmation that the telegram was indeed a "USNEG" document and even then he did so against his personal judgement.

By August 1953, the base agreement had two phrases left which were incomplete and some changes had been suggested by Spain in the Technical Annex. The military aid agreement had only one minor complication left. The economic aid agreement was acceptable to both parties and Washington still had to consider Spain's counter-proposal concerning taxes on construction imports.

The counter-draft by the Spanish negotiators dispelled speculation by Western Europe that the signing of the agreements was imminent.

In a meeting on 11 August, the Spanish Cabinet considered the agreement as proposed by the US and decided to reject it while making further minor changes. Consequently, in a meeting with General Vigón, Kissner was able to negotiate restoration of certain American proposals. Afterwards, Vigón was able to clear these changes directly with Franco. In order to consider the final Spanish revision, General Kissner flew to Washington on 23 August 1953.

Five days later the Ambassador in Madrid saw Artajo, who handed him a personal letter from General Franco to President Eisenhower. James Dunn took this letter personally to Washington on 30 August. In the letter Franco expressed his concern over the way in which the negotiations were developing. He considered that they were descending to an inappropriate level and that their slowness might create an atmosphere of mistrust and suspicion. According to the Spanish dictator, American negotiators seemed more interested in the texts of the technical agreements which referred to details which were of interest to the US but did not specify reciprocally the detailed provisions affecting Spanish aid. Franco wrote that the whole structure of the agreements would not be completed until it included an appropriate annex concerning the details of American aid towards the equipping of Spain's armies. The dictator very much feared the destruction of Spanish towns in the event of war. He believed that the US had not shown proper interest in Spain's defence preparations and urged Eisenhower to help Spain defend herself. It was quite apparent from his letter that General Franco aimed for early delivery of military equipment. Nevertheless, he did not at this stage insist on an annex setting forth the precise details of US military assistance.

James Dunn had been informed through Artajo, on 28 August, that Franco feared that the talks were being delayed by a group trying to block the arrangements or alternatively, that Franco feared that the US government mistrusted Spain's commitment.

In Washington, the question was raised which authority would be in charge of the construction of the bases in Spain. The Department of

Defense recommended that the USAF should have authority over the construction to provide better coordination on the American side, to cooperate with the Spanish authorities and above all to avoid direct clashes with the NATO structure. The proposal was accepted.

After consultation with the Secretary of State, Ambassador Dunn flew to Denver on 5 September to see the President. There Dunn delivered Franco's letter to General Eisenhower together with a draft reply concurred with the Defense and State Department. The reply, as later approved by the President, stated that he shared Franco's regret over the delay of the talks caused by the necessity to hold discussions in great detail. However, he claimed that this should not give rise to mistrust or suspicion. Many technical details in the negotiations arose from legislative practices in the US. The President informed Franco that US aid to Spain would give priority to military end-products but these could not equip Spain's land force more than the draft Defense Agreement allowed. Eisenhower confirmed that discussions would go forward regarding the programmes covering military and economic aid. He hoped that Ambassador Dunn, taking back to Madrid the last instructions, would be able to conclude all the agreements without further delay. The American head of state stressed the importance of Spain's air defence requirements and the fact that the US was aware of these. Finally, he tried to dismiss Franco's fears about the safety of Spanish cities.

Before their return to Madrid, Ambassador Dunn and General Kissner attended a conference over the wording of the texts and took with them the final US changes to the Mutual Defense Agreement, the Technical Agreement and schedules and the Tax Annex, together with authorization to conclude these agreements when they believed they had obtained the best position possible.

Concerning the Defense Agreement, Dunn was instructed to seek changes in the controversial wording of two paragraphs of Article I. Nevertheless, he was given the authority to accept the Spanish formulation if the Spaniards remained adamant. Finally, the Ambassador was to deliver a confidential note to the Spanish government which guaranteed, in connection with Article I of the Defense Agreement, a total aid programme to the amount of $466 million over a period of several years.

The last differences were ironed out in a series of meetings between the Spanish Foreign Minister and the American Ambassador to Spain. The first of these took place on 10 September 1953 at the Club Marítimo of Bilbao. The meeting, which was to start at 11.00 a.m. was delayed because Artajo, arriving from San Sebastian, was more than half an hour late. The meeting lasted until 3.15 p.m., by which time the two sides had almost settled the defence agreement.

In order to avoid a similar mishap by the Spanish Minister, the next meeting was held in San Sebastian on 17 September 1953. It was scheduled to start at 5.00 p.m. Arriving by car from Madrid, Ambassador Dunn left with plenty of time and arrived by 2.00 p.m., three hours early. During 75 minutes most complications in the other two agreements were solved, and, only minor issues remained. Ambassador Dunn reported on 14 September that he and the Spanish Foreign Minister had settled the Defense Agreement. One week later the other three documents, the Economic Aid Agreement, the Military Agreement and the Technical Schedules, were completed. These last three presented few difficulties.

Two days before the signing of the agreements, Dunn confirmed to Artajo that the US was planning to spend $465 million in Spain, of which $226 million had already been appropriated by Congress. The $465 million would be split $390 million in base construction costs and military aid and $75 million in economic aid. These funds would be available through the Department of Defense allocations for the armed forces overseas base programmes or alternatively, through the approval by the President of funds under the Mutual Security Act. Thus the Americans were able to guarantee the aid to Spain without causing legal complications.

There was a last-minute fear in the State Department that the wording in the Defense Agreement "to cooperate with the Spanish air force in air defense" committed US forces to Spain's air defence, which would have required Senate ratification. Bonbright, Deputy Assistant Secretary of State, argued that the insert "in air defense" should be taken out. Nevertheless, the Department of Defense was of the opinion that this was not needed, as no implication of military support for Spain had been made. On 25 September the Secretary of State decided that the analysis by the Department of Defense was to prevail. Cooperation did not necessarily mean military commitment, because the USAF would have the option of removing its personnel from Spain in the event of a military action in which it did not wish to be involved. Military cooperation with Spain was obviously very likely but certainly not mandatory. It was a legal, not a strategic matter.

In July 1954, after the agreements had been signed, Harold Stassen, Director Foreign Operations Administration made it clear that Spain could not be defended without defending the US air bases and vice versa. This removed the legal possibility of removing troops and planes from Spain in order to avoid defending Spain. Thus Spain had *de facto* received the final commitment by the US to defend her territory. The Executive had bypassed Congress and indirectly committed American forces to the defence of a foreign nation. This was done because the Department of Defense had argued that any changes would have further delayed and even jeopardized the conclusion of the agreements, planned for 26 September 1953.

On the last day before the agreements were signed, the President gave his final approval. Harold Stassen asked the President to give the green light under the Mutual Security Act 1951. This was required because it was possible that Mutual Security funds would have to be extended to Spain if Congress refused to appropriate funds. Eisenhower agreed and John F. Dulles sent a telegram to Ambassador Dunn instructing him to sign the Defense, Technical, and Economic Aid Agreement on behalf of the US government. General Kissner had already been authorized by the Deputy Secretary of Defense Keyes on 5 September to sign the four subsidiary Technical Schedules of the Technical Agreement.

14 Signing Off

On 26 September 1953, at 4:00 p.m., the agreements between the two countries were signed by James Dunn and Martín Artajo in the Salón de Embajadores of the Palace of Santa Cruz in Madrid. Spain was represented by the Foreign Minister Artajo, the General Staff General Vigón, the Minister of Commerce Arburúa, the Sub-Secretary for Foreign Affairs Navastúes, the Sub-Secretary of Foreign Commerce Argüelles, the General Director for Foreign Politics de las Barcenas and the Baron de las Torres for the Protocol. The US was represented by Ambassador James Clement Dunn, President of the Committee for Foreign Relations of the House of Representatives Robert C. Chipperfield, Member of Congress John Harman, General August W. Kissner as Chief of the Military Commission, Advisor to the Embassy Ivan B. White, Chief Advisor to the economic mission Richard S. McCaffery, Advisor to the Embassy Horace H. Smith, First Secretaries of Embassy Merril Cody and Stuart W. Rockwell, Civil Servants of the State Department Allen B. Moreland and Cdt Lennett, with Ramón E. Benedett from the military mission.

At the same time as the agreements were signed in Madrid, a press release was issued in Washington and Madrid which contained the texts of the three principal public documents. Letters were sent by the Department of State to those members of Congress who had expressed a special interest in the agreements, enclosing a copy of the press release. Finally representatives of the British, French, Italian, Dutch, Belgian, Turkish, Canadian, Australian and Portuguese Embassies in Washington were called in and briefed on this last chapter of the Spanish negotiations. The next day, in a press conference, President Eisenhower publicly confirmed that the deal was a quid pro quo.

The documents consisted of three separate bilateral agreements as opposed to treaties. The Spanish constitution did not distinguish between agreements, treaties, convention or protocols. The Cortes, the legislative chamber, had the right to intervene in agreements only if they were "objective of law". Its intervention had to be short and could not take place after any manifestations by the state. In fact the three documents were signed for Spain by Franco.

The first of these was a ten-year defence agreement. Through this agreement the US gained the right to develop, maintain and utilize for military purposes an unspecified number of military bases in Spain for its air force and navy. In return Spain received US war material and equipment. Spain became a strategic part of the NATO defence system even though she was not a member. The bases were to be used by both nations but remained under Spanish control. Apart from the construction of these bases, the US was also to construct a pipeline, necessary to supply these bases with sufficient fuel. Some of the construction expenditure had to be made in Spanish pesetas. In order to avoid the complicated Spanish foreign-exchange system, the exchange rate was fixed at 35 pesetas to the dollar, which was close to the black-market exchange rates.

Near Madrid, Torrejón became the most important US military establishment. It had only been an air-force experiment and a research centre for the Spanish Air Force and therefore needed extensive enlargement. Its runway was expanded from 4200 feet to 11 500 feet. The base itself was to be enlarged by 1500 acres. Similar construction had to take place elsewhere. El Copero was expanded from 617 acres to almost 2500 acres. Guadalquivir was an entirely new project and a new runway of 11 000 feet was constructed. The base at Moron was a fighter and night-flying school. Despite having two hard-surfaced runways, its size had to be increased from 900 acres to 1500 acres and one of the runways was to be enlarged to a total length of 10 000 feet. The base at Sanjurjo was a bombardment training base and was the only base where no plan of enlargement existed in January 1954.

Facilities for the US Navy also had to be improved. The planned naval base at Cádiz completed the "Radford Line" concept, as it anchored down the Navy at the eastern end of the Mediterranean, with strong areas of air and naval defences. For the USAF, the airfields in Spain were a third defence line in Europe. The first line ran through West Germany, Austria and Yugoslavia. The second line ran through Turkey, Greece, Italy and France. Finally, bases in Spain and Britain formed the third line and were considered outside the reach of the Red Army.

There were certain limitations in the defence agreement which limited the day-to-day use. These included a clause restricting US personnel to wear civilian clothes outside the base. The US wanted to avoid mistakes made in France and Germany where signs were appearing that part of the population was offended by the permanent stationing of troops in their country. In Spain, US military personnel were put under rigid control. In return each soldier received an extra $300 for civilian clothes. With an estimated 8000 soldiers stationed in Spain, this created annual additional costs of $2.4 million. US personnel only received one-third of their salary in pesetas to avoid inflationary effects on the Spanish economy.

At the bases, the US was in charge of personnel, technical aspects, operations and maintenance of military equipment. A military Assistance Advisory Group and an Economic and Technical Assistance Group were set up and reported. These two were to coordinate assistance projects in the future.

This first part of the agreements was a boost to the defence of the West and US military concerns about the failure to include German divisions in NATO were partially alleviated. The second agreement, concerning economic aid, was in concord with the Mutual Security Act. In return for economic aid, Spain was forced to practise an open-door policy towards the US. Article Two called for Spain to stabilize its currency, decrease inflation, balance its budget, disallow trade barriers and open its market to American goods.

Furthermore American investors in Spain were allowed to freely transfer profits. As a result capital invested in Spain increased after 1953. At the same time return on capital increased and by 1955 had almost caught up with average US returns elsewhere.

As important for foreign trade as the liberalization of Spain's economy was the third agreement. Raw materials, services and patent rights were exchanged without barriers and it was agreed to integrate Spain into the American trade policy. This meant that Spain had to join US embargo policies towards the East.

The agreements recognized the military threat to Spain and that in the event of general war, units of the US Strategic Air Command, based in Spain, would pose an immediate threat to the USSR. In view of this threat it appeared reasonable to expect that the Strategic Air Command bases would be attacked early in the war.

The same day as the agreements were signed, the Office for Diplomatic Information of the Foreign Ministry made a public statement in which these were described as agreements for peace and international security. Spain was to receive $226 million in the next year and $465 million over the next several years. The $226 million was composed of a $100 million credit, extended by $25 million, and the new $101 million. Of this, $85 million was economic aid while the rest, $141 million, was earmarked for military aid. Part of these funds went for the construction costs of the bases.

General Vandenberg recommended the formation of a Mutual Assistance Advisory Group, which would administer the bases under the Mutual Defense Assistance Programme as opposed to the USCINCEUR (US Commander in Chief Europe) or SACEUR (Supreme Air Command Europe). The latter two organizations were in charge of administration of bases in other countries. This was done to avoid political problems with European allies.

In confidential letters between Artajo and Ambassador Dunn in 1953/54 the use of the $465 million aid was settled. According to instructions by the Joint Strategic Plans Committee to the Joint Chiefs of Staff, the Mutual Defense Assistance Program stressed the importance of the air defence forces, ground troops and anti-submarine warfare. This was reflected in the allocation of financial resources.

Compared to other nations, the aid Spain received was unique. Normally 90 per cent of the aid would be economic while 10 per cent would flow back to the US for costs of administration. The construction costs for military facilities were usually met by the American service departments directly. In Spain only 30 per cent of the aid benefited the Spanish economy, 10 per cent covered administration costs and 60 per cent paid for the construction costs of the bases themselves. Despite this Franco seemed pleased and argued nine days after the agreements that Spain's anti-Communist attitude had made the agreements possible.

There also existed a secret annex to the agreements. Britain was soon informed through the Quai d'Orsay of its existence and of the fact that it was to remain hidden from the public. The information leaked from a marine officer and was later confirmed by statements in Congress. They gave America the right to freely use parts of the bases in peacetime as well as in wartime. In a sneak attack by the Soviet Union, the US government was not forced to consult with the Spanish government prior to the usage of the bases, thus limiting Spain's foreign policy.

The secret note was attached to the second paragraph of Article Three of the Defense Agreement. The military use of the bases was governed by two distinct scenarios. In the event of a Communist aggression, the US forces were to make use of the military facilities situated in Spain for action against military objectives, in such a manner as might be necessary for the defence of the West, provided that, when this situation arose, both countries communicated to each other their information and intentions. In other cases of emergency the two countries were to enter urgent consultation and action would be determined in the light of the circumstances.

This cast a shadow over Martín Artajo's statement that the agreements were an "indisputable success" and "occurred without the most minimum damage to our sovereignty and independence". Spain also gave tacit agreement to the stationing of nuclear weapons on its soil and the anchoring of nuclear submarines at Rota.

It had been argued even before the 26 September that the Spanish armed forces would lose control over Spain's national defence. What is clear is Franco's natural interest to pretend that Spain's sovereignty remained unharmed. Unfortunately for him, a few days after the signing of the agreements, the American press speculated that important matters were covered in secret agreements. To calm down the situation, James C. Dunn wrote to other diplomatic missions in Spain that the bases were under Spain's command at all times and that the US had no intention of stepping on Spain's sovereignty. He stressed this point during an address to the American Chamber of Commerce in Seville in November 1953. However, James Dunn knew that this was not the case. For Franco, retaining sovereignty was important due to possible internal challenges. At the same time, the US had good reasons to avoid great publicity on the topic. Firstly, Washington had just extended credits and was about to embark on military base constructions in Spain. Spain's internal conflicts and instability would threaten America's position. Secondly, America wanted to avoid being labelled imperialistic. On the other hand, the agreements without the secret clause would appear very weak to the American public.

In the US Department of State Bulletin, James C. Dunn wrote about the economic impact of the agreements. He argued that there was no immediate fear of inflation due to the system of mutually beneficial counterpart funds. The system worked straightforwardly. When a Spanish firm needed foreign credits, it could file an application with the Spanish and American governments for aid. After both governments approved, the company would receive the imports paid for by the counterpart fund. The firm would pay the equivalent in pesetas at a fixed exchange rate. These pesetas were placed in a special account of the Bank of Spain from which the US could withdraw funds for specific projects. Spain would retain full control over monetary policy while the US avoided complicated exchange regulations to convert dollars into pesetas.

Once the agreements were signed, interest in the development of the bases receded. There was no crash construction programme as in Morocco, due to public opposition to the waste of money. In fact the builders used construction equipment from base constructions carried out in Morocco. This further delayed the operation. The base construction took five years and consisted of three main airbases and one port and airbase at Rota. The three main airbases were situated near Saragossa, Torrejón near Madrid and Moron close to Seville.

Once the bases were constructed the shortcomings of the military surveys and constructions became obvious. For example, the Moron de la Frontera runway was crossed by a railway line! This led to an incident in February 1959 when two F-100s declared an emergency because of minimum fuel, as a result of two circlings ordered by ground control approach because a train was on the end of the runway.

The Chief of Naval Operations soon realized that the Matagorda strip was unsuitable, while the Rota base was satisfactory but 27 miles away from Matagorda, and thus required extensive road construction. The choice by the Navy for the airfield had been based on considerations for naval operations and not for air-force convenience.

The Navy was more successful in taking advantage of the agreements. Unlike the Air Force, the US Navy in Spain was under the Commander in Chief US Naval Forces Europe in London. Under his guidance, Rota soon developed into the headquarters of the American Sixth Fleet operating in the Mediterranean. Up to then the Sixth Fleet was stationed in Norfolk, Virginia. Its ships operating in the Mediterranean had been supplied by transport vessels and tankers. In addition to the extra expense, this posed political and security problems for fleet movements, especially for submarine operations in the Mediterranean. These problems were solved with the development of Rota.

From a strategic point of view, the value of Rota to the US was threefold. In a unilateral conflict in the Mediterranean, it could be used as a naval base. In a limited war in Europe between NATO and the Warsaw Pact, with conventional and tactical nuclear weapons, Spain was required as a platform for transportation via air and sea. In an all-out nuclear war, Rota would have been a vital nuclear base for American submarines.

Later the USS *Holland*, a repair ship, was to be permanently based at Rota to service all possible conceivable faults of submarines, both nuclear and conventional. This saved millions of dollars for the US Navy as it was no longer necessary to return submarines to the US for repairs. The base added greatly to the strategic value of the fleet.

In fact military experts like Jesse W. Lewis, the military affairs officer at the US embassy in Saudi Arabia, later argued that the Sixth Fleet was only superior to its Soviet counterpart, the Fifth Escadra, due to its extensive base system along the Mediterranean coast. This facilitated easy supply, land-based support and emergency repair facilities.

Rota had no bombers but operated as an aid to the Navy in

reconnaissance and communication as well as for basing aircraft units. Above all though, the base supported the nuclear strike power of the Sixth Fleet. The US saved an estimated $24 million per year per submarine, as the submarines did not have to return to Charleston or New London, a 14-day trip, for refuelling and maintenance.

Comparing the development, construction and assistance costs, with the money saved, the US bases in Spain were a good investment for the US Armed Forces. Spain's large standing army also provided a second defence line against a Soviet attack through Europe as well as a first European defence line against a thrust by the Soviets from the Balkans, across to North Africa and into Spain. It also opened the possibility of Spain's troops fighting north of the Pyrenees.

Nevertheless, the progress of technology influenced warfare and complicated the aims for military planners in the post-war period. From 1945 to 1948 the US had to rely on B-29s for the delivery of nuclear bombs. In 1949, the US had 500 B-29s capable of delivering more than 100 A-bombs. Their comparatively short range meant that they had to make use of overseas bases. By 1953, the US had more than 1000 A-bombs or H-bombs which could be delivered by a B-36 or B-47, two long-range bombers.

Already by 1957 this had changed. The US was in possession of 7000 to 10 000 bombs. These could be delivered by the Stratofortress B-52 which had a range of 10 000 miles and a capacity of 60 000 lb of bombs. At the same time the US developed tactical and strategic missiles. The Redstone missile had a range of 249 miles, but still lacked the capability to carry enough weight. The Pershing missile had a range of 400 miles. At the same time the US Navy developed the ability to launch missiles from submarines. The USS submarine *Nautilus* was commissioned in January 1955. The USS submarine *Halibut* was commissioned in 1956 and could carry three missiles. With the development of these new weapon delivery systems it was no wonder that overseas bases lost strategic importance.

Facilities in Spain, Greece and Turkey served as a connection to the Persian Gulf, and during the late 1950s the Moroccan base functions were transferred to bases elsewhere. Its operational functions were transferred to Spain. The logistic function was transferred to American bases in Spain, Italy and Portugal. During the 1960s bases in Libya were dismantled and as a result operations and logistics functions were transferred to Spain and Italy. Yet immediately after 26 September 1953, the Spanish air bases were planned above all to cope with operational function of the Algerian bases which had been dismantled during the late 1940s.

As the American base system was once more streamlined after the Korean conflict, Spain's new military facilities took over the function of other bases. Overall capital value of facilities in Spain in 1988 was estimated at $298 million, only behind Germany, Korea, Japan, Britain, Italy, the Philippines and Canada.

Spain had gained vital importance in two military aspects. According to a study by James R. Baker, Spain was for the US the sixth most important country for tactical air operations and naval operations. She had little importance for airlifts and no importance for ground operations. The two important areas, tactical air and naval operations, greatly enhanced US international power projection and thus worked as a deterrent. Given USSR real nuclear capability by 1954, the West had to put another deterrent against the Red Army. Up to 1954 the threat of US nuclear attacks countered the threat of the massive Soviet army. After 1954 when the Soviets had built up a delivery system for their nuclear weapons, the two superpowers' nuclear capabilities cancelled each other out. The Spanish bases were, according to James Baker, some of the best in the US base system to deter a possible sneak attack.

In order to fulfil this, the 16th Air Force was established on 15 July 1957. It was the largest overseas Strategic Air Command of the US. It operated in Spain and Morocco and reported directly to the HQ of Strategic Air Command at Offutt, Nebraska. The B-47 of the 16th Air Force in Spain could reach its target within six hours.

The concept on which the Spanish airfields had been planned was soon challenged by new military studies. In April 1954, the Rand Corporation published the R-266 study "Selection and Use of Strategic Air Bases" which concluded that the current US base system was the worst possible option compared to four alternative basing systems. Rand analysed the costs and military use of operating bases, overseas refuelling bases, strategic bases and air-refuelling systems. Operating bases would have bombers and fighter planes stationed on foreign airfields which would rotate with other planes at other operating bases as well as with planes stationed in the US. Overseas refuelling bases were designed to only refuel already armed planes on their way to their bombing targets. Strategic bases, on the other hand, were designed to have planes stationed there permanently to assure the defence and the bombing capability of the base itself. The idea of the air-refuelling system is well known and needs little explanation.

The report concluded that systems consisting of US operating bases and overseas refuelling bases were markedly superior to any other alternative. Overseas refuelling and operating bases were more vulnerable to Soviet attack compared to strategic airbases, but they could be run more cheaply by saving on AA-guns, early radar warning systems and fighter planes. Additionally, they did not require extensive personnel, housing and, above all, underground hangars. Another alternative, the US-based air-refuelling system, was considered but was found to be too expensive and risky. The time saved could not justify the extra costs of having several refuelling planes in the air. Thus the cheapest and most efficient way was to have the bombers stationed in the US and other safe bases. In case of attack they would take off, land at the refuelling base, refuel in as short a period as necessary, take off, complete their bombing mission, and return to the refuelling base before returning to the US. The extra costs for flying the whole route US–refuelling base–target and back easily outweighed the costs of overseas airports with stationed bombers as well as decreasing the risk of losing the bombers while operating from the overseas base. The fact that the bomber was a sitting duck while on the ground made it necessary to refuel in as short a period as necessary.

If the refuelling bases were overrun by the Soviets, the Americans could have easily fallen back on air-refuelling, and they would not have lost bases together with the planes. The Rand study also showed that it would pose no problem to convert the existing overseas bases into refuelling bases. Spain had not yet any bases constructed but those planned and later constructed were strategic airbases. By the time the bases were completed, the weapon arsenal of the US had changed and the Rand report itself was outdated. However at the Spanish bases the B-47 was the backbone of the strike capability until 1965.

The US expenditure on the base construction ranged between $300 and $420 million, out of which one-third was paid in the Spanish currency. In addition there was a yearly maintenance cost until 1963 of around $50 million. The construction was carried out by three companies, Brown & Root of Houston, Raymond International of New York City and Walsh Construction Company based in the UK. A total of 5000 Spaniards were employed directly and a further 15 000 through sub-contracts.

Military aid to Spain started with a delivery to Cartagena on 15 February 1954 of 1800 tons of military equipment. In ten years, US military end-products aid sent to Spain added up to around $600 million, of which two-fifths was received by the army and the rest was split between the other two forces. By 1963 the Spanish army had been fully restored to a modern fighting force.

Spain also received a large amount of economic aid. In order to administer this aid, a US Operations Mission was set up with 23 officers and supporting staff. It covered seven sectors including economic analysis, several industrial sectors and the infrastructure.

Between 1953 and 1957 Spain received $280 million in economic aid. Surplus commodities of the US valued at around $250 million were sold during the same period. On top of that, Spain was able to gain access to foreign credits. The Export–Import Bank credits, which accumulated to over $500 million in ten years, together with private credits of $1 billion, enlarged the Spanish market for American goods.

Spain had also gained recognition in the Western world and was integrated into the OEEC, as well as into the IMF. During December 1958, John F. Dulles visited Spain and one year later President Eisenhower did the same. The renewal of the Defense Agreement in 1963 was merely a formality. By then Spain was an acceptable international partner, even though the old regime of the 1930s was still in power.

Spain's totalitarian aspects had not changed. Franco was still the only legislator holding the main functions of the government. People were still jailed for threatening their head of state, advising Franco's incarceration, abusing the chief of government, distributing or producing illegal propaganda or belonging to an illegal society and participating in strikes. Military considerations had clearly overruled America's democratic and liberal convictions.

Bibliography

UNPUBLISHED PRIMARY SOURCES

National Archives/Washington, DC (NA Civil Branch; NA Military Branch)

ABC 092, Spain
ABC, Air Intelligence
ABC Decimal Files relating to Spain
ABC 336, Russia
Army Chief of Staff Decimal File 091, Spain, 1948–1953
CCS 092, US Joint Chiefs of Staff, Spain, 1946–1954
CD 091, 3, Defense Central Decimal Files, Spain, 1950–1953
CD 091, 3, MDAP, Spain
CD 92, Defense Correspondence Files, Spain, 1950, 1951
CD 92, 2, Spain
Classified Correspondence Secretary of Navy, Francis P. Matthews
CS 091, Spain
Forrestal General Records
G-3 091, Spain, 1950–1954
Lot Files 52–316, General Records Department State, Europe
Lot Files 53D444, General Records Department State, Dean Acheson
Lot Files 54D394, Office of European Affairs, Matthews
Lot Files 54D395, Office of European Affairs, Hickerson
Lot Files 55D105, General Records Department State, Miriam Camp
Lot Files 59D108, Subject Files Spain and Portugal, 1942–1958
Lot Files 64D563, Records of the Policy Planning Staff, 1947–1953
NSC 3, US Policy toward Spain
NSC 72, US Policy toward Spain
NSC 72, Background Information
NSC Meeting Minutes
NSC Actions
OIR Reports 4105, 4405, 5324.1, 5324.2, 6211
P-2, The Mediterranean and the Near East
PPS/12, Policy Planning Staff 1947–1953, US Policy toward Spain
R&A Reports 363, 532 (incl. IR Reports)
State Department Decimal Files 1945–1949, 600.528, 852.20, 852.24, 852.6362, 852.6363
State Department Decimal Files 1950–1954, 400.529, 452.00, 452.003, 452.006, 452.118, 752.56, 752.5622, 852.00, 852.000

Library of Congress/Washington, DC (LOC)

Microfiche Reports, Hearings for Congress
   H 1868 Survey
   H 1967 Report
   H 2287 Report
   H 2641 Report
   HFo-1 Hearing
   HFo-3 Hearing
   H.Rp.1834 Report
   S0062 Report
   S0343 Report
   S983-2 Hearing
   SFo-1 Hearing
   SFo-T.4 Hearing
   SFo-T.23 Report
   SFo-T.34 Hearing
   SFo-T.54 Hearing

Washington National Records Centre/Washington, DC (WNRC)

Army Intelligence, Project Decimal File, Spain, 1946–48
Records of the Army Staff, G–2 Intelligence, Spain, 1946–48

Other Libraries in the USA

Dulles, John F. Papers
Dulles, John F. Herter Collection
Dulles, John F. Oral History Collection
Earle, Edward M. Papers
Hughes, Emmet John Papers
Netherlands Information Service, "Dutch Press Divided on Franco Issue", 9 August 1951
Senior Thesis Collection Princeton
Sherman, Forrest P. Papers
Smith, Howard Alexander Smith Papers
Strategic Plan Division Records, US Navy (SPDR)
United States Naval Forces Eastern and Mediterranean Annual Reports, 1947–53

Public Record Office, London (PRO)

ADM223,51, 223–238
AIR040. 329
DEFE04, 1, 12, 13, 16, 17, 27–29, 32, 38, 52, 56
DEFE05, 12, 13, 17, 19, 26
   1, 5–7, 9, 13, 16, 19
DEFE07, 840
FO371, 60375–60377, 60407, 60427, 60441A, 60443–67878B, 67897, 73320–73323, 73341–73343, 73379, 79665, 79666, 79700–79702, 79706, 79719,

79721, 79739, 79767, 79775, 79777, 79752, 79809, 79815, 89479, 89480, 89491, 89492, 89494, 89496, 89497, 89499–89509, 89517, 89524, 89526, 89564–89566, 89568, 89571, 89576, 89613, 89614, 96153, 96154, 96169, 96170, 96172, 96181–96192, 96195, 96203, 96206, 102009–102011, 102014, 102017, 102018, 102022, 102024–102026, 102034, 102046, 102047, 102060, 102064, 107668, 107669, 107675, 107676, 107678, 107680–107688, 107691, 107693, 107696–107698, 107700–107704, 107710, 107712, 107714, 107715, 107717, 107719, 107730

PUBLISHED PRIMARY SOURCES

British and Foreign State Papers Her Majesty's Stationery Office, London
1948, Volume 151 (1956)
1948, Volume 152 (1956)
1951, Volume 158 (1961)
Chase National Bank of the City of New York, Spain: A Short Economic Review, State Department Decimal Files 852.000/4–2254, New York, 1954
A Decade of American Foreign Policy: Basic Documents 1941–1945, United States Government Printing Office, Washington, DC, 1950
Executive Sessions of the Senate Foreign Relations Committee, United States Government Printing Office, Washington, DC, 1976–1978
Volume 2, 81st Congress, 1st and 2nd Session, 1949–1950
Volume 3, 82nd Congress, 1st Session, 1951
Volume 4, 82nd Congress, 2nd Session, 1952
Volume 5, 83rd Congress, 1st Session, 1953
Foreign Relations of the United States (FRUS), United States Government Printing Office, Washington, DC, 1967–1988
1945, Volume V
1946, Volume I
1946, Volume V
1947, Volume I
1947, Volume III
1948, Volume III
1948, Volume I
1949, Volume IV
1950, Volume I
1950, Volume II
1950, Volume III₁
1951, Volume I
1951, Volume IV
1952–1954, Volume VI
Selected Hearings held in Executive Session before the Committee on Foreign Relations Senate, United States Government Printing Office, Washington, DC, 1972–1976.
Foreign Economic Assistance Programs
Relief Assistance, Act of
Reviews of the World Situation 1949–1950
The Vandenberg Resolution and the North Atlantic

Joint Hearings held in Executive Session before the Committee on Foreign Relations and the Committee on Armed Services Senate: Military Assistance Program 1949, United States Government Printing Office, Washington, DC, 1974

Hearings before the Committee on Foreign Affairs House of Representatives: Mutual Security Program, 1951–1953, United States Government Printing Office, Washington, DC

Hearings before the Committee on Foreign Relations and Committee on Armed Services Senate: Mutual Security Act, 1951–1953, United States Government Printing Office, Washington, DC

Hearings before the Subcommittee of the Committee on Appropriations House of Representatives: Mutual Security Appropriations, United States Government Printing Office, Washington, DC, 1953, 1954
1952
1953

Public Papers of the Presidents of the United States of America: Containing the Public Messages, Speeches and Statements of the President: Harry S. Truman, Volumes 1945–1953, United States Government Printing Office, Washington, DC, 1961–1966

Public Papers of the Presidents of the United States of America: Containing the Public Messages, Speeches and Statements of the President: Dwight D. Eisenhower, 1953, United States Government Printing Office, Washington, DC, 1960

Public Papers of the Secretaries General of the United Nations, Trygve Lie, 1946–1953, Volume 1, Columbia University Press, New York, 1969

Published Hearings Senate: United States Foreign Aid Programs in Europe, United States Government Printing Office, Washington, DC, 1951

Report on Spain, Spanish Embassy, Washington, DC, 1946

Spain and the United Nations Accusations, Diplomatic Information Office, Madrid, 1949

Weekly Political Intelligence Summaries (WPIS), 4 July 1945–29 October 1947, Nos. 300–415, Kraus International Publications, Millwood, NY, 1983

Ferell, Robert H., ed., *The Eisenhower Diaries*, W. W. Norton & Co., New York, 1981

Johnson, Walter, ed., *The Papers of Adlai E. Stevenson, Vol. 2, Washington to Springfield 1941–1948*, Little, Brown & Co., Boston, MA, 1973

Mills, Walter, ed., *The Forrestal Diaries*, Viking Press, New York, 1951

Rand Report, by A. J. Wholstetter *et al.*, "R-266: Selection and use of Strategic Air Bases", April 1954, in Marc Trachtenberg, ed., *Writings on Strategy 1952–1960*, Vol. 1, Garland Publishing, New York, 1988

Ross, Steven T. and Rosenberg, David A., eds, *American Plans for War against the Soviet Union 1945–1950 (APWSU)* Vol. I–VII, Garland Publishing, Inc., New York, 1990

Siegfried, André, ed., *L'Année politique 1946*, Paris, 1947

Truman, Harry S., *The Memoirs of Harry S. Truman, Vol. 1, Year of Decision: 1945*, Hodder & Stoughton, London, 1955

Truman, Harry S., *The Memoirs of Harry S. Truman, Vol. 2, Years of Trial and Hope: 1946–1953*, Hodder & Stoughton, London, 1956

218 Bibliography

MAGAZINES, PERIODICALS AND NEWSPAPERS

Business Week, 14 July 1951
Catholic World, Vol. 167
Christian Century, Vol. 70
Commonwealth, Vol. 46
Congressional Digest, March 1953
Contemporary Review, Vols 150, 152
Digest of US Practice in Government, 1977
European Review
Foreign Affairs, Vols 31, 41
Foreign Policy Bulletin, Vols 28, 29, 31
Foreign Policy Report, Vol. 23
Fortune
Forum, Vol. 110
Harper's Magazine, Vol. 196
Nation, Vols 167, 169, 173, 175
Netherlands Information Service, 9 August 1951
New Republic, Vols 121–5, 129
New York Times
Newsweek, Vols 32, 34, 42
Reader's Digest, Vol. 62
Reporter, Vols 8, 9
Saturday Evening Post, Vols 221, 225
United Nations World, Vols 2, 7
United States News and World Report, Vols 25, 26, 31, 35, 36
United States Department of State Bulletin, Vols 20, 25, 26, 29

SECONDARY SOURCES

Akehurst, Michael, *A Modern Introduction to International Law*, 5th edn, George Allen & Unwin Ltd, London, 1984

Ambrose, Stephen E., *Rise to Globalism: American Foreign Policy since 1938*, 4th edn, Penguin Books, New York, 1985

Arango, E. Ramón, *The Spanish Political System: Franco's Legacy*, Westview Press, Boulder, CO, 1978

Arrarás, Joaquín, *Francisco Franco*, Geoffrey Bles, London, 1938 (trans. J. Manuel Espinosa)

Baker, James R., *United States Overseas Basing*, Praeger, New York, 1990

Barbé, Esther, *España y la OTAN*, Editorial Lai, Barcelona, 1981

Bidwell, Percy W., "Ideals in American Foreign Policy", in *International Affairs*, Vol. XXII, University of Toronto, Toronto, 1946

Bin Ahmed, Qasim, *Britain, Franco and the Cold War 1945–1950*, New York, 1992

Blaye, Edouard de, *Franco and the Politics of Spain*, Penguin Books, Harmondsworth, Middlesex, 1976 (trans. Brian Pearce)

Brewer, Sam Pope, "Spain: How good an ally", in *Yale Review*, Spring 1952, Vol. 41, No. 3

Bullock, Alan, *Ernest Bevin: Foreign Secretary 1945–1951*, London, 1983

Calvocoressi, Peter, *World Politics since 1945*, 6th edn, Longman, London, 1991

Calvocoressi, Peter, ed., *Survey of International Affairs*, Oxford University Press, London, 1952–56, Volumes on 1947–1948, 1949–1950, 1951, 1952, 1953

Campillo, Manuel, *Las inversiones extranjeras en España 1850–1950*, Gráficas Manfer, Madrid, 1963

Carr, Raymond, *Spain: Dictatorship to Democracy*, 2nd edn, Harper Collins, London, 1981

Carr, Raymond, *Spain 1808–1975*, 2nd edn, Clarendon Press, Oxford, 1982

Carr, Raymond and Fusi, Juan Pablo, *España de la Dictadura a la Democracia*, Editorial Planeta, Barcelona, 1979

Carreras, Alberto, *Industrialización Española: Estudios de Historia Cuantitativa*, Espasa-Calpe, Madrid, 1990

Cava Mesa, María Jesús, *Los diplomáticos de Franco: J. F. de Lequerica, temple y tenacidad*, Bilbao, 1989

Chamorro, E., *et al.*, *Las Bases Norteamericanas en España*, Euros, Barcelona, 1976

Chandler, Geoffrey, "American Opinion and Foreign Policy", in *International Affairs*, Vol. XXXI, University of Toronto, Toronto, 1955

Chavkin, Samuel, *et al.*, eds *Conference on Spain: Implications for United States Foreign Policy*, Greylock Publishers, Stamford, CT, 1976

Cleugh, James, *Spain in the Modern World*, Alfred Knopf, New York, 1953

Coletta, Paolo E., *American Secretaries of the Navy, Volume II*, Naval Institute Press, Annapolis, MD, 1980

Condit, Doris M., *The Test of War, Vol. II, 1950–1953*, United States Government Printing Office, Washington, DC, 1988

Cortada, James W., "The United States", in James W. Cortada, ed., *Spain in the Twentieth-Century World*, Greenwood Press, Westport, CT, 1980

Crozier, Brian, *Franco: A Biographical History*, Eyre & Spottiswoode, London, 1967

Cuadrado Roura, Juan R., *Las Inversiones Extranjeras en España: Reconsideración*, Gráfica URANIA, Malaga, 1976

Duke, Simon, *Military Forces and Installations in Europe*, Oxford University Press, Oxford, 1989

Einhorn, Marion, *Wer Half Franco*, Akademie-Verlag, Berlin, 1983

Eleta, Juan S., *Spain's Role in the Defense of Allied Security in NATO*, US Army War College, Carlisle Barracks, 1986

Espadas Burgos, Manuel, *Franquismo y Política Exterior*, Ediciones Rialp SA, Madrid, 1988

Esteban, Joan, "The Economic Policy of Francoism", in Paul Preston, ed., *Spain in Crisis*, Harvester Press, Hassocks, Sussex, 1976

Feis, Herbert, *From Trust to Terror: The Onset of the Cold War 1945–1950*, London, 1970

Fernández, Carlos, *Tensiones Militares durante el Franquismo*, Plaza y Janes Editores, Barcelona, 1985

Fusi, Juan Pablo, *Franco*, Unwin Hyman, London, 1987 (trans. Felipe Fernández-Armesto)

Gallo, Max, *Spain under Franco*, George Allen & Unwin, London, 1973

García, M. G., "The Armed Forces: Poor Relations of the Franco Regime", in Paul Preston, ed., *Spain in Crisis*, Harvester Press, Hassocks, Sussex, 1976

Garriga, Ramón, *Franco-Serrano Suñer*, Editorial Planeta, Barcelona, 1986

Gibernau, Joseph A., *Triumphs and Failures of American Foreign Policy from Roosevelt to Reagan 1936–1986 with Spain as a case history*, Phoenix Books, Phoenix, AZ, 1986

Gilbert, Martin, *Winston Churchill, Never Despair 1945–1965*, Houghton Mifflin, Boston, MA, 1988

Greene, John Robert, *The Crusade: The Presidential Election of 1952*, University Press of America, Lanham, MD, 1985

Griffis, Stanton, *Lying in State*, New York, 1952

Grimmett, Richard F., "An overview of the Formative Years 1953–1970", in John W. McDonald Jr., *U.S. Base-Right Negotiations*, Dep State Publications, Washington, DC, 1988

Halstead, Charles R., "Spanish Foreign Policy 1936–1978", in James W. Cortada, ed., *Spain in the Twentieth-Century World*, Greenwood Press, Westport, CT, 1980

Hamby, Alonzo L., *Beyond the New Deal: Harry S. Truman and American Liberalism*, Columbia University Press, New York, 1973

Hayes, Carlton J. H., *The United States and Spain: An Interpretation*, Sheed & Ward Inc., New York, 1951

Hillman, Jordan J., *The Export Import Bank at Work*, Quorum Books, Westport, CT, 1982

Hills, George, *Franco: The Man and his Nation*, Robert Hale Ltd, London, 1967

Houston, John A., "The United States and Spain", in *Journal of Politics*, Vol. 14, University of Florida, 1952

Jenkins, Roy, *Truman*, William Collins, Sons & Co., London, 1986

Kaufmann, William W., *Planning Conventional Forces 1950–1980*, Brookings Institution, Washington, DC, 1982

Kennan, George F., *American Diplomacy*, University of Chicago Press, Chicago, IL, 1984

Keylor, William R., *The Twentieth Century World An International History*, 2nd edn, Oxford University Press, New York, 1992

Langer, William L., "The Mechanism of American Foreign Policy", in *International Affairs*, Vol. XXIV, University of Toronto, Toronto, 1948

León, Girbau, "España y la Guerra Fría", in *Cuadernos Americanos*, Jul./Aug., Sep./Oct. 1960, Vol. 62, Mexico

Lewis, Jesse W., *The Strategic Balance in the Mediterranean*, American Enterprise Institute for Public Policy Research, Washington, DC, 1976

Lleonart y Anselem, J., "España y la ONU: La cuestión española 1945–1950", in *Revista de Política Internacional*, Jul./Aug. 1977, Vol. 152, Madrid

Lloyd, Alan, *Franco*, Doubleday & Co, Garden City, NY, 1969

Lowi, Theodore J., "Bases in Spain", in Harold Stein, ed., *American Civil-Military Decisions*, University of Alabama Press, Tuscaloosa, AL, 1963

Luzárraga, Francisco Aldecoa, "La política exterior de España en perspectiva histórica 1945–1984. De la Autocracia al Estado de Derecho", in *Sistema*, Nov. 1984, Vol. 63, Madrid

McCauley, Martin, *The Origins of the Cold War*, Longman, New York, 1983

McCullough, David, *Truman*, Simon & Schuster, New York, 1992

Marquina Barrio, Antonio, "Aspectos relevantes en las negociaciones entre España y los Estados Unidos", in Buhigas, José Luís *et al.* eds, *Bases y Reducciones: Las Negociaciones España-EE.UU.*, Instituto de Cuestiones Internacionales, Madrid, 1987

Marquina Barrio, Antonio, "The Bases in Spain", in Thomas Veremis and Yannis Valinakis, eds, *US Bases in the Mediterranean: The cases of Greece and Spain*, ELIAMEP, Athens, 1989

Marquina Barrio, Antonio, *España en la Política de la Seguridad Occidental 1939–1986*, Ediciones Ejército, Madrid, 1986

Matthews, H., "Spain Today", in *Virginia Quarterly Review*, Vol. 28, No. 1, 1948

Maxwell, Kenneth, ed., *Spanish Foreign and Defense Policy*, Westview Press, Boulder, CO, 1991

Miller, Merle, *Plain Speaking: An oral biography of Harry S. Truman*, Coronet Books, London, 1974

Nadal, Jordi, *et al.*, eds, *La economía española en el siglo XX*, Editorial Ariel, Barcelona, 1987

Nicholas, H. G., *The United Nations as a Political Institution*, 5th edn, Oxford University Press, London, 1975

Oronoz, Javier, *Transformación del sistema capitalista y evolución de la formación social española*, Editorial Lur, Donostial, 1980

Payne, Stanley G., *The Franco Regime: 1939–1975*, University of Wisconsin Press, Madison, WI, 1987

Pollack, Benny, *The Paradox of Spanish Foreign Policy*, St Martin's Press, New York, 1987

Portero, Florentino, *Franco Aislado: la cuestion Española 1945–1950*, Aguilar, Madrid, 1989

Potter, E. B., *Admiral Arleigh Burke*, Random House, New York, 1990

Preston, Paul, *The Politics of Revenge: Fascism and the Military in the 20th Century Spain*, Unwin Hyman, London, 1990

Preston, Paul, *Franco*, Harper Collins, London, 1993

Preston, Paul, ed., *Spain in Crisis*, Harvester Press, Hassocks, Sussex, 1976

Preston, Paul, and Lannon, Frances, eds, *Elites and Power in Twentieth-Century Spain: essays in Honour of Sir Raymond Carr*, Clarendon Press, London, 1990

Ramírez, Luís, *Francisco Franco: La obsesión de ser, la obsesión de poder*, Ruedo Ibérico, Châtillon-sous-Bagneux, 1976

Remiro Brotons, Antonio, *Las Cortes y la Politica Exterior de España*, Gráficas Andrés Martín, Valladolid, 1977

Ren, Williamson de Visme, *Culture and Policy: The United States and the Hispanic World*, University of Tennessee Press, Knoxville, TN, 1949

Roberts, Frank, *Dealing with Dictators: The Destruction and Revival of Europe 1930–70*, Weidenfeld & Nicolson, London, 1991

Rubottom, R. Richard, and Murphy, J. Carter, *Spain and the United States: Since World War Two*, Praeger, New York, 1984

Rupérez, Javier, "Spain, the United States and NATO: Political and Strategic Dilemmas", in Lasky Joyce Shub and Raymond Carr, eds, Spain *Studies in*

Political Security, Georgetown University Press, Washington, DC, 1985

Sherwin, Martin J., "The Atomic Bomb and the Origins of the Cold War", in Leonard Dinnerstein and Kenneth T. Jackson, eds, *American Vistas: 1877 to the Present*, Oxford University Press, New York, 1979

Shubert, Adrian, *A Social History of Modern Spain*, Unwin Hyman, London, 1990

Stanford Research Institute, *Las Inversiones Norteamericanas en España*, Câmara de Comercio Americana España, Barcelona, 1972

Suárez Fernández, Luís, *Francisco Franco y su Tiempo*, Tomo IV/V, Fundación Nacional Francisco Franco, Madrid, 1984

Sufrin, Sidney C. and Petrased, Franklin A., *The Economy of Spain*, Headline Series, Sept.–Oct. 1952, Vol. 95, New York, Foreign Policy Association

Vázquez Montalbán, Manuel, *La Penetracíon Americana en España*, Divulgacíon Universitaria, Madrid, 1974

Viñas, Angel, *Los Pactos Secretos de Franco con Estados Unidos: Bases, Ayuda Económica y Recortes de Soberanía*, Editorial Crítica, Barcelona, 1981

Viñas, Angel, "8. La Conexión entre Autarquía y Política Exterior en el Primer Franquismo 1939–1959", in, Angel Viñas ed., *Guerra, Dinero, Dictadura*, Editorial Crítica, Barcelona, 1984

Viñas, Angel, "10. El Plan Marshall y Franco", in *Ibid.*

Viñas, Angel, "11. La política exterior española durante el Franquismo y el Ministerio Exterior", in *Ibid.*

Watson, Robert J., *The Joint Chiefs of Staff and National Policy 1953–1954*, US Government Printing Office, Washington, DC, 1986

Welles, Benjamin, *Spain: The Gentle Anarchy*, Praeger, New York, 1965

Whelan, Richard, *Drawing the Line: The Korean War, 1950–1953*, Little, Brown & Co., Boston, 1990

Whitaker, Arthur P., *Spain and Defense of the West*, Harper & Brothers, New York, 1961

Whitfield, Stephen J., "The 1950s: The Era of No Hard Feelings", in Leonard Dinnerstein and Kenneth T. Jackson, eds, *American Vistas: 1877 to the Present*, Oxford University Press, New York, 1979

UNPUBLISHED THESES

Barrett, John William, *A Study of British and American Foreign Relations with Spain 1942–1945*, Ph.D. thesis, Georgetown University, 1970

Bengal, Saint Callista, *The United States and Spain 1939–1946: A Study in Press Opinion and Public Reaction*, Ph.D. thesis, Fordham University, 1959

Bergin, Thomas F., *Franco Spain from 1939 to 1948*, MA thesis, Princeton University, 1948

Bin Ahmad, Qasim, *The British Government and the Franco Dictatorship 1945–1950*, Ph.D. thesis, University of London, 1987

de Garmo, Peter Henry, *Beyond the Pyrenees; Spain and Europe since World War II*, Ph.D. thesis, University of California, Davis, 1971

Dorley Albert J., *The role of Congress in the Establishment of Bases in Spain*, Ph.D. thesis, St. John's University, 1969

Dura, Juan, *United States Policy Toward Dictatorship and Democracy in Spain 1936–1953: A Case Study in the Realities of Policy Formation 1936–1953*, Ph.D. thesis, University of California, Berkeley, 1979

Dwight, William, Jr., *United States Foreign Policy and Franco Spain 1945–1951*, MA thesis, Princeton University, 1951

Ellis, C. Allen, *United States Foreign Relations with Franco Spain 1945–1951*, MA thesis, Princeton University, 1952

Goodrich, Hunter, Jr., *Spain and Western European Defense*, MA thesis, Princeton University, 1953

Hadian, Ronald Franklin, *United States Foreign Policy Towards Spain 1953–1970*, Ph.D. thesis, University of California, Santa Barbara, 1976

Hourtoule, Gilbert O., *The Case of Franco Spain before the United Nations 1946–1950*, Ph.D. thesis, Pennsylvania State University, 1953

Jones, Randolph Bernard, *The Spanish Question and the Cold War 1944–1953*, Ph.D. thesis, University of London, 1987

Safian, A. Chester, *Relations between Spain and the United States 1945–1953*, MA thesis, Princeton University, 1955

Sandson, Theodore M., *Spain and Western Defense*, MA thesis, Princeton University, 1955

Scowcroft, Brent, *Congress and Foreign Policy: An Examination of Congressional Attitudes towards the Foreign Aid Programs to Spain and Yugoslavia*, PhD thesis, Columbia University, 1967

Seymour, Christopher H., *Ostracism: The United States and Spain 1945–1950*, MA thesis, Princeton University, 1976

Sharp, Benjamin Cameron Jr., *NATO and the Mediterranean 1949–1979: Deterioration on the Southern Flank*, Ph.D. thesis, University of Maryland, 1981

Smith Cornelius C., Jr., *United States Policy in Spain and the Mediterranean Area: An Analysis of the Economic and Military Agreements of 1953*, Ph.D. thesis, Claremont Graduate School, 1956

Watson, Bert A., *United States–Spanish Relations*, Ph.D. thesis, George Washington University, 1971

Weeks, Stanley Byron, *United States Defense Policy toward Spain, 1950–1976*, Ph.D. thesis, The American University, 1977

Willson, John Paul, *Carlton J. H. Hayes in Spain 1942–1945*, Ph.D. thesis, Syracuse University, 1969

Index

224